THE FICTION OF
RAJA RAO
CRITICAL STUDIES

Edited by
RAJESHWAR MITTAPALLI
PIER PAOLO PICIUCCO

ATLANTIC PUBLISHERS AND DISTRIBUTORS

Published by
ATLANTIC PUBLISHERS AND DISTRIBUTORS
B-2, Vishal Enclave, Opp. Rajouri Garden, New Delhi-27
Phones : 5413460, 5429987

Sales Office
4215/1, Ansari Road, Darya Ganj, New Delhi-02
Phones : 3273880, 3285873, 3280451
Fax : 91-11-3285873
e-mail : info@atlanticbooks.com
web : www.atlanticbooks.com

ISBN 81-269-0018-0

Typeset at
APD Computer Graphics, Delhi
Printed in India at
Nice Printing Press, Delhi

PREFACE

Raja Rao is undoubtedly the most brilliant writer that modern India has produced. His contribution to Indian fiction in English is manifold. He is a master stylist and in terms of style, with the possible exception of Salman Rushdie, he is unparalleled in India. His fictional technique derives from the hoary wisdom and time honoured traditions of India. He made a creative use of the resources of the English language for portraying Indian sensibility and modes of thought, feeling and behaviour in his very first novel *Kanthapura*.

Raja Rao is a careful and conscious artist. He is disciplined in his expression, almost to the point of being a perfectionist. He allows himself plenty of time for his ideas to take a definite fictional shape and only then sits down to write a book. That perhaps explains his meagre fictional output and the long gaps between any two of his books.

Raja Rao is singularly credited with philosophising the Indian novel in English with the publication of *The Serpent and The Rope*. Even *The Cat and Shakespeare*, which is artistically flawed to some extent, portrays his philosophical concerns, albeit in a comic light. One might say that while Swami Vivekananda directly interpreted Indian philosophy, specially the Vedanda, Raja Rao did it creatively and artistically and perhaps in a much better way than the great Swami. His fondness for Vedanta issues from his Brahmanical upbringing. It is not without reason that his protagonists are mostly Brahmins. But they gradually evolve from being caste Brahmins, with the attendant encumbrances, into transcendental beings, as Raja Rao himself surely did.

His *The Cow of the Barricades and Other Stories* fictionlises his patriotic and social concerns. For Raja Rao, India is not a geographical entity. It is a metaphysical and spiritual reality transcending geographical and temporal barriers. He spent all his formative and productive years in the West but his spirit has always remained Indian. He is firmly rooted in India, and absolutely does not suffer from a sense of alienation. His vision is holistic because it includes both the physical and the transcendental. For him the physical world is just a part of the vast cosmos, which lies outside the scope of human comprehension.

Given Raja Rao's phenomenal achievement and contribution to Indian fiction in English and given his range, sweep and philosophical depth, no attempt at critically assessing his works can be complete. Still the articles contained in this volume perceptively treat all the important concerns, themes and techniques of his fiction. A significant number of them focus on his style and his handling of the English language for artistic and creative purposes. His vision and philosophy are treated in an equally big number of articles. Themes such as identity, myth and Ganhian ideology have been the central points of discussion of yet another group of articles.

Raja Rao's small fictional output has been of advantage to us the editors in that we could accommodate articles on every one of his novels and collections of short stories in this volume. With somebody like Narayan this would not have been possible. The contributors, most of whom are highly respected scholars, have dealt with various facets of Raja Rao's fiction so ably that it has been a pleasure editing them. Our thanks are due to them. Their ready willingness to contribute to this volume greatly encouraged us. We also wish to thank Dr. K.R. Gupta of Atlantic Publishers and Distributors whose fondness for Indian Writing in English seems to know no bounds.

EDITORS

CONTENTS

1

Raja Rao: A Philosophical Novelist

MALLIKARJUN PATIL*

Like R.K. Narayan and Mulk Raj Anand, Raja Rao is a 'Raja of the Indian English fiction.' He is as renowned as the other two stalwarts. His literary product and philosophical stand has brought him the status of a classical writer.

Born in Mysore, Raja Rao studied in Europe and began to write stories when he stayed at Paris, France. He wrote several novels of excellence and short stories of importance. *Kanthapura* is his well-known novel—a masterpiece. Others include *The Serpent and the Rope, The Cat and Shakespeare, Comrade Kirillov* and *The Chessmaster and His Moves.* His collections of short stories are *The Cow of the Barricades* and *The Policeman and the Rose.* His works are greatly acclaimed both in India and abroad. Much of Raja Rao's life seems to have been spent abroad. At present he is a Professor at the University of Texas, U.S.A.

Mr. Raja Rao is a philosophical writer. Mohinder Pal Kohli calls him 'a Vedantist,' while P. Dayal says he is also 'a Tantrist.' Many Indians are of the view that Raja Rao, the writer is a Gandhian. Still there is a section of critics who thinks that Raja Rao writes like an European in some aspects. What made these to say this is the fact that Raja Rao was greatly influenced by many western philosophers. Therefore, he has been all of these.

Raja Rao was greatly influenced by Hinduism. Born a Brahman, he learnt most of the Vedant philosophy and the Vedant schools influenced him. The basic tenets of Vidantic philosophy are explicit

---

*Lecturer, Dept. of English, Gulbarga University, Gulbarga (Karnataka).

in his novels and stories. Principles such as devotion to God, surrender of the self, meditation, sexual abstinence and ascetic rigour are reflected in his fictional output. Non-attachment and desire to get liberation from the cycle of birth and death are special features of his vedantic views.

As earlier stated, Raja Rao's works show his affinity with tantric literature. The ideas about Siva and Parvati, the union of them, the primal need of Sakti are reflected. Tantra recommends the worship of the mother goddess, invoked by various names such as Lakshmi, Saraswati, Maha Kali, Durga, Kenchamma or Tripurasundari. In his works, the quest for truth does not entail sexual restraint but involves the search of extra-marital Tantric love.

Raja Rao, a pure Hindu in so far the vedantic principles such as love, truth, nonviolence are concerned, was greatly influenced by Mahatma Gandhi. His first novel *Kanthapura* holds a mirror to this fact. Influenced by the Gandhian notion of purity of means and ends, Raja Rao advocates truth and non-violence. However, as P. Dayal opines, the philosophical dimensions of Gandhian philosophy are, therefore, limited in his works. Indian epics the *Ramayana* and the *Mahabharata* too made their own impact on Raja Rao. In an article entitled "Books which Have Influenced Me," Raja Rao himself admits to have been influenced by the ancient Indian epics such as the *Ramayana* and the *Mahabharata* which, according to the author, epitomise the Indian tradition and wisdom.

Another remarkable influence on Raja Rao is the European writers such as Charles Baudelaire, Fyodor Dostoevsky, Roman Rolland, Andre Gide and Paul Valerie. Inspired by the congenial ideas of Gide and Baudelaire, the expatriate writer Raja Rao speaks also for the affirmation of the flesh. It is argued that, "However, it may be pointed out that his expatriation to the west is merely an accident; he is essentially an Indian in regard to his personal propensities and artistic preferences; and his novels primarily revolve round Gandhism, Vedanta and Tantra."[1]

Raja Rao is a great writer of Indian English fiction. However, he greatly differs from R.K. Narayan and Mulk Raj Anand, both in theme and treatment, he has his own place in Indian literature in

English. Unlike Anand and Narayan, Rao does not write about life in terms of social realities. Instead, he portrays man's spiritual aspects, his relationship with his self, and finally his quest for selfhood. Rao gave to his novels rather a philosophical colouring. M.K. Naik remarks "Raja Rao has lent a philosophical depth to Indian novel in English."[2] Indeed, Raja Rao is a novelist of philosophical consciousness and approach.

Kanthapura, Raja Rao's first novel written in 1938, is a classic of its own kind. It portrays the Freedom Movement launched by Mahatma Gandhi in the 1920s to liberate India from the imperialistic hegemony of the British. In P. Dayal's view, India's struggle for independence, with its powerful impact on Indian sensibility, forms the nucleus of the novel.

Already the theme of freedom struggle and Gandhism is depicted in the works of Narayan and Anand. Narayan's novel *Waiting for the Mahatma* (1955) and Anand's *Untouchable* (1935) display Gandhism as vividly as Rao's in *Kanthapura*. Similarly K.A. Abbas refers to Jallianwala Bagh tragedy, Salt satyagraha and Gandhi-Irvin pact in his novel *Inqilab* (1955). But Rao's exploitation of Gandhism is more lucidly brought out to the light. His use of mythical analogy that Gandhi is Krishna, British are Ravan, Nehru, Bharata, etc. adds its own adornment to the tale. Besides Gandhi is treated as a divine figure. Rao's faith in Gandhian thought led him to idealise Mahatma Gandhi as a veritable God—a divine persona and an incarnation.

Similarly the Gandhian hero, Moorthappa has been idealised as an extraordinary person. Gangamma describes him as "Moorthy, the good, Moorthy, the religious and Moorthy, the noble" (144). Moorthy, the major character of the novel, is a Brahman, a graduate and a clean chap.

Inspired by Gandhi's principles truth, non-violence and the Harijan movement, he participates into the freedom struggle. Like any sincere leader of the time, he does not believe in superstitious mode of life and money-mindedness. Nor does he remain a traditional minded Brahmin either. He advocates his people to speak truth and commit violent deeds no more. What brings domestic disaster to him is his reformation of Hindu-Harijan relationships. This hurts the orthodox Hindus and the leading Brahmins threaten him of excommunication. Even hurt by her son's radicalism, his mother dies. His community abstains from him. But Harijans love and respect his nobility and greater consciousness.

Later with Patel, he starts the freedom movement actively. He becomes a leader and asks his people to contribute towards the movement by spinning and other village works. But the British arrest him. Meanwhile strikes at the nearest coffee estate worsen the situation. Amidst these India gets freedom and all goes peacefully.

The novel is an enchanting story of how the independence movement becomes a tangible reality in a tiny and secluded village in South India. It is the story of young Moorthy, stormy and idealistic and his fight against conservative forces. The novel has the flavour of an epic as it emerges through the eyes of a delightful old woman who comments with wisdom and humour on the variety and complexity of village life.

E.M. Forster enjoying the reading of its style and matter is said to have remarked "*Kanthapura* is the finest novel to come out of India in recent years."[3] The novel is apprised as 'a classic of resurgent India told in a poetic almost mythical style.' Another writer Santha Rama Rao opined, "It has all the content of an ancient Indian classic, combined with a sharp, satirical wit and a clear understanding of the present."[4]

Some words about the language and style that went in making *Kanthapura*, a classic of its own kind, must be said. The writer has used very archaic and colloquial Indian English, and more words are used where some would suffice. Another feature is bombastic diction and phraseology. Look at the following extract:

> Meanwhile Rachanna's two grandchildren come in, and gazing at Moorthy, they run into the back yard, and then Madanna's children come, and then Madanna's wife, pestle in hand, and Madanna's wife's sister and her two months old brat in her arms, and then all the women and all the children of the pariah quarter come and sit in Rachanna's central veranda and they all gaze silently at Moorthy, as

though the sacred eagle had suddenly appeared in the heavens (105).

The Serpent and the Rope, published in 1960 established Raja Rao's reputation as a philosophically complex novelist. The novel is deeply rooted in Indian philosophy and tantricism. It depicts man's quest for self-realisation. The theme of the novel, as Raja Rao observes, is "the futility and barrenness of man in human existence when man has no deep quest and no thirst for the ultimate. Man's life here in Samsara is an august mission to find the Absolute."[5] Ramaswamy, the hero of the novel expresses his irrepressible quest for God. For this purport, Raja Rao advocates us to follow Vedanta, which is truth. In Vedanta, everything is revealed. According to the hero, the world is an illusion, life is unreal, only Brahman or God is real, true and loveable. In his view, "the world is either unreal or real—the serpent or the rope. There is nothing in between the two and all that's in between is poetry, is sainthood" (335). In the light of futile worldly glories, both Ramaswamy and the author insist upon salvation. Since man's life is mortal or temporary, he must aspire for moksha or liberation from the fetters of life. Death is compulsory for all. Ramaswamy speaks much about death. His ideas on it are taken from the Upanishads. Death affects him neither. He argues that soul is unperishable and it aspires to join Brahman. In his view soul and God are one and the same.

> Not hearing nor tasting nor smelling or seeing,
> But Form of Consciousness and Bliss;
> Shiva I am, I am Shiva (114).

But the wonder is that although he speaks much about Vedantic philosophy, observance of brahmcharva and virtues, Ramaswamy, a graduate in London does not practise anything. In fact, he suffers from several human frailties such as sexual morbidity, craze for material advancement and sense of possessiveness. So he appears a confused character. He wants to enjoy life and aspires to be praised.

Ramaswamy, an Indian who undertook a project in France and England for nearly eight years settles down there. He marries Madeleine, a French lady who is weak in sexual compatibility but quite interested in Vedanta and Tantric cult. Ramaswamy is an Europeanised Brahmin who finds it difficult to practise vedantic asceticism. His doctoral investigations involving the study of metaphysical influences on the Albigensians arouse in him a sense of appreciation for the European cultural tradition. It is significant to observe that Ramaswamy's pilgrimage in the novel culminates in his misery and suffering, because he became rootless without a home, temple, city, climate and age. He is a rootless figure always in search of questhood. First he tries to get self-realisation through Vedant. But his carnal desires take him to Tantric cult.

Though Ramaswamy marries Madeleine, he fails to get any real satisfaction. He possesses an extra marital relationship with Savitri. Not only that, he always thinks of Saroja, his sister's beauty. He finds that many women including his sister better should have been his wives. There are critics who see his infatuation with his sister. He says that in remote antiquity in Greece, brother and sister marriages were not only tolerated but were a mark of aristocracy. Hence, he believes that most of the ascetics develop concupiscence despite their loincloth, Kamandala and their stick or naked feet (172). He thinks that most of the monks who observe celibacy become ghosts in their next life. Here one fact must be born in mind that Raja Rao emphasises the importance of sex as a physiological necessity. No doubt, sex is the source of pleasure and ecstatic bliss. But it should not be man's mission to attach great importance to it forever. What happens here is that Ramaswamy, a spoilt child, indulges in it and he follows Shakti or Tantric cult for that sake alone. P. Dayal says, "'Since Ramaswamy suffers from sexual repression, he follows the path of tantra which promises the fulfilment of his carnal love as well as the attainment of truth" (31).

By Shakti or Tantric cult, it is observed, man can attain not only entertainment but also enlightenment. Bhoga or the pleasures of the world, the propounders of this cult say, is a means for salvation. Besides, by Tantric cult many miracles can be created and enjoyed. Ramaswamy observes that the Black Virgin of Saint Oven still cures dreadful diseases; and Madeleine propitiates Black Madonna who answers all her questions. Further, Ramaswamy dreams of wonderful performances:

I can think that a building may just decide to fly, or just Stalin may become a saint, or that all the Japanese have become Buddhist monks, or that Mahatma Gandhi is walking with us now. I sometimes feel I can make the railway line stand up or the elephant bears its young one in twenty-four days; I can see an aeroplane float over a mountain and sit carefully on a peak, or I could go to Fateh-Pur-Sikri and speak to the Emperor Akbar. It would be difficult for me to think when I am in Versailles, that I hear the uncouth voice of Roi Soleil, or in Meayx that Bossuet rubs snuff in the palm of his hand, as they still do in India, and offers a pinch to me I can sneeze with it, and hear Bossuet make one more of his funeral orations (6).

Ramaswamy, Madelaine, Savitri, Saroja, all the characters who believe Tantric cult, think that it controls all the elements of life and death. The hero's desire for magical accomplishments in the novel are essentially Tantric in import.

In the light of Tantric cult, the followers of it, invariably assume that sexual happiness or love, brings man not only happiness but also liberation. Woman, in Tantric cult, is nothing but Devi, Shakti, Adishakti. If she blesses man she attains heavenly bliss. The exaltation of women in *The Serpent and the Rope* has Tantric connotations. In this novel, woman is personified as a goddess as she is considered 'the priestess of God' (57). No doubt, Raja Rao's principal characters idealise their beloveds and worship them as the emblems of Sakti or the Female Principle. His belief that woman is the source of sensuous and aesthetic pleasure to man has Tantric contours. Another remarkable thing is that Rao portrays woman as a mystery. He says woman is a baffling mystery. Often and again sexual union is said to be fruitful for contentment. On an occasion, Ramaswamy explains to Savitri how truth can also be acquired through the Tantric experience of the biunity of the male and the female.

The Cat and Shakespeare is Raja Rao's third novel. As the novelist remarks this novel is a sequel to the preceding novel *The Serpent and the Rope*. As the theme of the novel is a continuation of Tantricism from the earlier novel and as it is more complicated here, it is very difficult to offer a critical appraisal of it. *The Cat and Shakespeare* is an enigmatic work, for it combines both comic and serious and amorous and metaphysical. In P. Dayal's view, "The juxtaposition of the apparently heterogeneous elements interwoven in the text and the representation of the cat as a goddess add complexity to the novel" (P. Dayal, 60). The novelist's own explanation of the book is also curiously complex.

> It is a metaphysical comedy and all I could want the reader to do is to weep at every page, not for what he sees, but for what he sees he sees. For me it is like a book of prayer.[6]

The criticism on Raja Rao's novel is quite intriguing. Many critics like C.D. Narasimhaiah and M.K. Naik are of the view that the novel tantalises the reader, for the philosophical seriousness disseminated therein is inscrutable. C.D. Narasimhaiah has found in the novel the traces of ego, illusion and three gunas enumerated in the Gita, while M.K. Naik affirms Ramanuja's modified non-dualistic philosophy is enshrined in it. Others have interpreted the cat-kitten theory expounded in the novel as symbolic of the doctrine of *prapatti* or self-surrender enshrined in Visistadvaita. However, the novel greatly utilises Tantric cult and it is in this light a study of the novel is desirable.

Ramakrishna Pai is the major character here. Saroj is his wife. There is no domestic happiness between them. As a result, he lives with Shanta, a schoolteacher ever not at all afraid of the society. He is a radical, a believer of Tantric cult, and a womaniser. His ambition in life is to live as happily as possible. He never cares for 'means and ends' theory. Totally his aim is to live happily.

The novel is an indulgent glorification of the supreme goddess. Most of the characters such as Govindan Nair, Shantha, Shridhar, Usha, Mudali and Ramakrishna Pai are the worshippers of the goddess who is the supreme deity of the Hindu Tantric Cult. The cat in the novel is symbolic of the female deity. It is not an ordinary cat, because it has the sense of discrimination. The cat knows what is right and what is wrong, for mysterious are the feline ways. But what meaning is attached to the title word 'Shakespeare' is not at all hinted at in the novel. This has led many readers astray. However, those who loved, admired and worshipped cat attain bliss, and those who disgraced it found themselves discontented. For evidence, men experience the ineffable joy once the deity blesses him. The child Shridhar, who professes his faith in the goddess and converses with Usha over the wall, is carried by the cat and enters a three-storeyed house, which is symbolic of nirvana, the release from the cycle of earthly fetters. On the contrary, characters like Bhoothalinga Iyer who lack faith lead a meaningless existence. Iyer who considers the cat a pariah animal faces despair, death and damnation. Characterisation of Shakti cult is at its height here. Woman is supposed to be goddess in whatever form she appears *i.e.* daughter, wife, mother and the like. Ramakrishna Pai pays the richest tribute to Shantha, his beloved. Though he did love his wife Saroja, as he loves Shantha. To him Shantha appears an embodiment of love, beauty and truth,—all divine features. He says: "What is woman you may ask. Well, woman is Shanta.... I am just a man. And Shanta is not just a woman, she is woman" (22). Shantha for him is symbolic of goddess. She gives meaning and recognition to Pai's life. P. Dayal asserts, "The woman in *The Cat and Shakespeare* is delineated as wife, mother and deity. All the diverse forms of womanhood coalesce into a single being. This treatment of the woman here is consonant with the Tantric faith which considers all women earthly representatives of the supreme goddess."

Another aspect so much focussed upon in the novel is that woman appears to be a mystery. Shantha too admits that woman is the biggest puzzle. And it is emphasised that woman is a must for man's salvation and *vice versa*. Ramakrishna Pai believes that the male attains awareness only through his affinity with the female. He realises his identity and attains selfhood only through his cordial relationship with woman. Similarly, women get awareness because of their family life and men.

Comrade Kirillov is Raja Rao's another novel. This was written in 1950's. But it was published in 1976. Meanwhile its French version was produced in 1965. But the novel was originally written in French. However, the critic's opinion on the novel is not positive and favourable.

All know that Raja Rao, as a novelist is preoccupied or much attached himself with Gandhism, Vedanta and Tantricism, but no such philosophical strands are dealt with here. The novel *Comrade Kirillov* is purely 'a critique of communism.' Some critics describe it as a 'slender and inconsequential expose of ideas.' D.S. Maini calls it an insignificant 'brain-spun thing...sadly out of tune;' with the rest of the author's work. He finds a grievous decline in style, fabulation and rhetoric and points out that the "failure of technique is, in fact, a failure of vision and values."[7] The novel is totally deficient in the depth of thought that characterise Rao's later or earlier fiction.

The theme of the novel is communism and its far-reaching impact on the laity. But despite Kirillov's ideological commitments, the novel remains a parody of an Indian's protestations of communism. This parody of communism is heightened as Kirillov is projected as a hypothetical Buddha. And Raj Rao's comparison of Kirillov's communist logic with the anonymity of Sanyasis is satirical in the sense that it exposes the hollowness of the protagonist.

Raja Rao's latest novel *The Chessmaster and His Moves* is set in the background of Vedanta philosophy and Tantricism. It is a well-written classic. So it brought the novelist a worldwide fame. He has, because of this and his other works, been awarded the tenth Neustadt International Prize for Literature. While accepting the prize at the University of Oklahoma, U.S.A., on June 4, 1988, Raja Rao observed, "I would like to be completely nameless and just be that reality which is beyond all of us who here me—that reality which evokes in me you, and I in each one listening to me this evening, that there be no one there but light. And it is of that reality the sages have spoken."[8]

The title of the novel is autotelic 'Chessmaster' is God, the Almighty and 'His Moves' means, his *lilas* or activities. The novel displays Rao's interplay of Vedanta and Tantric as far as God and his role in shaping human existence is concerned. Another aspect of this is Shakti or Tantric cult, which pays way to attain salvation through the worship of woman, an incarnation of Shakti. In this regard, there is less dissimilarity between the two novels. *The Serpent and the Rope* and *The Chessmaster and His Moves.*

The Chessmaster and His Moves is the story, of Sivaram Sastri's unfulfilled love. Sivaram Sastri, an Indian mathematician goes to Paris, as a research scholar. He settles down there. Though a Brahman and a man greatly interested in Vedanta, he falls in love with a variety of women,—Indian and French. He falls in love with Suzanne Chantereux and feels attracted by her physical beauty. Frequent meetings between them bring them close to each other. Her love for Indian lover compels her to get an attachment with him. As a result, she develops both an intellectual and emotional affinity with Siva (Sivaram Sastri). However there is a sense of holiness about her, Siva's relationship with Suzanne is characterised by his physical encounters with her:

> Here was a woman in her firm womanhood, her thighs and bust so perfectly made for surrender, for union, biological greases pulling you so forcefully to your inner adventure. As I held her firmly in my arms, and adjusted myself to her breath and hold, I felt not a Caliban, not even Ariel, but a prince. How royal my long and alive body seemed, almost to shine in its own glow, and the tender cries, the gentle caresses of Suzanne seemed a miracle, the first and last miracle that woman gives to man (197-98).

When Suzanne goes away from Siva, Mireille enters in his life with a sense of greater freedom. Her emotional attachment makes Siva worship her. They develop understanding between them. Siva considers Mireille the source of his enlightenment while she proclaims to have discovered "her kingdom—her man she had been searching for since ages. So Mireille's love for Siva acquires 'fullness' and satisfaction.

Of all the women, however, Siva is most fascinated by is Jayalakshmi, an elegant and sophisticated princess, married to Raja Surendar Singh. He develops an immense liking for Jaya, for she possessed a similar taste and temperament, he had had. In the novel, though they do not marry each other, Jaya and Siva have been portrayed as true lovers.

The novel offers probable solutions to the metaphysical

propositions raised in the preceding works. The title of the novel is symbolic. Sivaram asserts that all the events of man's life are governed by the rules of the game of chess which has not "four orders of pawns, but a million" (195). Besides, the novel has the Tantric thought, interspersed in its texture. Raja Rao believes that the goddess can grant liberation to man if he develops faith in her. Another aspect of the novel is that several characters of it criticise loveless conventional marriages. Thus, the novel *The Chessmaster and His Moves* has philosophical overtones and an encyclopedic sweep.

NOTES

1. P. Dayal, *Raja Rao*, New Delhi: Atlantic Publishers, 1991, 4.

2. M.K. Naik, *Raja Rao*, *Ibid.*, 160.

3. E.M. Forster, Front Page, *Kanthapura.*

4. *Ibid.*

5. Raja Rao's letter to M.K. Naik.

6. Raja Rao, *The Cat and Shakespeare*, New York: qt. from the publisher's blurb.

7. D.S. Maini, "Raja Rao's Vision, Values and Aesthetics, *Perspectives on Raja Rao*, ed. K.K. Sharma, Ghaziabad, 1980, 17.

8. Raja Rao, "Laureate's Words of Acceptance," *World Literature Today,* 62, No. 4, 1988, 528.

2

Rope in the Serpent: Comments on Raja Rao's Indian Vision and Voice

M.S. PATI*

It might have appeared at one time that critical dichotomy over *The Serpent and the Rope* issued from a cultural polarisation involving two different approaches to reality. With critics like Walsh[1] and McCutchion[2] expressing acute discomfort with this 'Indian' cerebralisation of the novel-form—McCutchion found in it a paradox, the 'Brahmin novel'—as against high adulation accorded by Indian scholars like Iyengar,[3] Narasimhaiah,[4] and Naik,[5] it seemed as if the novel worked as a catalytic agent precipitating biases latent in the Indian and Western traditions. It is not as if generous appreciation was absolutely scarce in the West,[6] and it was roses all the way in the home country. But one could see that even those Indian critics who had strong reservations about the 'metaphysical propositions' novel were far less vehement in their disparagement than were those with a European background—Mulk Raj Anand or Meenakshi Mukherjee[7] could be matched with McCutchion[8] to make the point. In more recent times, however, there have been signs of a changes the value of Raja Rao's intellectual wares today appears to be undergoing a sharp slump among Indian critics as well. Although voices are still being raised in defence of his style,[9] more and more of his country, men in the recent past seem to be losing patience with his 'intellectual garrulousness.' The latest full-length study to come out on the novelist, Dr. K.R. Rao's *The Fiction of Raja Rao,* may be cited to note a possible change in

*Department of English, Sambalpur University, Sambalpur.

Indian reactions. In contrast with authoritative Indian voices on the subject less than a decade ago, Dr. K.R. Rao's indictment is rather strong and unequivocal.[10]

In this context the present essay attempts to make two main points. First, it discusses how the narrative voice in the novel is designed to function as a high-romantic medium to 'dissolve' the philosophical, social and psychological realities and 'recreate' them as a visionary outlook, to gather everything into a new plastic form and stimulate in the mind of the reader a kind of fluid sentience. Secondly, it argues that because of its peculiarly 'Indian' perspective and its poetic, mythical mode, certain of the traditional critical approaches are likely to prove here misleading. It is suggested that Raja Rao's narrative comes off as distinctively Indian not only in terms of certain of its grammatical features, philosophical attitudes, or patterns of social convention, but on the basis of something much deeper, namely, aesthetic mood. Since the novel engages itself in the 'serpent' while advancing towards the 'rope,' it naturally calls for a special aesthetic mood that should conduce to a fluid, allusive communication. While laying a suitable base for its theme of growth into wisdom it does, of course, grapple with a number of dualistic, and the dialectical possibilities inherent in them. But to cogitate over its intellectual asides and philosophical reflections instead of responding to the evocative poetry of their utterance is to do the novel wrong: the haunting, esoteric quality which constitutes the very essence of its twilight message would then vanish in the garish daylight of critical enquiry.

The narrative voice furnishes an unmistakable indication of Raja Rao's approach to his subject. An alert, yet languorous, mood of reminiscence and introspection predominates: punctuated by stretches of action and movement, this stream of memory—individual and traditional—imparts to the novel a certain dreamy, poetic fluidity. There is much philosophical debate, no doubt; but except on a few very rare occasions they do not appear as acts of cerebralisation. The novel strikes one rather as a long plaint of wintry introspection, broken by intermittent bursts of reminiscent spring-time excitement hearkening unto a new autumnal serenity in its final stages. Since the novel is concerned with human sorrow in its widest possible ramifications, and with the way to deliverance, it was only natural that it should have some such structure. A sense of brooding sorrow, of quiet melancholy, hovers over almost its entire length. The scene shifts across vast geographical territories, a number of finely realised characters presenting a beautiful mosaic of outlooks and habits, and a large body of themes and motifs is handled, but there is one continuous burthen, Now muted and now amplified, running through them all. From Little Mother and Soroja to Madeleine and Savithri, the same haunting strain breaks forth, again and again, orchestrating in Ramaswamy's consciousness a certain ineffable poignancy. The use of rather old-fashioned narrative media—long epistles, diary, small parables, legends, and the like—acquire a startling effectiveness because of the special tone the novel maintains with an unremitting, quiet power.

The quality of its voice is not grounded simply on an autobiographical structure that provides for a constant blending of story with reminiscence and reflection. It functions in a far more fundamental way in projecting an extraordinary kind of mood and vision. Indeed, the voice may be said to constitute the very essence of the novel, namely, a poignant experience of the 'Serpent.' It is as one long stretch of rumination, therefore, that the novel has its shape. There are no chapter-headings; not even bare numeral indicators of the different stages of action are provided. The novel does, of course, have several chapters, but the entire thing is sought to be presented in a fluid, caterminous state, the state in which it exists in the mind of the protagonist. And the brooding, meditative tone has a natural quality about it, for the protagonist is portrayed as a consumptive, hypersensitive individual, an intellectual with a poetic disposition. But even this would not adequately explain the quality of the narrative voice here: one cannot, that is to say, understand *The Serpent and the Rope* as a variation on *The Magic Mountain* style with Ramaswamy as an Indianised Hans Castorp. As may be seen, the narrative voice meanders through long digressive passages, not so much for psychological or intellectual elaboration as for poetic transformation. Every now and then the story pauses so that a certain poetic, mythical colouring of the moods and ideas organised in the sequence may be facilitated. No doubt, some of these sequences are sought to be framed into a strong intellectual-metaphysical structure, but the framework has a gossamer quality too. A complex network of finely spun evocations is stretched across the entire length of the novel, so that some of the elusive meanings it is pursuing might be captured and made tangible. Its meditations—both philosophical and psychological are sought to be realised more as poetic apprehensions than as lucid thoughts. Myths, puranic legends, fables and ancedotes are, therefore, inducted in profusion, thereby to abrade the rough edges of historical narration and convert the novel into a complex romantic-metaphysical lyric of epic dimensions.

One might examine its limpid plasticity of discourse and its constant involvement of a fluid, poetic state of consciousness by choosing a sequence which, to start with, promises to keep to utterly precise, pointed narration:[11]

> I took Savithri back to Cambridge. At the station we jumped into a taxi and I left her at Girton College, then I went ....

A few sentences later we move into the library with Ramaswamy and hear him making certain interesting observations on the place. These lead him to the question of the relationship between a writer's physique and his style, a question which sets him establishing connections through a number of authors: Shakespeare, Goldsmith, Maupassant, Proust and even the Vedic seer. Apparently this is a typical mannerism of Raja Rao, to whom every ordinary situation in the novel seems to furnish an excuse for launching into intellectual and metaphysical discussions. But the important thing to note is how such movements are saved from degenerating into pedantry. For one thing, they are made to function as natural, dramatic experiences in the context of the characters. Thus in the present instance, there is affirmed, first of all, a certain psychological basis:

> With my poor lungs a library is always a place of a broad, propitious breath, and so books are not only my professional need, but also my respiratory, my spiritual need.

Moreover, Raja Rao makes of discursive reasoning a kind of intellectual runway to soar into higher poetic realms in search of sore elusive, but more valuable, meanings. Thus Ramaswamy proceeds from the question of literary style to talk of the wisdom concealed in the 'silences' between lines and behind books, and leads the discussion back to the original point, namely, the elusive truth symbolised by Savithri. The 'digression' on language and books, we now note, had a very precise direction. A richly evocative passage is then introduced to round off and clarify the entire movement, and the real, complex significance of this discourse is gathered in a compact form by projecting the Feminine Principle through the character of Savithri. As one reads the following one realises how concentrated and economical, and not rambling and prolix as one might have suspected, has been the narration:

> She was the source of which words were made, the Mother of sound, Akshara Lakshmi, divinity of the syllables; the night of which the day was the meaning, the knowledge of which the book was the token, the symbol—the prophecy.[13]

This is typical of the use to which Raja Rao puts historical, intellectual, and philosophical references in the novel: they are almost always a means to gear up the narrative towards some profounder poetic apprehensions. To discuss them for their intellectual value or philosophical relevance alone would, therefore, be to work against the very design of their organisation. One may follow up the narrative stretch under discussion to find something illustrative again.

Ramaswamy, we see, continues with his myth-making mood, and goes on to reflect on the Cam in terms that remind one of the Indian philosophical concept of Prakriti, the Primordial Reality that is ever seething with creative transformations but still remains an unchanged, Original Manifestation. These reflections lead him back to what has been centripetally under reference all along, namely, Savithri, and he concludes by saying:[14]

> I might call Savithri, but Savithri speaking to Savithri did not call herself Savithri. The sound is born of silence and the river is of space. Love has nothing to do with loving, for 'I' itself is love.

Once again, poetic economy rather than mannered garrulousness strikes the reader as the special quality of the narration. He is made aware of an incisive artistic purpose at work in the apparently circumlocutory, pedantic talk on the Cam: It prepares the ground for a special experience of the protagonist's involving a visionary outlook rather than a 'philosophical' argument. The two passages that follow present Rao's mythical technique at its best, converting objects and persons into media for certain profounder explorations. As may be seen, Savithri, Girton College and Cam continue to be the objective points of reference, but a powerful romantic imagination is set to work in transforming them and offering a controlled, tantalising, dreamy evocation of transcendent places of experience and meaning. Many of the generalisations which, for a novel, Eight appear to be rather too bold and inept outside their contexts are seen to be invested here with a peculiar evocative charm. Thus the discussion leads to the following:[15]

> Just as reading poetry at break of day is like remembering the feel of one's dream, but not the acts of one's dreams, to know Savithri was to wake into the truth of life, to be remembered—unto God.

Removed from the context, such a statement could appear outrageously pompous and vague, but here it comes off as a logical consummation to a certain sequence of ideas; it is intended, that is, to act as poetic evocation and not as philosophical construct.

It is, of course, clear that Raja Rao is not so such narrating a story as weaving a romantic myth imbued with a variety of intellectual insights and spiritual apprehensions. There is a constant tangential flights off the action or story, compelling the reader's mind to hover over them with the feel of a new knowledge and new vision—something shadowy, yet authentic and real. It is this which reveals the author's deepest contact with the Indian tradition, both philosophical and aesthetic. Ancient Indian art, as is well known, did not aspire to be a social document or a rational study of man. As Richard Lannoy in *The Speaking Tree* summed up the nature of this art,[16] and as H.W. Wells in his perceptive study of Indian drama discussed,[17] it functioned more in an oneiric, evocative style than as precise, clearly articulated feelings and ideas. A close interaction of body, mind and spirit could be discerned, but the work of art was made to function in a plastic manner somewhere above the conscious mind, though not removed from it. The main objective of Indian art was to produce joy and illumination at some rarefied aesthetic and metaphysical heights rather than the delight attendant upon imaginative appreciation of socio-cultural realities as they impinge on a particular consciousness. The synthesis one comes across in Raja Rao belongs to that superior order, involving what may be called both immanence and transcendence, and not merely integration at the level of the conscious mind. He seeks to insinuate a paradoxical state of sentience in the reader; the perceptual faculty is both stimulated and lulled by means of special poetic devices, and the reader is made to transcend the ordinary mental plane and get sensitised to a more subtle cognitive mechanism within. This is but an artistic necessity for a novel that sought to treat history as vision.

We may hear discussions on Marxism, Nazism, Vedanta, Masculine and Feminine principles, history and individual identity, and so on: we may have legends and fables of various kinds culled from different cultures, and we may note a variety of objects being processed through the mythical imagination: but the effort is always the same: to convey a special vision with the aid of evocative philosophical suggestions and poetic insights and by inciting a fluid state of sentience in the reader. A kind of cross between symbolic poetry and philosophical meditation, the novel, therefore, involves constant shifts from assertion to suggestion and from evocation to statement.

But this has by no means been an easy task to carry through. As Coleridge confessed, and as Arnold too keenly realised, poetry and philosophy have a natural tendency to neutralise each other in the creative mind. A novelist who tries to present a metaphysical vision in the form of poetic discourse runs the risk of furnishing strings of mannered statements that would not adequately stimulate or clarify. Such utterances may still have some appeal but they may not always succeed as effective aesthetic presentation of visionary experiences. Achieving neither the coherence of a philosophical statement nor the supple evocations of a poetic discourse, they could end up merely as a lump of ungainly, viscous, ambivalent narrative material.

The Serpent and the Rope is not entirely free from blemishes of this kind. For example, at certain points in the section dramatising the mutual 'discoveries' of Ramaswami and Savithri at London— discoveries that are of crucial importance to the novel—Raja Rao appears to be more conceptually interesting than artistically convincing. The debate on Communism (pp. 180-190) has an obvious importance; it is to serve as an intellectual substructure for Savithri's awakening into profounder implications of her feminity, an awakening which in its turn would prepare the grounds for the enchanting consummation of an archetypal love—Queen and King, Mira and Gopal, Radha and Krishna—between her and Ramaswsmy. But the debate between Marx and Yagnyavalkya does not really achieve a proper grip. With all the enticements Rao has at his command striking references to history and culture, 'puranic' stories, patches of Socratic dialectic interspersed with aphoristic 'utterances' in the manner of the Upanisads, exciting bursts of romantic fancy— the sequence grows somewhat dreary. That the author himself might have felt uncomfortable about it may be inferred from the manner in which he abruptly suspends the argument, and concentrates instead on emotionally more exciting reflections on Savithri.

Rao's mythical style does not have the same kind of intensity and assurance at all places in the novel. For instance, the mythologising of the advent of a new Queen to the English throne which is quite effective earlier on in the novel when offered in small doses, as occasional asides, later grows into a theatrical gesture. One does, of course, understand Rao' fascination for the subject. Here was something from contemporary history which furnished an epic symbol of feminine ascendance something that could be effectively linked with a dialectic that is at the very heart of the novel, namely, resurgence of an active benign, feminine principle of 'Life' through its interaction with the hard, detached, masculine principle of 'Death.' The author felt naturally drawn to the symbolic potential of the Queen's coronation. But contemporaneity was precisely the bane here; for events from the immediate milieu are not always felicitous subjects for epic enlargement and mythical evocation. The sequence dealing with the coronation, therefore, does not succeed in gaining the symbolic potency Rao wished to invest it with. But such gaps between promise and performance are too few to irreparably damage the poetic discourse of the novel.

Such occasional arid patches could, however, have been avoided if the author had restrained his impulse at those places to state the intellectual background of his mythic vision in the form of lucid thoughts. As can be seen, the novel's ideational greatness resides more in its areas of implicit, unspelt experiences than in directly articulated arguments. Some of those deeply embedded emotions and insights function with exquisite precision and power. Indeed, so organic, so indissolubly iconised is their existence in the novel that to elucidate them in conventional terms is bound to result in a critical falsification of their import. The Feminine-Masculine opposition, for example, is worked out across an expansive space, Oriental and Western; but critical annotations in terms of Tantra mysticism, Sankhya, Vaisnavism, Plato, Kant, Freud, Jung, Arthurian romances and ancient epics, to all of which the novel makes direct allusions or implicit references in the context of that dualism would not, by themselves, have much relevance for the obvious reason that what is being attempted here is poetic vision and not an intellectual construct. Whenever, therefore, the novelist tries to achieve a total clarity of intellectual formulations[18] and whenever a critic tries to reduce the 'arguments' to clear, logical statements, a proper appreciation of the mythic vision gets thwarted. There is a special semantic of art, one notes here more than elsewhere, which ranges beyond the pale of dictionaries and encyclopaedias. Particularly in this novel, where a profoundly traditional Indian soul with a cosmopolitan, modern mind functions as the perceptual centre, an oblique, poetic method of communication is made obligatory by the ingrained ambivalence of consciousness. The bipolar perspective of its protagonist, who operates by straddling widely different cultural ethos and metaphysical positions, forces him to resort to the universal language of myth and fable. References to different intellectual traditions that are inducted in the interest of inclusiveness and authenticity of treatment are meaningful only in the total poetic context of the novel. Unifocal magnification of these materials would, therefore, constitute a travesty.

The special cultural matrix within which Rao seeks to organise various elements in his novel has its own peculiar compulsions, and criticism is likely to go berserk if it is not in conformity with the attitudes and responses germane to that culture. We see how deeply the entire experience of the novel is embedded in a traditional Indian taste. Thus Ramaswamy is presented as a liberal, cosmopolitan

mind, a person who by education and choice has made himself heir
to the entire human tradition, but one whose value judgements and
responses continue to be pervasively 'Indian.' This forces upon the
reader a certain critical discipline. For instance, one might suspect
the presence of an abundance of suggestions in the novel demanding
a Freudian explication of Ramaswamy's mind. But the actual
business of critical analysis reveals that they are all a false scent.
Certain passages relating to Ramaswamy's reactions on Saroja
attaining the age of puberty may be examined to make the point:

> Saroja's presence now obsessed me sometimes, like
> one of those nights with the perfume of magnolia.
> Rich and green seemed the sap as it rose, and it has
> a night of its own and a day—I would myself pluck
> flowers for her hair and take her out on long walks....
> I was intoxicated with Saroja's presence, like a deer
> could be before a waterfall, or an elephant before a
> mountain-peaks something primordial was awaking
> in a creature. There was something of the smell of
> musk, of the oyster when the pearl is still within, of
> the deep silent sea before the monsoon breaks. There
> was, too, a feeling of temple sanctuary, and I could
> now understand why primitive people took the first
> blood of menstruation for the better harvesting of
> their fields. And why the Indians told us how
> Malavika when she poured water made the Asoka
> flower of Shakuntala the Karnikara blossom. What a
> deep and reverential mystery womanhood is—I could
> bow before Saroja and call her Queen.[19]

This is a typical Ramaswamy discourse; dense, complex and lyrical.
To many, the temptation to introduce Freud and discover suppressed
incestuous leanings in the protagonist may be quite a natural response
to this passage. But it should not take one long to appreciate that
such a reading goes counter to the fundamental intention of the text.
Ramaswamy's 'intoxication,' as is unambiguously emphasised, is
caused by his encounter with a primordial reality, an experience
which with greater accuracy may be linked with the Jungian 'anima'
and 'collective unconscious,' if at all, than with the Freudian
subconscious. Responses spanning primitive ritual and super-

civilisational customs are introduced to portray the extraordinary sensation Ramaswamy experiences in the presence of Saroja. But the dominant strain is one of religious fervour, something nearer the mystical than the sensual. The references, again, subserve a peculiarly Indian philosophical outlook by helping to dramatise Ramaswamy's initial awakening into the eternal creatrix, Prakriti, mirrored in the present instance in Saroja's growth into womanhood. It is important to recognise that the focus is on Ramaswamy's attainment of self-knowledge; the emphasis is on a mystical, poetic apprehension and not on any psychological complex. Raja Rao does not really leave his intentions in doubt:[20]

> That Saroja was my sister made the knowledge of her womanhood natural to me—natural to see, to observe, and even to breathe—I prayed for Saroja, and knew in the eye of my eye, somewhere in the interstices of my being, I had named something I had not known yet—it was the absence that had become presence again; it was not Saroja I felt that I smelt, but something of the Ganges and the Jumna that rose into my being. Benares was indeed nowhere but inside oneself: 'Kashi Kshetram, Shariram tribhuvanam jananim.'

Clearly, what is witnessed here is not a Freudian landscape but an engaging transformation of similar looking vistas into an Indian inscape.

Critical ineptitude becomes even more glaring in the case of purely 'intellectual' approaches to the novel, Cerebration in Raja Rao, as distinct from the same in Mann or Rolland, does not have a rational, humanistic thrust, an inspiration for clear, logical presentation of ideas. This is not to imply that Mann or Rolland is less aesthetically motivated or imaginatively reassuring than is Rao. But, whereas Mann is often seriously engaged in arguing out the validity of a certain intellectual position, Raja Rao is concerned finally with revealing the 'serpent' quality of much of his discourse. The novel is occupied with a 'poetic,' 'saintly' task of delineating a certain way to truth; the narrator might profess an objective historian's approach,[21] but his subject matter by its very nature (neither 'unreal' nor 'real,' but what is in between the two—

'poetry,' 'sainthood'[22]) demands a more plastic, more poetic rendering. The fundamental thing to note about this novel is its deliberate choice of an a historical, mythical approach:[23]

> This happened, this happened so long ago, oh, as long ago as I have known myself be. Ever since being has known itself as being I have known it. It is the gift that Yagnyavalkya made to Maitreyi, it is the gift Govinda made to Sri Sankara. It is the gift He made to me, my Lord.

It is necessary to keep in mind the temper and experience reflected in this extract as one goes to evaluate the intellectual content of the novel.

At this point where the dynamics of action and thought in the novel are finally resolved, the protagonist comes to achieve only one knowledge, that of his ignorance heretofore, and has only one action to perform, that of dedicated inaction. All that is described and debated earlier has been coloured by this realisation. It is to be noted that neither a simple rejection or *vairagya,* nor a straightforward acceptance of some distinctly articulated intellectual position describes this culminating gesture. It may also be seen that many of the Indian philosophical and spiritual ideas which are reiterated in the novel do not receive any definite philosophical elaboration through the story. For instance, *vairagya* has has been invoked and dramatised on a number of occasions and in a variety of ways, but the Buddha remains only a haunting prospect. *Vairagya* as a developing spiritual theme is not dramatised, as is done in Hermann Hesse's *Siddhartha;* it is rather a poignant mood with which the story is reminisced. The tone of the novel would have been different if, either, the inherited, latent spirit of renunciation in Ramaswamy's 'Brahmin' consciousness had led him into positive non-attachment—not as a reaction but as a stimulus to Madeleine's *vairagya,* for instance—or, if the novel had been reminisced from a point when his establishment in *vairagya* with the aid of his *sadguru* was firm and secure. Similarly, reflections which connect themselves to Sankara's monism are perpetually kept under focus, but the realisation of its essence is confined only to a certain distrust of dualisms—I and thou, he and she, history and the moment, presence and absence, and so on. A positive monistic assurance is only hinted at as a liberating possibility, but not dramatised as an achieved, aesthetically articulated state. That is why a definite philosophical realisation does not constitute the climax for the novel. Not even the other alternative is advanced—the one emphasised in Forster's *Howard's End,* for instance—the view that truth may be apprehended only through a continuous process of integration and balance.[24] For Raja Rao it may be discerned somewhere behind and beyond the world of dualities.

And so *The Serpent and The Rope* is prepared as an epic evocation of certain attitudes and values, and not as a story of clear dialectical progression issuing from the certitude of positive synthesis. To that extent all the events and characters in it have a certain provisional, symbolic quality about them. They might appear to have been framed in a simplistic manner—just a study in contrasts—but in reality they are organised as a compact, interpenetrating body of references to project truth by indirection, through the togetherness of a number of tentative, poetic suggestions rather than as isolated pieces of definite assertion. That is why the novel achieves its logical consummation by leading Ramaswamy to the feet of his guru, a development which attests to Raja Rao's profound understanding of the Indian spiritual tradition (contrast the more humanistic organisation in *Siddhartha).* And only on this basis should its affirmations and intimations be evaluated. The presence of a clear body of ideas and values in it is not in doubt, but it occurs as an outlook, a received tradition and not as a developed logical structure. Once again, *Siddhartha* furnishes a helpful contrast: equally lyrical and meditative in its impulse, one can see how the story of *Siddhartha* is contrived against the background of a definite, logical development of a concept and a schema.

At the culminating point of the story where the restless voyage of Ramaswamy appears to come to an end and he casts anchor in the calm waters of the haven offered by the *Sadguru,* his sensitive intellectual faculty is meekly cast aside: he no longer tries to talk wisdom, but affirms in the action of his surrender the promise of a growth into wisdom. He solemnly declares that only now does he find himself on the threshold of truth which operates as a mystery of wordless wisdom, of action in repose. All the vast network of

ideas and words he had so prolifically spun in the past and all the
activities and relationships he had kept himself busy with, are now
reduced to a false vision—'the serpent.' The novel does not seek to
present any intellectual philosophical resolution of these dualities,
it emphasises instead the manner and necessity of their transcendence. All the emotionally charged situations, arresting intellectual
debate and pithy aphorisms through which Rama thought he was
making progress towards the truth now reveal their emptiness. The
description of his *Sadguru* is thus significant:[25]

> It sits on a riverbank, it sits as the formless form of
> truth, it walks without walking, speaks without
> talking, moves without gesticulating, shows without
> naming, reveals what is known. To such a truth was
> I taken, and I became its servant.

This is where the passion and the voiding of Savithri and Madeleine
have their proper resolution, and all that has been described in the
novel takes on a new significance from this height—only now, is
the rope in the serpent attested.

In a sense nothing radical takes place at the conclusion. For the
Indian spiritual tradition which is emphasised there as the way to
truth is already foregrounded from the beginning as the basis of
Ramaswamy's identity. But, significantly enough, the South-Indian
Brahmin has to wed a French girl and plumb the depths of European
cultural and religious traditions (to the extent of leaning towards
Christianity at one stage) in order that he may have a proper
awakening into the 'Krishna'-consciousness through his relationship
with an Anglicised North-Indian princess. He has to experience
Madeleine's Buddhistic renunciation and Savithri's Vaisnavite
enactment of the passion of a gopi, each case involving total
surrender of the self, a sacrifice of both the inherited and the
acquired identities, and a deep urge to fulfil oneself at some higher
plane of being. There are a variety of other experiences he has to
pass through, and discard, before he can achieve the right perspective
on the 'serpent.' These leaps from one cultural, psychological,
metaphysical position to another produce a complex emotive and
ideational pattern, intensifying the sense of multivalence generated
by constant shifts in the narrative voice. The basic design of the
novel consists of the projection of such a dense, complex universe

which should finally give place to a profound, controlled simplicity—from History to Guru. It is this which renders the novel so intimately Indian. The poetic, dream-like intimations, the view of life offered from a position above the conscious mind, the mythical scaffolding, and, finally, the surrender of a liberal-humanistic emphasis on human reason and personality, are the truly revealing qualities of its Indianness.

REFERENCES

1. 'Raja Rao does go on and on, and being curious and lively he thrusts upon us bits of scholarship, and innumerable reflections on masses of subject.'

   William Walsh, *Commonwealth Literature*, Oxford University Press, London, 1973, 10.

2. 'The question might arise: is this a novel at all? Is it not rather .... a compendium of interminable commentary and philosophising a book of discursive enquiry rather than narration?'

   'Since all is subjective illusion, there is no fixed reality upon which to build a novel, only a flux of impression and interpretations.'

   David McCutchion, *Indian Writing in English,* ('The Novel as Sastra'), Writers' Workshop, Calcutta, 1973, 86-87.

3. 'Never before has the subtle and tortuous mind of the cultivated Indian who is caught in the narrows of the ambiguous agonizing present been presented so engagingly and excitingly in a work of fiction—it is an attempt really to make the imponderables of 'inner' life seen reasonably logical and concrete, and it is besides, an attempt—a bold, adroit, sustained attempt—to set the English language to a prolonged articulation of Indian modes of thought and speech —.'

   K.R.S. Iyengar, *Indian Writing in English* (Second Edn.), Asia Publishing House, Bombay, 1973, pp. 405-406.

4. 'Where in any creative writing on the Indian scene before and after Raja Rao has one witnessed such high cerebration: wide-ranging intellectual interests, the shapely spirit of imagination which integrates the enormous reading, and the ability to bring it creatively so as to enlarge the sphere of interests and provide a perspective to our thinking —?' C.D. Narasimhaiah, *Raja Rao,* Arnold Heinemann, New Delhi, 1972, 126.

5. 'Its philosophical profundity and symbolic richness, its lyrical beauty and descriptive power—are of the stuff great classics are made of.' M.K. Naik, *Raja Rao,* Twayne's publishers, New York, 1972, 113.

6. '—a truly contemporary work—one by which on age can measure itself, its values.' Laurence Durrell, quoted in the Jacket of *The Serpent and the Rope*, Orient Paperbacks, New Delhi, 1968.

7. 'Raja Rao unearths metaphysical proposition everywhere ... abstract truth is

read into the smallest action, hence the interweaving of myths merely adds to the flux of general observations about cosmic truth.' Meenakshi Mukherjee, Twice-born Fiction, Heinematm Educational Books Ltd., New Delhi, 1971, 150.

'But Raja Rao growingly defies the novel form and uses it for philosophical essay, thus seeking to revive the *Yoga Vasistha* methods, with its pale cast of thought-exhorting men and women to seek salvation: Old theme New Myth, Recital *versus* N Novel,' Mulk Raj Anand, *Indian Literature of the Past Fifty Years*, C.D. Narasimhaiah (ed), University of Mysore, 1970, 119.

8. *Op. cit.*; 'Stinging edge,' 'self indulgent,' undiscriminating, pretentious, sentimental, vague, messiness, are some of the typical expressions liberally strewn across McCutchion's' essay.

9. R.K. Kaul, '*The Serpent and the Rope* as a Philosophical Novel,' The Literary Criterion, Vol. XV, No. 2, Mysore, 1980.

10. In his search for truth, Raja Rao gets out of touch with reality in its concrete modes. This is largely true of his character also. Rama, Nair, Savithri and Madeleine are all philosophers engaged in the pursuit of the impersonal reality. They often indulge in vain spiritual rigmarole ....

Raja Rao disinters metaphysical propositions everywhere (in *The Serpent and the Rope*) and the solid defining ties of human relationship are lost in the haze of philosophical abstraction and speculation. K.R. Rao, The Fiction of Raja Rao, Parimal Prakashan, Aurangabad, 1980, 25, 29.

11. *The Serpent and the Rope*, p. 166. (All references to the novel in this essay are to the Orient Paperbacks Edition, New Delhi, 1968.)

12. *Ibid.*, 167

13. *Ibid.*

14. *Ibid.*, 168.

15. *Ibid.*, 169.

16. 'The Indian aesthetic sense is based on an intuition of order which differs, for example, from the Euclidean harmony, of Greek and Renaissance order— I will tentatively suggest oneiric (Greek word—dream) as the most appropriate term to describe Indian art as a whole. We do not 'see' dream, but experience them as a simultaneity of multiple sensory impression and memories. Indian art is generally synaesthetic a mixture of media combined in a manner which resembles oneiric experience.'

Richard Lannoy, *The Speaking Tree*, Oxford University Press, London, 1971, 21.

17. 'Sanskrit drama from the Western point of view is that ultimate paradox, a Successful contemplative drama. It is psychological and spiritual rather than social, ethical, or intellectual.' 'Its ideal form is neither narratory, dynamic, nor centrifugal but metaphorically speaking, musical, plateresque, and magnetic.... A surprising part of their thought is metaphysical.' 'Repeatedly characters are presented as confusing reality and illusion. Dreams are of much importance. Time is relative, life is much more mobile than the

Western man has conceived it to be.' Henry W. Wells, The Classical Drama of India, Asia Publishing House, Bombay, 1963, 30, 32, 33, 92.

18. 'Raja Rao's refusal to temper the wind of his meaning to the shorn lambs of the reading public has made many a Western reviewer accuse the novel of obscurity.' M.K. Naik, 'The Serpent and the Rope: The Indo-Anglian Novel as Epic Legend,' Critical Essays on Indian Writing in English, Macmillan & Co. Delhi, 1977, 303.

19. The Serpent and the Rope, 69.

20. Ibid., 49, 50.

21. 'I am not telling a story here, I am writing the chronicle of a life—with the objectivity: the discipline of the historical sciences, for by taste and tradition I am only a historian.' Ibid., 231.

22. 'The world is either unreal or real—the serpent or the rope. There is no in-between the two—and all that's in-between is poetry, is sainthood. You might go on saying all the time, "No, no, it's a rope," and stand in the serpent. And looking at the rope from the serpent is to see paradises, saints, avataras, gods, heroes, universes. For, wheresoever you go, you see only with the serpent's eyes.' Ibid., 335.

23. Ibid., 403.

24. E.M. Forster, Howards End (Ch. XXIII): 'No, truth, being alive, was not half way between anything. It was only to be found by continuous excursion into either realm.'

25. The Serpent and the Rope, 403.

3

Stylistics in Raja Rao's *Kanthapura:* An Indian Response

PREM PRAKASH*

That Indian scholars of English should not use Western theoretical models in the study of Indian literature in English is made amply clear by many distinguished scholars. The significance and originality of Indian literary theory is now being gradually realized as an independent and mature discipline. In the changing conditions of modern life and literature, the time is ripe for the reorientation of literary theory. In such situations Indian (Sanskrit) literary theories could prove rather helpful and appropriate in comparison to Western theory in the study of Indian literature in English because in it are embedded the Indian ethos and mores of life and culture. These could be explored and understood well by the application of Indian literary theory. As Ganesh Sripad Balashastri observes:

> Our comparison of Eastern Methodology with the Western one, doubtless, proves that the former is in no way inferior to the latter, but is more fundamental and subtle from the philosophical and psychological points of view. Again it will be repeatedly noticed that the 'Hindu Schools of Thought' too have their own psychological ideas, on the basis of which they propound their linguistic theories and try to explain the process of verbal comprehension.

The Western critics have used historical, comparative and

*Department of English, Kashi Vidyapith, Varanasi.

analytical methods to examine *Kanthapura,* which throw light only on its outward features; the inner unity of the novel puzzles them as it grows and develops in our ancient oral tradition and culture with which they are not familiar. It was only in recent times that some of the critics and linguists tried to discover the inner vitality of such a work of art, using Indian methods about which some of the scholars have spoken in the following manner:

> Some were apologetic about Indian English as it was not British English or BBC English, Others asserted that Indian English was Indian English with a distinct vocabulary, phonology and syntax and not a pale imitation of British English. Indian English writing, one said, should not be judged by British standards but by Indian standards.

The need for the use of Indian methods in the study of Indian English literature is now being felt. But these methods have not yet been fully applied in its study. My endeavour, however, in writing this paper is to explore the stylistic features of *Kanthapura,* using our Indian methods which will throw fresh light on Raja Rao.

My focus is essentially empirical and linguistic. In the first part, I propose to Indicate how my stylistic study relates to certain literary theories and principles of Indian Acharayas and Sanskrit theoreticians, such as Shankarācharya, Gaudpadācharya, Bhartihari and Pānini, who have used linguistic theories of the Indian schools of thought to elucidate literary texts. In the second part, I shall apply these principles to *Kanthapura.* The third part would gather and generalize the findings.

I

Shakarācharya and Gaudpadācharya, among others, of the *Advaita Vedānta* say that a word is an illusionary form of the Absolute and that the distinctions between individual and genus are simply the conceptions of the mind. According to them the most expressive words pass beyond all distinctions of the individual and genus, etc., helping one to merge in the all-pervading silence of the Absolute. But according to the *Upanishadic* theoreticians such as Bhartrihari, Patanjali and Pānini, sound-essence symbolically called on *om* is the source of all names and forms of the universe. This sound as the compound of the three letters अ—उ—म indicates the three states: Wakefulness, dream and deep-sleep respectively. All human beings with their thoughts and speech have to pass through them.

A word, therefore, is a collection of sounds. It shows the transformations of thought or motif produced in relation to objects according to a particular order by the internal effort of the speaker. It consists of four attributes of an individual in language, viz., genus, quality, action and noun. Considering these attributes, Pāninī says that the sense of a word is both genus and individual. Out of these four attributes, genus is an attribute inherent in a thing which gives life to it. In other words, a word denotes an individual and connotes the genus, distinguishing the individual from dissimilar individuals by its peculiar form or configuration.

There are two popular methods which are used in the study of the words in a whole sentence: synthetic method and analytical method. The synthetic method represents the whole sentence with its various parts and sections using the vertical punctuation mark in order to denote the completion of a sentence. Thus, the construing of words in a complete sentence standing between vertical marks is designated as synthetic. Obviously, in the synthetic method all the words in a complete sentence are arranged according to their grammatical function and syntactical relation.

In the synthetic method, the subjects are generally picked up first and the verb afterwards; while in the analytical method, the verb, which is picked up first, is connected with the subject and the object by framing suitable questions. These two methods are based on the principles laid down by the *Naiyāīkas, Mimānsakas* and *Vaiyākaranas*. The *Naiyāīkas* are of the opinion that the subject is the principal word in a sentence; the *Mimānsaka* asserts that the verbal form is the principal word to which all other words in a sentence are related; and the *Vaiyākarana* holds the root meaning of a verbal form to be the most important. So the synthetic method seems to have its source in the theory of the *Naiyāīka* while the analytical method owes its origin to the theory of the *Mimānsaka*.

Shankaracharya was one of the most eminent and versatile luminaries of the ancient Indian tradition. His outlook was comparative. First, he realized the importance of combining the principles of words, sentence and logic for the exposition of the Vedantic philosophy, applying synthetic method. He was greatly influenced by Badarāyana who first systematized the Upanishadic philosophy in his *Brahmsutra,* and to his great Guru Gaupadāchārya also, who in his *Kārikā* on the *Mandūkyopanishad* showed the main outlines of synthesis. This is why Shankarāchārya accepts good points from all Indian systems and assigns to them a proper place in the wider scheme of his analytico-synthetic methodology. Thus, he concludes his *Bhashya* by saying that in the hypothesis of word-essence there is a negation of facts that are actually perceived and an assumption of what is not perceived.

With the same view Shankarāchārya observes that words are related to the eternal genus and not to the non-eternal individuals. According to the Vedāntas, there is an identity between an attribute and the thing possessing that attribute, *i.e.* between genus and individual respectively. The same cognition, therefore, that can cognize the genus can also cognize the individuals. The Vedāntins consequently maintained that the foregoing independent power of a word resides in an individual as well as in a genus, though in different degrees. In an individual it is latent or unknown though existent while in a genus it is expressed or known.

The most important point to be noted in the *Bhāshya* is that the unification of single letters into aggregates (words) is made by our synthetic mental activity and the meaning arises from such words in relation to things in the universe. The synthetic mental activity is continuously engaged in unifying letters into words, words into sentence, sentences into paragraphs, etc. and it helps us to apprehend the connected sense of a passage.

The Upanishadic philosophy embraces Bhartrihari's philosophical aspects of grammar. According to him, a sentence is the unit of language and that the analytical method of separating the form and affix of a word is an imaginary and artificial process of facilitating the understanding of beginners. Similarly, Patanjali has adopted in his *Mahābhāshya* the methods of etymology, dialogue and deduction. On the basis of Pāninī's 'Sutras,' he says that the sense of a word is for the genus and individual. The dialectic method of explanation followed by Patanjali throughout the whole of his *Mahābhāshya* assumed in the later commentaries on literature the definite form of analysis.

After Patanjali's *Mahābhāshya,* two important grammatical works were taken into consideration; the *Vakyapadīya* of Bhartihari and the *Kashikāvritti* of the joint authors Jayāditya and Vāman who were Buddhists. The *Vakyapadīya* mainly deals with the philosophical aspects of grammar and expounds in detail the theory of word-essence.

Kāshikāvritti is the best commentary on the *Astādhyāyi.* It explains each *Sūtra* with many suitable examples. Pāninī discusses in *Astādhyāyi* the analytical method of separating stem and affix of a word deriving it from a root. He availed himself of Yask's etymological method. Thus, he, being influenced by him, concentrates his attention on the verb as the ultimate element. His idea of the Nominal style of his *Sūtras* may be characterized as the omission of verbs and the significant use of case-relation. It was greatly appreciated by his followers.

In the light of the foregoing discussion on the literary theories and principles of the *Upanishads* and the Vedāntic systems, we shall see how far these principles can be successfully applied to the study of Raja Rao's *Kanthapura.*

II

Kanthapura is a monumental work. It describes the Gandhian movement against the British rule in India and how it reaches a south Indian village, Kanthapura. This movement quickens the process of social change in Indian villages from which starts the action of the novel centred on Moorthy who is the confluence of the three strands of experience that make up the action of *Kanthapura* : the political, the social and the religious. These three ideas of the movement are deeply rooted in the culture and motive of the people. Thus the entire atmosphere of the novel bristles with the Gandhian struggle and movement which increases the frontiers of human consciousness in India and later on assumes the form of global consciousness.

Gandhian consciousness is conveyed through Moorthy who transforms the life of an entire community, but the fact is that the story is narrated by Rangamma, an old lady who is able to evoke the Indian spirit of folk-epic, the *Puranas.* She uses typical local language and reacts to things directly and vividly.

Moorthy, as a Gandhian, organizes *bhajan, Hanikathā,* fasting and religious functions at Kanthapura Swami Temple. Through these religious functions, he creates national feelings in the minds of the uneducated villagers. These social functions became popular at that time and are performed by the major characters in *Kanthapura.* Raja Rao has used religious words from Sanskrit and modern Kannada literature in keeping with the context and bringing about some change in the formal English syntax. These words have a direct relationship with epic or *Purānic* myth (polarities between good and evil as exemplified in Rama and Ravana) which Raja Rao uses to describe the Gandhian struggle against the brute forces of the red-demon in *Kanthapura.* Moreover, Pan-Indian myth and the rites and rituals serve as a frame of reference, weaving in myth, legends and rituals which constitute the structural design of *Kanthapura.* Its study clearly shows that the villages in India are inveterate myth-makers; the gods of tradition, the heroes and heroines of epics jostle with historic personalities. The following lines testify to the fact:

> They say the Mahatma will go to the Red-man's country and he will get us Swaraj. He will bring us Swaraj, the Mahatma. And we shall all be happy. And Rama will come back from exile, and Sita will be with him, for Ravana will be slain and Sita freed, and he will come back with Sita on his right in a chariot of the air, and brother Bharatha will go to meet them with the worshipped sandal of the Master on his head. And as they enter Ayodhya there will be a rain of flowers.

Gandhi is an incarnation of Rama and the red-foreigners represent the ten-headed Ravana. The *Satyāgrahī'* (votary of truth) in prison is the divine Krishna. The novel portrays the whole drama of the Gandhian revolution, mixing politics with mythology, using ancient mythological devices in order to mix up south Indian folk-idiom with the emotional excitement of the characters in *Kanthapura.* These ideas are mixed up with the theme of *Kanthapura* and are writ large on its story. It contains a common heritage drawn from a common subject or theme. It is related to Raja Rao's outlook, culture and history which reflect his spiritual bent of mind, preoccupation with the national history, patriotism, and the simple Indian village, expressed through such words as *Bhajan, Upanishad, Sanyāsi, Harikathā, Panchāyat, Inquilāb Zindābād; Vande Mātaram; Maistrī, Mahatma Gandhi ki jai, Lāthi, and Pandāl,* etc. These are some of the common factors related to the remarkable features of his style which need to be isolated and studied. The study is, above all, concerned with Indian personality, lying deep in the mind of Raja Rao. There is reason to believe that the novelist has thought about the problems involved in the use of language and has made a deliberate effort to represent our national spirit. The issue is clearly set out by the novelist in the preface to *Kanthapura*:

> The telling has not been easy. One has to convey in a language that is not one's own the spirit that is one's own. One has to convey the various shades and omissions of a certain thought-movement that looks maltreated in an alien language. I use the word 'alien,' yet English is not really an alien language to us. It is the language of our intellectual make-up-like Sanskrit or Persian was before—but not of our emotional make-up.

Raja Rao's aim is to create a style which will reflect the rhythms and sensibilities of the Indian psyche, and since it is in Sanskrit that the Indian mind has found its most consummate linguistic expression; he has tried to adapt his English style to the movement of a Sanskrit sense.

Indian literary theories and principles forge insight into the various facets of literary writing—the personality of the author, his socio-cultural and historical background, his creativity in language, his attitude to life, and above all, the general flavour of his artistic personality. Raja Rao makes choice of linguistic items to suit his artistic personality and gives expression to his cultural bias reflected in his choice of vocabulary, in his typical Indian expression and idiom and in his syntax. Moreover, Raja Rao has made an extensive use of verbal illustrations in *Kanthapura* in the forms of parables, legends, myths, word-picture; familiar expressions and allusions which appeal to the imagination of his major characters, colouring the entire atmosphere of the novel. These catch up Indian sensibility and build up its form, covering linguistic aspects, such as style, felicity of words, phrases and rhythm. Besides, certain linguistic choices are related to Indian mythology, spiritual and cultural relations. These allusions might appear to be disgressive but they cohere with the total artistic milieu.

The conversion of a word should be understood with reference to an individual, since it is the individual alone that can become the object of sense-perception which is concerned with any concrete object or thing affecting the live senseorgans. Raja Rao has made use of a large number of words and expressions in order to express the Indian sensibility and ethos. A few of them may be taken here into account as examples from *Kanthapura*:

1. the ghats (1), 2. sandal and of sal (1), 3. 'he-ho' (2), 4. Zamindar (33), 5. Maharaja (32), 6. Bhajan (29), 7. Lathi (46), 8. Yoga (147), 9. Panchayat (103), 10. Hari-Om (102), 11. Karma (129), 12. Charka (27), 13. Vidya (146), 14. Patwari (33), 15. Goat-eyed (65), 16. Badmash (205), 17. Coolies (65), 18. Mandap (87), 19. Laddu and pheri (113), 20. Veranda (110).

Moreover, the author combined the local words to give a new structure. Pre-modification is more frequent than post-modification in *Knnthapura*. For example:

1. The Temple-square-Tamarind (41).

2. Dung-eating curs (212).

3. Corn-distribution Barber Venkata (134).

4. A Moon-Crowned god (191).

5. The bang-bang of the lathis (197).

6. Front-House Suranna (33).

7. Corner-House Narsamman's son (9).

8. Post-Office-House people (31).

9. Front-House people (33).

10. Your fire-tailed Hanuman (188).

The author has moulded the syntax to suit his artistic purpose. In *Kanthapura,* at several places, we find the literal translation of local dialects and proverbs. The following examples may be given from the novel:

1. If rains come not, you fall at her feet and say (2).
2. The air is empty (11).
3. How are the rains in your parts (34).
4. I'll drop a word in your ear (39).
5. Rangamma, you are a sister to me, and (41).
6. Every squirrel has his day (110).
7. I am no butcher's son to hurt you (41).
8. May be Ratna would be at the well (57).
9. You will take to evil ways (50).
10. You know you said you did not want daughter for your son (52).
11. Helpless as a calf (55).
12. Sons of concubine are planting well (19).
13. You sons of my woman (15).

At some Places in *Kanthapura,* we find typical expressions and local idioms which the author has translated into English in order to reveal the true nature and feelings of the characters. The following are a few examples:

1. Moorthy had gone through life like a noble cow (6)
2. Otherwise Brahminism is as good as kitchen ashes (40)
3. He was as honest as an elephant (12)
4. Why do you seek to make our stomach burn (2)
5. A crow and sparrow story (22)
6. Stitch up your mouth (84)
7. He wanted me to be his dog's tail (97)
8. Go and ask the squirrel on the fence (58)
9. I shall squash you like a bug (21)

Besides the above literal translations, the following lines contain some typical expressions in the form of abuse. Raja Rao has translated the traditional expressions and local *idioms* which appear rather unobtrusively in *Kanthapura.* For example:

Meanwhile Vasudev has arrived, and behind him Gangadhar and the men and the women, and from behind the bamboo cluster the maistri too, and the butlers from the bungalow, and then there is such a battle of oaths—'son of concubine'—son of a widow'— 'I'll *sleep with your wife*'—' *you* donkey's husband'—'you ass'—'you pig'—'you devil'—and such a shower of spittle and shoes, and 'Brother, stop there—'No, not till I've poured my shoe-water through his throat 'No no, calm your-self—'Oh you bearded monkey'—'Oh, you pariah-dog,' and as Moorthy forces himself up.

In the above passage, such linguistic factors as 'son of concubine, 'son of widow,' and 'I will sleep with your sister' are used. These are related to extra-linguistic factors; as culture, atmosphere, dialects and states of mind of the characters. They are an unavoidable component of Raja Rao's style. Their use is quite un-English. He has used them as part of an inbred idiom as there are no suitable expressions for them in English. Thus the novelist has tackled the problem of language by taking cultural words which his characters use in *Kanthapura* in their daily life. Such expressions refer to Indian myth and rituals. They may refer to epic or *Purānic myth*. The "sthala Purāna" (in the words of the author) and the rituals like that of natural *Ārti* with *Kumkum* and camphor censer. The story revolves round these three important elements of the narrative which determine the artistic design of *Kanthapura.*

The poetic account of the deeds of Gandhi and India's past history refer to Puranic myth because in it are mixed fact and fiction, myth and history, and the Indian atmosphere echoes through various ceremonies, rites and rituals—hair-cutting ceremony, rice-eating ceremony, marriage ceremony, and death-anniversary, from which emanate the social conditions of our villages, religion and spiritual resources of our people in the remote parts of India.

Raja Rao has moulded the dimension of language to distil the raciness and poetic non-stop narration in *Kanthapura* which create rhythmic and poetic quality in its fabric. Its unique pattern is based upon traditional Hindu culture, adopting current and political hymns which stir consciousness among the people in the country. These are expressed through extra-linguistic factors which show the upsurge of the people. For example:

> And as we began to march, it was not 'Satyanarayan Maharaj ki jai' that came to our throats but 'Vande Mataram'; and we shouted out 'Vande Mataram-Mataram Vande'; and then suddenly from the darkened Brahmin Street and the Pariah Street and the Weavers' Street and the lantana growths came back the cry 'Mahatma Gandhi ki jai,' and the police were so infuriated that they rushed this side and that, and from this courtyard and that garden, from behind this door and that byre, and from the tops of champak-tree and pipal-trees and tamarind-trees, from beneath—.[7]

'The Indian Schools of Thought' describe the common linguistic principle under the verbal testimony to the oral as well as the written tradition of intellectual and emotional subjects. The application of the interpretative methods of *Pada*, *Vākya* and *Pramona* shows the external linguistic signs or symbols of inner ideas, perceptual or conceptual, helping us to recall them. The *Meemānsaka*, in general, recognises the theory of class connotation of words which can be reconciled with the usage of 'Elders.' In *Kanthapura*, we find such concepts present in the talks of several characters, more particularly in Moorthy whose entire life is involved in the contemporary problems of the villages. More or less, he is an embodiment of the author's personality, and his language reveals the remarkable features of Raja Rao's style.

The use of Indian idioms, rhythm, tone and the distinctness of its vernacular make the style of Raja Rao unconventional. These are present in the natural speech of rural folk and have been translated into English. The fabric of *Kanthapura* is woven round this translation which creates seductive rhythm and power. The speech of the characters in the novel coils itself round one inextricably involving one in experience. The words which they use form streams of suggestions, creating waves of sound which make haunting music and develop a unique style.

There are three types of Nominal Style mentioned in the

Shāstras. The first is 'dialgoue type' which is essentially nominal and simple, chatty and lively. The second is 'Lecture Style' which, though nominal, is yet fluent and free from any kind of artificiality, and the third is the most 'artificial type' represented by the later works such as the *Shāstras.* The following passage exemplifies the Nominal style:

> Then once again Rangamma shouts 'Gandhi Mahatma ki jai !' and we all rush forward and the crowd rushes behind us and the gate creaks and breaks and we all rush towards the trees, one to this and one to that, to saplings and twisted trees and arched trees and anthills crumble beneath our feet, and the leaves tear and crunch, and the lathis break on our backs and hands and heads. And stones are thrown at the tree-trunks and pots break and spatter down and someone cries out 'Mahatma Gandhi ki jai !' and we rise with it, and we see up there on the top of the toddy tree is someone and he is cutting down branch after branch of the toddy tree and men after men gather them like sanctified flowers and women slip in here and crouch along there, and policeman after policeman tries to climb the tree, and one falls and everybody laughs and another goes up proudly and he slips down again, and the Police Inspector says, 'Moti Khan, you'd better try,' and as he is trying to go up the other policemen fall on us again, and we rush to this side and that, while somebody pulls down Moti Khan and the man on the top spits down on him, and a wave of laughter whirls up the toddy grove.

Raja Rao has made the use of short sentences which are involved or complex. Relative clauses in them are simple and frequently used. All these make his style nominal because in it case-relation is more important than the finite verb and it also shows the abundant use of noun-forms and its equivalents, scarcely of verb forms. At some places, we find the purposeful use of participles and case-forms like those of the ablative, the instrumental and long compounds. Compound words are somewhat freely employed. Raja

Rao exhibits lengthy compounds and complicated sentences. The order of the words, however, is not wholly arbitrary, since in the sentences, language-units (words, etc.) are used according to the natural sequence of thought. As thoughts change and recur, words are also repeated—such as 'here' and 'there.' Thus it appears that the recognition and repetition of separated words in the language and their combination into a sentence is made by the synthetic process. That is to say, in the beginning of a sentence, the words are first arranged, then they are repeated again and again.

III

Raja Rao asserts that the epic method is the most suitable for the individual temperament. "And our paths are interminable— Episode follows episodes and when our thoughts stop our breath stops, and we move on to another thought."

Specific quotations from *Kamthapura* show that the author's personality is deeply imbued in the literary-cultural complexes of a particular context. They also show the author's linguistic orientations. Raja Rao is given to those contexts in terms of syntax, vocabulary and a distinct register of language. The author evinces a strong interest in myth, in fact, he seems to be creating one specially infusing Gandhian ideas in an almost virgin soul. All this is done through collocation, derivation, and compounding of words, so basic to Indian stylistics. Three types of Nominal styles emerge— the dialogue, the lecture and the verbose. A glance at Raja Rao's syntax would show that it lengthens itself with the help of connectives. This only bespeaks the inexhaustibility of the content that would like itself to be incorporated at a single stroke of the imagination. And Raja Rao, of course, does it beautifully and comprehensively.

As we have said, the aim of the paper was to make an Indian response to the study of *Kanthapura*. This response embraces analytico-synthetic method, demonstrating that the episodic dimension characterizes its story as made out of events. Such events as Moorthy offering a dinner for each day of the month and collecting money for observing different festivals to unit people for social regeneration abound in the parallelism of identical occurrences which unify past and present. Likewise, Rangamma's story-telling, in a dramatic way, functions as a major source of parallelism and motif of occurrence. These artifices shape the narrative of *Kanthapura*.

The past mingles with the present and the gods with men in *Kanthapura*. Their mingling creates a powerful emotional flow in people involved in the freedom struggle. At that time there was a need of emotional integration to solve the problems of the country which created a great popular excitement. To express their emotional ideas, in their totality, in an alien language was a difficult problem. Raja Rao tackled this problem because he was well acquainted with the cultural traits and social conditions from which our language has evolved. He tried to express subtle nuances and emotional feelings by deviating from the accepted norms of language. Purposely he chose local typical expressions, idioms, collocations and symbolic words which were in common practice. These were appropriate to the changing conditions of the contemporary society. Meenakshi Mukherjee observes:

> She talks of the "pumpkin moon" (236), the streets "milk splashed" on a moonlit night (240), young boys "bright as banana trunks" (245), of "hearts tied up in sari fringes" (235). The metaphors are taken from familiar phenomena which would come naturally to a village woman. The character also enables Raja Rao to achieve his professed aim of reproducing the rhythm of Indian speech in English as well as of coming closest to the oral tradition of story-telling. In the now well-known preface to *Kanthapura* Raja Rao has stated that the meandering, repetitive manner of story-telling is not only an oral tradition but is also part of the literary tradition in India.

The choice of vocabulary, typical Indian expressions and new forms of syntax constitute the artistic personality of Raja Rao distinguishing his individual style from the styles of other Indian fiction writers in English. The English vocabulary achieves an Indian ontology and words evoke an Indian locality and an Indian tradition. Kenneth Burke said of Freud that Freud is a lexicon and it is not easy to contradict him unless one invents another lexicon.

The same could justifiably be said of Raja Rao who has created an idiom where the trans-temporality of words has become his own.

NOTES AND REFERENCES

1. These include Gowdah Aniah, C.D. Narashimhaih, M.G. Krishnamurthi, Meenakshi Mukherjee, Janet Powers Gemmili, William Clifford, Dorothy Spencer, Prof. William Walsh, David Mc. Cutchion, Hayden Moore Williams.

2. Huparikar, Ganesh Sripad (Balashastri), *The Problem of Sanskrit Teaching*, Bharat Book Stall, Kolhapur City, 1945.

3. Mohan, Ramesh (Edited) *Indian Writing in English*, CIFL. Hyderabd, Preface XVIII, 1978.

4. *Kanthapura*, First published, George Allen & Unwin Ltd. London, 1938, 258.

5. Preface to *Kanthapura*.

6. *Kanthapura*, 84.

7. *Ibid.*, 236.

8. *Ibid.*, 185-86.

9. Mukherjee, Meenakshi, *The Twice-Born Fiction*, Arnold Heinemann, India (Pvt. Ltd.), 1974, 39

10. Ricoeur, Paul, *Narrative Time, Critical Inquiry*, Autumn, 1980, 178.

11. Huparikar, Ganesh Sripad (Balashastri), *The Problem of Sanskrit Teaching*, published by Bharat Book Stall, Kolhapur City (India), 1949, 543.

12. Ali, Ahmed, *Illusion and Reality, The Art and Philosophy of Raja Rao*, The Journal of Commonwealth literature V, 1968.

13. Mukherjee, Meenakshi, *Raja Rao's Shorter Fiction*, Indian Literature, X3, 1967.

14. Patanjali, *Mahabhashya*, Mahamohopadhya Sri Gridhar Sharma (Edition), 1981.

15. Panini, *Astadhyayi* (Bhashya)-1-Bralunadatta 'Jigyasu Krit Hindu Tika' (1-3 'Bhag'), Chaukhambha Orientatia, Varanasi, Delhi, 1981.

16. Bhartrihari, *Vakyapadiya* (1-3 'Bhag'), Helraj, Virdhit Prakashan 'Vayakhya,' 1981.

17. Lodge, David, *The Novelist at the Crossroads and other Essays on Fiction and Criticism*, Routledge and Kegan Paul, London, 1971, 119.

4

"Raja Rao and Arundhati Roy's Indianization of English in Their Fiction"

MALLIKARJUN PATIL*

However, Albert C. Baugh, the English critic thinks that "Few people ever master a language not their own, and writings done in an alien speech rarely rise above the level of school exercises,"[1] now and then, it is true, some geniuses transcend these limitations and create literary works of universal merit. Indeed, writers like Joseph Conrad, Chinua Acheba, Mulk Raj Anand, Arbindo Ghose, Raja Rao, R.K. Narayan and many others have created an enjoyable body of literature in a language not theirs own.

Here the problem is of two dimension—one is related to the goods to be delivered, and the other, the way of its deliverance. No doubt, every writer has his own themes good or ill and he presents them coherently. But here the crux of our problem lies with the way of presentation, the use of language, the stylistic structures and the final effect. It is true, any work of art in literature should have a form and substance. As earlier said, here our concern is about form, say, how a writer should write a novel, or an essay. So it is all about the use of language.

No doubt English is the global language used by people across the world. People in England and America where English is the first language use it freely and properly. But in other countries, say

*Lecturer, Department of English, Gulbarga University, Gulbarga.

in South Africa, Pakistan or in India. English cannot be used as graciously as it is done in the UK and the USA.

However, people across the oceans write in English. They master the English idiom and employ it for their varied literary purposes. But in this regard at times what goes wrong is that sometimes English language is nativized or pidginized. In our context to put it in a nearer way by far, for good or ill, English is Indianised. Writers like Raja Rao, G.V. Desani and Arundhati Roy have used English in their own rights. Admittedly this is more so in the case of Raja Rao and Arundhati Roy.

Whatever might be the theme in his first novel *Kanthapura* (1938), in it, Raja Rao Indianizes English. The novel which is summed up as 'Gandhi and our village,' is but a Gandhi Purana in its narrative details. *Kanthapura*, being allegorical, is presented in a style that is exclusively Raja Rao's own. Here Indian sensibility is portrayed so brilliantly in an Indian idiom. In C.D. Narasimhaiah's view 'the words are English, but the organization is Indian and the novelist had to organise it himself.' Look at the following passage of the novel:

> And more and more women joined us, and children followed them, and old men followed the children, and there was a close silence, and everybody sat looking at the tight hall door, when suddenly it opened, and there was Ratna, and she said something to Seethu and Seethu said something to her neighbour and the neighbour said something to us, and we all gathered our sari-fringes and we waited, and the door opened again, and one of the boys came out, and with him was Pariah Madanna, and we said, 'So, he's back, he?' and we looked at each other and we looked at Madanna's wife and Madanna's wife smiled back at us knowingly, and we said, 'So, he, too, was only in the jungles,' and we said surely there are many others that have come back, and our stomachs heaved with joy. And more men came out of the hall, and there they were Puttanna and Chandrayya and Seethanna and Borappa and Potter Sidda—and the city boys, they were like princes fair

and smiling and firm, and one of the volunteers, the
one stood by the threshold, and said 'Sisters' there
is nothing to be frightened about.[1]

Mr. Raja Rao's English is Indianized here; his sensibility is
shown in its bones and blood, raw, rife, safe and sound, almost
evocative, startling but original. Phrases and expressions like Fig-
Tree-House people, Nine-beamed House Range Gowda, Moorthappa,
Waterfall Venkamma, pregnant second daughter's seventh-month
ceremony, 'If you are the sons of year father, Corner-house Moorthy
are nothing but Indian in colouring. In this regard, C.D. Narasimhaiah
says, "The emotional upheaval that overtook Kanthapura could
only find expression by breaking the formal English syntax to suit
the sudden changes of mood and sharp contrasts in tone, by
establishing a correspondence between perceptions and the images
he could readily lay his hands on in the life around and by a fresh
emphasis on old images and a completely different, in this case
Kannada, intonation to the English sentence. In other words, it had
to be a highly original style, a technical innovation indistinguishable
from an essential Indian sensibility.[2] The literal translation of images
like 'Maddur Seetharamu' or 'our Seetharamu,' plastic use of English
language like 'crush it in the seed' for 'nip it in the bud,' the native
expression and the Indian stylistic devices to suit a wide range of
human emotions are Raja Rao's pure contribution for the enrichment
of General Indian English (GIE). C.D. Narasimhaiah is right when
he says, "an outstanding contribution of Raja Rao to Indian writing
in English is to have struck new paths for a sensibility which is
essentially Indian."[3]

Similar is the case with Arundhati Roy. True, John Berger
should be accepted when he utters "Never again will a single story
be told as though it's the only one,"[4] because, though it is the old
wine, Roy has well displayed it in a new bottle—a bottle that can
tempt the reading public of any description to think over the use of
language. What a marvellous story Roy tells us here! In Sunil
Sethi's words, it is "A work of unusual range and depth and feeling,
all the more remarkable for finding expression in a first novel. It is
so well-paced, evocative and densely-plotted that it sustains the
tension and tautness of a thriller."[5] The story of the novel is that
Veluta, a dalit falls in love with Ammu, a Kutti of the Kerala

Syrian-Christian neighbourhood. But the social circumstances, or to put it in Roy's own image "'History-House' devours him, for he had violated the Love-Laws *i.e.,* that lay down who should be loved. And how. And how much..." Roy also makes use of biased communist politics of Kerala. In all, she tries her best to portray the themes of upper-class people's exploitation of lower, male-chauvinism and poisonous politics. *The God of Small Things is* certainly a break through novel, a novel about a tragic event but told a new, a 'banquet' for our reading. The Booker Prize cites "The book keeps all the promises that it makes" while in *Independent,* Boyd Tonkin writes, *"The God of Small Things* is an ancient drama played out against an unmistakably modern backdrop. It turns the clash of tongues and histories in Kerala into the motor of its comedy, its lyricism and its fine intelligence. And in doing so, it makes the remarkable Arundhati Roy a fitting standard-bearer for the immensely rich literature of India today."[6] True the subject of the novel as well as the master craftmanship of the novelist, particularly in regard to the native use of language, style and other literary devices, is unusually exceptional. There is the artistic, innovative and original imprint of the author in every sound, every word and every page of the book and the story resounds with the novelist's inner voice. The breathtaking beauty of the theme and the author's lawlessness in using language are both amazing and astonishing, original and chaotic, praiseworthy and condemnable. However, we cannot forget, Arundhati Roy has written *The God of Small Things,* a novel that brought her a big Cheque.

O.K.! Regarding the theme of the level, we have no head ache. But the use of language, or the utilization of stylistic inversions, or Roy's deviation from the standard language, has angered most of us—more specially the critics who are quite aware of the standards of language. Like William Wordsworth's breakthrough of the tradition of versification in his *Lyrical Ballads* or in its 'Preface,' in her novel, Roy has broken the ethics of language, or to put it mundanely, she has violated the norms of language as much as Ammukutty and Veluta violated the 'Love-Laws.' Roy has sufficiently forgotten the existence of a 'History House' in regard to the use of English. Of course, one has to use a living language, one cannot, or should not, brake the mode of a good means. Or can it be said that no writer is supposed to transgress the common limitations that are imposed by the standard English. For example, Kings English or RP is used by native speakers, while the English language users outside the UK and USA, follow either RP or American English. Or, they may, at the least or last, change this standard slightly. But only few writers have daringly violated the 'Love-Laws' of standard language.

'Alas! Arundhati Roy has broken the tradition of language' wrote Prof. C.D. Narasimhaiah, but people across the world, appreciated Roy for her erratic use of language. No wonder, John Updike tells, "A novel of real ambition must invent its own language, and this (Roy's *The God of Small Things*) does...."[7] Whatever might be the controversy upon the great success or downright failure of Roy's work, it is true, Roy has enriched English language by her bold innovations, breakthroughs, mishandling and verbal virtuosity.

A linguist, I hope, can timidly say that in her novel Roy has made a linguistic experiment. Roy's art of writing is new, surprising, incongruous but skilful. Here we find her deftly and daring rebellion against the accepted norms of language. The novel, however is full of newliness. Descriptions in part due to the lively words, phrases and expressions are really splendid. Roy's narration, because of her using of everyday speech, is Indianized. For example she writes:

> On the back seat of the Plymouth, between Estha and Rahel, sat Baby Kochamma. Ex-nun, and incumbent baby grand aunt in the way that the unfortunate sometimes dislike the co-unfortunate, Baby Kochamma disliked the twins, for she considered them doomed, fatherless waifs. Worse still they were Half Hindu Hybrids whom no self-respecting Syrian Christian would ever marry. She was keen for them to realize that they (like herself) lived on sufferance in the Ayemenem House, their maternal grandmother's house, where they really had no right to be. Baby Kochamma resented Ammu, because she saw her quarrelling with a fate that she, Baby Kochamma herself, felt she had graciously accepted. The fate of the wretched Man-less woman. The sad, Father Mulligan-less Baby Kochamma. She

had managed to persuade herself over the years that her unconsummated love for Father Mulligan had been entirely due to her restraint and her determination to do the right things.[8]

This passage of the novel consists of nine sentences. But three of them are ungrammatical while in the fourth (Half, Hybrids), in the seventh (Man-less), in the eighth (Mulligan-less) and in the ninth, glaring mistakes abound. However, these linguistic incongruities are judiciously used by Roy to heighten the effect of story. For example, the capitalization of 'Half-Hindu Hybrids' and hyphenization of 'Ex-nun' and 'Mulligan-less,' a proper noun are used exclusively for emphasis, while bracketing (like herself) is done for the sake of clarity. Besides, twice italicization of the word 'her' in the last line is meant for reiteration. This is not all. Everything is Indianized. Lively descriptions, meaningful statements, comic dialogues recur throughout the novel. Heartfelt expressions and sayings surely go in making the novel an interesting piece of art. See Roy's sentence or prose pattern in the following:

Who was he?

Who would he have been?

The God of Loss

The God of Small Things.

The God of Goose Bumps and Sudden Smiles.

He could do only one thing at a time.

If he touched her, he couldn't talk to her,

If he loved her he couldn't leave, if he spoke he
  couldn't listen, if he fought he couldn't win.

Ammu longed for him. Ached for him with the whole of
  her biology.[9]

Besides, there are passages and poems that can amuse any linguist:

> Fast faster fest
>
> Never let it rest
>
> Until the fast is faster,
>
> *And the faster's fest.*[10]

The implications of the word 'Police' are spelt thus:

Politeness

Obedience

Loyalty

Intelligence

Courtesy

Efficiency.[11]

An incursion of cookery wisdom:

Add the Pectin to concentrated juice. Cook for a few (5) minutes. Use a strong fire, burning heavily all around. Add the sugar. Look until sheeting consistency is obtained. Cool slowly. Hope you will enjoy this recipe.[12]

This recalls us a cook's modest guidance.

Certainly the novel's every para and page is full of linguistic absurdities exploited by Roy for her idiomatic presentation. Typical words, phrases, sentences, words wrongly constructed, sentences-broken and ungrammatical, or wordy, deliberate errors, needless brackets, italics, wrong structures of lines, syntactic inversions, beating the bush sensations, reverse words, repetitions, words running into other words, cliche, distorted words, coinages, foreign words, obscure expressions, typical imagery, vague abstractions all are there in *The God of Small Things*.

However, grand the tale of Roy's novel is, her Indianization of English has created much furor—namely we think that Roy has enriched English language but as a standard-bearer or trend-setter, she will mislead our future writers as well as language users. However, both Raja Rao and Arundhati Roy Indianized English, Raja Rao's experimentation does not misguide us as it is in the confines of our standards. But certainly Arundhati Roy's use of English is more harmful than any others.

REFERENCES

1. Albert C. Baugh, *A Literary History of England* (London: Routledge and Kegan Paul Ltd., 1950), 12.
2. Raja Rao, *Kanthapura* (London, George Allen, 1938), 226-27.

3.   U.D. Narasimhaiah, *Introduction to Raja Rao's Kanthapura* (London, George Allen, 1938), xvi.

4.   John Berger, The first page, *The God of Small Things* (Delhi, India Inc., 1997).

5.   Sunil Sethi, *"Outlook."*

6.   Ian Jack, *Independent on Sunday.*

7.   John Updike, *The New Yorker* "(cover page)."

8.   Arundhati Roy, *The God of Small Things,* 45.

9.   *Ibid.*, 330.

10. *Ibid.*, 104.

11. *Ibid.*, 304.

12. *Ibid.*, 196.

5

A Plea and a Cheer for Indian English: A Note on Raja Rao

ALESSANDRO MONTI*

In the opening pages of the novel *Kanthapura* (1938) by Raja Rao, the intradiegetic teller narrating the events speaks of the young hero Corner-House Moorthy as a "noble cow, quiet, generous, serene, deferent and brahamanic; a very prince."[1] Popular Hindu wisdom speaks through the voice of the brahmin widow, seen in her capacity as a witness-narrator. She draws her comparison from the sacred nature of cows, compressing the identity of the character into a few masterly and suggestive strokes of strongly idiomatic language, including the deflected use of verbal tenses, "Moorthy who had gone through life...."[2]

However, the "swadeshi" nature of her cow-oriented metaphor can be semantically arranged within a wider gamut of loan translations percolating from Standard English to Indian English. Later in the text, the same narrative voice comments on the favour the old mother Narsamma lavishes on her youngest son Moorthy, "the youngest is always the holy bull, they say, don't they!."[3] The idiom holy bull here at hand should be equated with the notion of a spoilt child in Western culture, minus the sting of deprecation.

The movement from the quotation of the usual Hindu devotional discourse to the more intimate sphere of the family circle is grounded in the field of a collective consciousness, embodying the "communal" voice of the village. To engraft the personalised idiom "holy bull"

* University of Turin, 10124 Turin, Italy.

onto a wider pattern of deflective usage, the intradiegetic narrator reports the direct transcription of a metadiegetic collective voice, introducing a "they say" form (structurally enhanced by the colloquial tag "don't they") as a marker of reliability, both in the biographical rendering of the character and in the verbal organisation of the mimetic discourse.

A reader ought to remember the analogous "people said" pattern Virginia Woolf makes use of in Chapter 5 of *To the Lighthouse* (1927). In both instances an authoritative but unspecified voice ("people" and "they") is introduced to add or to confirm information about a seminal character in the book. As a result, the level of narration is commuted into a second-degree narrative, which automatically draws attention to previous ellipses. The gaps such very concise or, rather "implied," retrospective analeptic fill in might be summarised as the following minimal story-lines: (a) Mrs. Ramsay and her former lover, (b) Moorthy and his doting mother.[4]

The hypodiegetic texture of the two passages is quite different, the former instance featuring an analeptic segment (or straight "flash back") which covers an ellipsis in the story-line regarding Mrs. Ramsay, the latter helping to confirm the narrator's account by means of a common linguistic consciousness she shares with the other inhabitants of the village. Instead of positing a mere retrospective segment as does Virginia Woolf, Raja Rao modifies the fixed rate of narration by going beyond the explicative function the hypodiegetic level usually takes care of. In his case, the words used to narrate the story-line are more important than the information we receive through them, the emphasis falling on the idiom "holy bull," rather than stressing the feeling a mother has towards a son.

In Raja Rao, the "don't they" tag marks the transition from a possible Standard use of English to its lexically and stylistically deflected Indian version, the textual echo of the encroaching violation being embedded not in the category of specific authorial innovations, but in the common voice of the rustic Kannada people. As a "holy bull," Moorthy is inscribed into the intimate and inner circle of traditional village life and of its untrammelled and timeless discourse.

The new measure yielded by the relocated idioms "noble cow" and "holy bull" is intensified and brought to major significance in the "Harikatha" sequence. The "Harikatha" (a folk spectacle mixing song, dance and recitation) is introduced into the novel to assess the genealogical lineage of Gandhi as a mythical fighter for the freedom of his own country ("deshi"). The peculiar flavour ("rasa") the passage is imbued with stems from the indirect quotation, in *Kanthapura*, of a similar tale of divine birth, found in the huge *Kathasaritsagara* by the medieval Kashmiri poet Somadeva.[5] In the old text the gods complain to Siva that the fiends "asuras," being reborn as "mlecchas" or barbarous foreigners, desecrate India and make waste of the land. Then Siva sends a "gana" (one of the host of his heavenly followers, whose chief is Ganesa, the god with the head of an elephant) to set things aright. In Raja Rao the sage Valmiki asks Brahma for a similar boon,

> since men have come from across the seas and the oceans to trample on our wisdom and to spit on virtue itself. They have come to bind us and to whip us; to make our women die milkless and our men die ignorant. O Brahma! Deign to send us one of your gods so that he may incarnate on Earth and bring back light and plenty to your enslaved daughter.[6]

The folk segment concerning the birth of Gandhi goes beyond the mere analeptic quality of a biographical sketch, giving information about the birth of a character; rather, it establishes the past event not as a fictional point of return from the present, but as an everlasting (or endlessly flowing) statement of truth which cannot be fractured into a "before" or an "after." Thus the figure of Gandhi is directly carved into the tablets of unbroken lore and literature. Consequently, the story told in the village of Kanthapura by the "Harikatha-man" is a further drop added to the eternally flowing and increasing "Ocean of stories," within which the British "rednecks" are but the last offshoot in a long line of "mlecchas" invading Mother India.

Despite its mythical setting and mode, the "Harikatha" passage conjures up a past which is *inside* the starting point of the fabula. Here the analepsis includes a hypodiegetic collective voice, a cluster of second-degree tellers which maintain, *via* their common identity, homogeneity of theme between the present and the tradition of the past. Moreover, the language of myth Raja Rao makes use of is skilfully rooted by him in the polite discourse of the Indian social setting, thus equating the everyday speech of the unsophisticated Hindu people with the words addressed to the gods or spoken by the gods themselves.

There is no difference in discourse and tone between the answer Brahma gives to Valmiki in the "Harikatha" passage and the "matchmaking" considerations of the brahmin woman speaking of Moorthy. If Brahma pronounces "O Sage, it is greater for you to ask or for me to say 'Yea'?," the brahmin voice mirrors with striking exactness the polite Indian way of capping with a request, "Achakka, you are of the Veda Sastra Pravina Krishna Sastri's family, and it is greater for you to ask something of me, or for me to answer 'Yea'?"[7]

A further instance of polite specific discourse, replacing Standard formal offers of the "would you like?—Won't you?" pattern with "deshi" forms of "courteous coaxing" may be found when the rebellious villagers of Kanthapura are *de facto* marooned by the British in the wilderness of the nearby mountains. Helped back to a friendly village, they are offered food and hospitality.

> And we all sit in the hall, and Subbayya's wife, Satamma, says, " 'Oh, take only this much milk, aunt!—Oh, only this banana, aunt!—Just this handful of puffed rice!,' and we are so tired that we say 'Yes, yes.'"[8]

A different kind of "coaxing" is brought to service when Moorthy has to persuade the brahmin women to hire a "Harikatha-man" to celebrate a string of Hindu festivals. He argues that these professionals are not too proud or too exigent in their requests, they don't ask for palanquins and howdahs. The sentence deploys two transfer insertions ("palanquin" and "howdah," the latter being "a covered passenger seat strapped on an elephant's back").[9] Both means of conveyance suggest royal pomp and honour, with a touch of effeminacy in the case of the palanquin (or palankin), if we consider such illustrative examples as the Portuguese remonstrance against its use, "In the territories of the Portuguese in India it is forbidden to men to travel in palankin as in good sooth effeminate a proceeding."[10]

A similar reference to the palanquin as an opulent passenger vehicle is made by Raja Rao in the first story in *On the Ganga Ghat* volume (1989), when the Indian university professor comes back to India and to Benares.

> 'Palanquin, Palanquin, leave the way, ho, for His Honour, the Palanquin'—this is how we should have been received at Mughal Sarai Station, but we're met by self-selling, high-turban adjusting taxi drivers, their chariots betoken of a forgotten dignity.[11]

The "incipit" focuses attention on the idiomatic quality of the narrated event, shifting back the rhetoric of language from Imperial English to Indianized English, with a finishing touch of "literary coinage."[12] Indian and European conveyances are perennially at odds in the British discourse on India; to quote an early Anglo-Indian source, on touring Benares Bishop Heber observes that

> No Europeans live in the town, not are the streets wide enough for a wheelcarriage: Mr. Frazer's jig was stopped short almost in its entrance, and the rest of the way was passed in tonjons, through alleys so crowded, so narrow, and so winding, that even a tonjon sometimes passed with difficulty.[13]

A "tonjon" (vulg. a "tomjon") is, or was, of course, "a kind of palanquin, *i.e.* a sort of sedan or portable chair...carried like a palankin by a single pole and four bearers."[14] The coinage a "chariot" for a taxi adopted by Raja Rao might be induced from the intermediate Anglo-Indian form "palkee-garry," "palki-gari" in old Hindustani speech, "gari" being the general Indian term for every wheeled conveyance. A "Palkee-garry" was "a carriage shaped somewhat like a palankin on wheels" thus the humble Oriental ancestor of our contemporary taxi-cabs.[15] As a result, the slightly puzzling idiom "chariot" translates the Hindi word "gari," which in its turn may be easily linked (through "palki-gari") with the more traditional "palankin," in a continuous lineage mixing by means of change and modification Standard (formerly Imperial) English and Indian Languages.

To conclude, it would be useful to make a brief observation on the heuristic quality the act of oral narration entails, either as a concise segment in *To the Lighthouse* or as a major function of voice in *Kanthapura*. The "people said" pattern of presentation in Virginia Woolf elevates gossip to the high status of truth, by which I mean the reliable reporting of past information. The trick recurs a few pages later again in Chapter 5, when the author shifts the scene from Mrs. Ramsay, sitting in the shabby room in her Skye house, to Mr. Bankes being previously on the phone with her in London. In the circumstance Mrs. Ramsay achieves a sort of sacred identity when Mr. Bankes focuses her in his thoughts as a mythical figure full of feminine grace and beauty.[16] The abrupt passage from trite everyday reality to the glamorous vision of an Olympian world of gods and semigods reverses the then-and-there perception the reader might have of Mrs. Ramsay as a middle-aged and rather worn out housewife. To catch the spark of the eternal Venus burning within Mrs. Ramsay, Virginia Woolf has to move backward in time and elsewhere in space.

It goes differently with Raja Rao. In this short preface to *Kanthapura* he connects the "unsophisticated" act of narration of the brahmin widow with a "sthala-purana," *i.e.* an old local story, amounting to a Greek myth of foundation.[17] Raja Rao claims that mythical tales are the seminal model for the narrative discourse of *Kanthapura*. His novel replaces the fragmented individualism of the modernist writer with a notion of shared experience and common heritage, both values being embodied in the perennial "hic et nunc" quality immanent in every Indian locality, whose soil has been trodden by real gods in their holy and manifold wanderings.[18]

In *Kanthapura* the vision of myth is not conveyed or suggested through the private vision of a single character (actually, a likely mouthpiece of the implied author, such being the case with Mr. Bankes in *To the Lighthouse*), but it is the expression and the consequence of a communal "genius loci," deeply rooted in the unbroken frame of timeless Indian tradition, in which past and present live together, since "time does not flow," to misquote Raja Rao.[19]

NOTES

1.   Raja Rao, *Kanthapura* (1938; Orient Paperbacks: New Delhi, 1971), 12.

2.   See R.N. Srivastava & V.P. Sharma, "Indian English Today," in S. Gupta and

Kapil Kapoor, eds., *English in India—Issues and Problems* (Academic Foundation: Delhi, 1991), 202. "IE is part of this exploding universe of English. There are two ways of looking at the non-nativeness in English. One way is to look at it as inadequacies and imperfections (mistakes) in second language acquisition, which call for immediate rejection or rectification. The other way is to accept them as deviations which are manifestation of the pragmatic needs of speech communities that employ English language for their social interaction. They may be called 'deflections.'"

3. *Kanthapura*, quoted, 51.

4. See Shlomith Rimmon-Kenan, *Narrative Fiction* (Routledge: London, 1991), the whole chapter "Text: Time." See 16 for a definition of a story-line.

5. The title means *The Oceans of the Rivers of Stories*. It was written between 1063 and 1081. See v. 2 XVIII lambaka, first taranga Visamasila. Cited from *"L'oceano dei fiumi dei racconti"* (Einaudi: Turin, 1993).

6. *Kanthapura*, quoted, 21.

7. *Kanthapura*, 12-13.

8. *Kanthapura*, 190.

9. *Kanthapura*, 18. For a definition of 'howdah,' see S. Muthiah, *Words in Indian English* (Indus: New Delhi, 1991), 82.

10. See Henry Yule and A.C. Burnell, *Hobson-Jobson—A Glossary of Colloquial Anglo-Indian Words and Phrases* (1886; Routledge and Kegan Paul: London, 1985), 660.

11. Raja Rao, *On the Ganga Ghat* (Vision Books: New Delhi, 1989), 9.

12. See "Indian English Today," quoted.

13. Reginald Heber, *Narrative of a Journey through the Upper Provinces of India*, 3 Vs. (John Murray: London, 1828), Vol. I, 371-72.

14. *Hobson-Jobson*, quoted, 390-91.

15. *Hobson-Jobson*, 664.

16. Virginia Woolf writes: "How incongruous it seemed to be telephoning to a woman like that. The Graces assembling seemed to have joined hands in meadows of asphodel to compose that face."

17. *Kanthapura*, quoted, see "Foreword." "There is no village in India, however mean, that has not a rich sthala-purana, or legendary history, of its own. Some god or godlike hero has passed by the village—Rama might have rested under this pipal-tree, Sita might have dried her clothes, after her bath, on this yellow stone, or the Mahatma itself, on one of his many pilgrimages through the country, might have slept in his hut, the low one by the village gate. In this way the past mingles with the present, and the gods mingle with men to make the repertory of your grand-mother always bright. One such story from the contemporary annals of my village I have tried to tell."

18. See C.D. Narasimhaiah, *No for Nobody: Autobiography of an English Teacher* (B.R. Publishing Corporation: Delhi, 1991), 1. "I grew up in a small town called Closepet on the Bangalore-Mysore highway. [...] Legend says that the

exiled Sri Rama rested on the hill wearied with wandering in the woods. And as Devi Sita felt thirsty, the valiant husband charged an arrow into the rock which opened to the gushing waters from the bowels of the earth below. And the fresh cool water formed into a pool with sturdy rocks holding it on the sides. It still glimmers in the sun while no one has dared to know its depth—an impious thought!."

19.   See quotation at the beginning of *On the Ganga Ghat* stories, "Water Does Not Flow," Sri Atmananda Guru.

6

Kanthapura: A Stylistic Feat in Indian English Novel Writing

GAJENDRA KUMAR*

Raja Rao's profound and philosophic knowledge of Indian life, his passionate attachment with the Indian National Movement and his literary quest to search a soothing and inspiring language for delineating his thought have got expression in his debut— Kanthapura. Kanthapura—a cohesive whole comprises the three distinct strands of experience—the political, the religious and the social are so dovetailed into one another as to present a panoramic picture of the revival in the 20s of this century. Rama Jha rightly analyzes the novel in her critical perspective and says:

"If the humanistic aspect of Gandhian thought influenced Mulk Raj Anand's treatment of social problems in his novels it is the metaphysical and spiritual aspect of it that shaped Rao's creative vision. Not that Rao is completely unaffected by the humanistic aspect of Gandhian thought, but he assimilated more deeply its spiritual and religious aspect."[1]

Theoretically *Kanthapura* deals with Gandhi, Gandhian revolution, its impact and Nehru on a small South Indian village caught in trouble and turbulent happenings of the national movement. The story covers the very volatile phase of Indian freedom struggle between Gandhi's Dandi March in 1930 to Gandhi-Irwin Pact in 1931. Raja Rao has presented the story in the puranic "Akkhyan Style"[2] which he terms in the 'Foreword" as Sthala Purana in which

---

*Lecturer in English, Rajendra College, Chapra.

"the past mingles with the present and the gods mingle with men..."[3] relieving and mingling the contemporaneous socio-political history with the rich and religious mythology. Iyengar makes it a point, "what happens in Kanthapura is by no means a unique experience, but the telling of the story gives the whole affair an itihasic—at least a Puranic dignity."[4] The entire action is set in a village, thus, the novel is at its best, considered to be a village novel having a record of its changeless and ever changing choice. The story of Kanthapura is beautifully narrated by a typical Indian grandmother—Achakka with her own idiosyncratic norm. Symbolically "Kanthapura is India in microcosm: what happened there is what happened everywhere in India during those terrible years of our fight for freedom."[5] In his de-facto analysis of the book Iyengar rightly summed up the stylistic feature of Raja Rao in his own way. He says, "Gandhi and our village, but the style of narration makes the book more a Gandhi Purana than a piece of mere fiction. Gandhi is the invisible God, Moorthy is the visible Avatar."[6] Moorthy, a prudent protagonist came under the spell of Gandhi while he was a college student. The author himself was bristling over with tantalising developments so he got himself involved in Gandhism as well as in search for a Guru. Psychologically the novelist's own self or psyche is projected so extensively projected in the mind and make up of Moorthy which becomes, however, inescapable and inevitable.

In the heart of the village there is a temple dedicated to Kenchamma, Great Goddess, Benign one. The organic picture of the village, ipso facto, is being constituted by a river, a hill and a temple with the presiding and all pervasive deity. The folk song pertaining to Kenchamma evokes in us images and attitudes meant for the people of Kanthapura. Kenchamma, the blood and bone of the village presents the core and cure of their lives and makes everything meaningful, There is a colourful context of the money-lender (Bhatta), the priest (Swami) and the Zamindar (Bhatta) which focus the traditional forces of oppression and exploitation. Moorthy, the Satyagrahi, the leader of the non-violent movement belongs to Gandhi in Kanthapura. Bade Khan is the embodiment of oppression, Bhatta stands for false orthodoxy. Range Gowda, indubitably, epitomises sense, sanity and honesty in the village. The village has been charged with deep and dense, abiding and all pervading localised colour and Charishma. To Raja Rao, literature is meant for spiritual experience, it is for him a theological thirst. Raja Rao himself argues:

"For me literature is Sadhana (spiritual discipline)... my writing is mainly the consequence of a metaphysical life, what I meant by Sadhana. And by man I mean the metaphysical entity. So the idea of literature as anything but a spiritual experience ... is outside my perspective."[7]

Gandhi is of the view that politics and religion are inextricably mated together, Kanthapura evinces this divine truth that man's status in the society is spiritual as much as it is political. In the ontological framework the theme of Kanthapura is the liberation of Indian spirit by Gandhian ideas while Brahma Dutta Sharma pinpoints that 'here Gandhism and Nehruian socialism have been presented as two alternatives... and there comes a stage when the protagonist and his followers resolve to embrace the political philosophy of the Nehruvian Socialism."[8] Kanthapura appears to be a dynamo of the Gandhian thought and theory. The leitmotif of Raja Rao in Kanthapura is his acute awareness of the spiritual "ideals and values of ancient India and its place and impact on the emotional make-up of the inhabitants of this South Indian Village during the period when Gandhi's personality and thought was a force to be reckoned with."[9] The novel is, in fact, as Iyengar says, "a veritable grammar of the Gandhian myth."[10] In Kanthapura religious fervour is blended with social realism in such a way that the ideas of Gandhiji are easily comprehended by the villagers. The impact of Harikathas is ennobling and innovating and even the old women cannot remain detached. Gandhiji had been a divine phenomenon. "He is a saint, the Mahatma, a wise man and a soft man and a saint" (23). It is worthwhile to suggest that the Dandi March has been portrayed as a pilgrimage. This is Moorthy, the Gandhian who keeps the village people *au fait* with the day-to-day activities of the Mahatma while he was on the Dandi March.

Gandhi rejected the tenet of Hindu Caste System, The opening of the temples to the pariahs whom Gandhijee called Harijan is an event of historical importance in the novel, Untouchability was considered to be a scar on the face of the society. It is, moreover, a revolutionary gusto in Kanthapura that the Brahmin boy Moorthy who becomes the spokesperson of Gandhian idealism and ideologies. In the Kanthapura, the chants of 'Satya Narayan Maharaj Ki Jai' changes into the shouts of '*Inquilab Zindabad*' and Gandhi Mahatma has come on this earth "to slay the serpent of the foreign rule" (22). When the Village Panchayat Committees are constituted Range Gowda finds Seenu as the "fire-tailed Hanuman" (111). In Kanthapura, all the plans and programmes of Gandhiji have been taken into account, such as non-violence, untouchability, prohibition and the way in which the women of Kanthapura under the leadership of Moorthy, Rangamma and Ratna came forward in the wake of the struggle. Such is the spirit of women of Kanthapura that their faith in Gandhi and in their goddess Kenchamma benign and bounteous, sustains their life spirit. It is, however, captivating that the spiritual force of the mother goddess is invoked again and again to enthuse people to action. This is the only language through which the political idea of India's liberation can be transmitted to the villagers. In fact, the novelist "locates the action of the novel in historical time, not in illusory space, for it provides a concrete representation of a significant aspect of Indian freedom struggle, in which the accent is on demonstrating Gandhi's main achievement of arousing the consciousness of the Indian masses against the British. Rao, of course, mythicises Gandhi and his mission, for purely strategic reasons."[11] In the theoretical stimulation of Kanthapura tradition and modern sensibility absorb each other and flow to foster society.

In Kanthapura both the matter and manner are equally good and grand. The use of tone and tenor, cadence and diction, the irony and humour and the sublimity in a language make the novel dazzling and delightful. The whole of the Indian tradition is brought up to date, along with its pertinent persuasions for the present, flows into the villagers, because it is rendered in and recommended to the villager's own idiom. Kanthapura proves to be a milestone in combating the colonial complex and winning respect for the Indian— Indian in form and content. Hence, it becomes a potent weapon for creative use of English for the expression of a truly Indian sensibility. Nowadays the novel has become a bright book of life and one of the effective means of education of the sensibility of the young,

Kanthapura is a breathless story, or stories illustrating a story, in the age-old Indian tradition of story telling. Structurally the novel operates on the village level and all the knowledge and wisdom that come to it or go out of it can only be at that level. It is a tale told by a grandmother from her rich repertoire, Thus, it can be said that, "Kanthapura is a supreme example of Raja Rao's grand style; it is an excellent realisation of his own dictum."[12]

The novel discusses the distinctive Indian sensibility with peasant sensibility even in the second language situation, The words are English, but the organisation is Indian and the novelist had to organise it himself. It helped him escape from the cliches and the elaborate prose style of the novel that had come down to us from the Victorian novelists. There is no linguist who wishes to keep abreast of current developments in his subject can afford to gloss over Raja Rao's theoretical pronouncements. Like philosophers and psychologists Raja Rao can draw upon in his discussion of the relationship that holds between language and thoughts. In fact, it is part of Raja Rao's case that linguistics, psychology and philosophy are no longer to be regarded as separate and autonomous disciplines. Man is clearly distinguished from other animal species, not by the faculty of thought or intelligence but by his capacity for language. Raja Rao's native use of the English language is to describe the ever-enlarging spheres of our relationships for example, "He is my wife's elder brother's wife's brother-in-law." Kanthapura reflects the whole of the social milieu of Indian women just in One coinage 'Kitchen Queen.' Stylistically the syntactic structure of long sentences, repetitions of names and words make the novel an archetypal. The authors in no way, suffers from the penury of the stylistic devices to suit a wide range of emotional or mental constructs. To Raja Rao, Kanthapura is inspired by a reading of Ignazio Silone's 'Fontamara.' The narrative mode used in both the novels perpetuates the oral tradition which is in consonance with the rural background of the novels. In 'Kanthapura' the story has been narrated in the first person narrative like 'Fontamara.' Raja Rao in 'Kanthapura' by using the spirit of 'Sthalapurana' highlights the esoteric significance or the local legendary history of a particular places. Silone also says in the 'Foreword' to Fontamara, "Let everyman then have the right to tell his tale in his own way" (16) and he further says:

"The art of story telling, the art of putting one word after another, one sentence after another resembles the ancient art of weaving, the ancient art of putting one thread after another one colour after another, clearly, tidily, plainly for all to see."[13]

Silone in 'Fontamara' has used the oral tradition of story-telling in his own way. In an interview Raja Rao explores the Puranic strain in his novel Kanthapura:

"The aesthetic is that, sometimes, I like to write like a Purana. I like the Puranic conception, that is the only conception of novel for me. I don't want to compare my novel with any foreign novel. I am very much an Indian and the Indian form is the puranic form. Form comes naturally to me."[14]

A close textural analysis of the novel crystallises this fact that linguistics is an empirical sciences whose purpose is to construct a theory of human languages. Raja Rao employs a daring and highly meaningful experiment in language, a language deliberately adapted from the archaic Sanskrit tradition of story telling. In order to catch the full flavour of the Indian speech and rhythm in English, Raja Rao has put the whole story in the mouth of an old widow, different from the intonations of the King's English. In the opening of the novel Rao says:

"Our village—I do not think you have ever heard about it—Kanthapura is its name, and it is in the province of Kara" (7).

Raja Rao's spiritual doctrine presented in 'Kanthapura' has a Puranic pattern fundamentally suits the socio-spiritual cosmic insight articulated in the novel. The epigraph on the title page of the novel is full of Vedantic nuances focusing the doctrine of incarnation as nucleus of the philosophy of Avatar. The novel has a consistency in its narratology and prophetic utterances without any subsequent chapterisation. In 'Kanthapura' Raja Rao has, ably, shown "an epic breath of vision, a metaphysical vigour and philosophical depth, a symbolic richness, a lyrical fervour and an essential Indianness of style."[15] Therefore, it would be relevant to comment that. "The experimentation that Raja Rao hinted at was of the creation of a mode of expression which could give the real flavour of Indianess to the Western readers besides the meanings and values of Indian life in a language comfortably accessible to Indian people."[16] The description of the pastoral life and the linguistic use of the Puranic form for all the facts of language behaviour adequately purports Raja Rao's critical venture to evolve a literary form rooted in the indigenous soil. C. Paul Verghese explores the stylistic facets of Raja Rao in his own words:

"It (*Kanthapura*) is a novel written entirely in a manner that is the author's own; it has, because of the skilful adaptation of the English language to incorporate the idiom and rhythm of the regional language and because of its theme and local colour, the texture of a novel written in an Indian language—a rare feat in English."[17]

NOTES AND REFERENCES

1. Jha, Rama, *Gandhian Thought and Indo-Anglian Novelists*, Chanakya Publishers New Delhi, 1983, 86.

2. Rao, K.R., *The Fiction of Raja Rao*, Aurangabad, 1980, 60.

3. Rao, Raja, *Kanthapura*, Orient Paper Back, Delhi, 1972, (Foreword). All Subsequent references are to this edition.

4. Iyangar, K.R.S., *Indian Writing in English*, New Delhi, 1962, 392.

5. Narasimhaiah, C.D., Raja Rao's Kanthapura: An analysis in *Critical Essays on Indian Writing in English*, Karnataka University, Dharwar, 1968, 273.

6. Iyengar, K.R.S., *Indian Writing in English*, 391.

7. An Interview in *The Illustrated Weekly of India*, 'Raja Rao, Face to Face' January 5, 1964, 44-45.

8. Sharma, Brahma Dutta, Raja Rao's Kanthapura: A plea for the Nehruvian Socialism in *Points of View*, Summer 1999, Vol. VI, No. 1, Ghaziabad, 84.

9. Prasad, Anil Kumar, *The Village in Indo-Anglian Fiction*, Novelty and Company Patna, 1994, 50.

10. Iyengar, K.R.S., *Indian Writing in English*, 396.

11. Dhar, T.N., History, Myth and the Post-Colonial: The Indian Context in *Interrogating Post-Colonialism, Theory, Text and Context* ed. by Harish Trivedi, and M. Mukherjee, Shimla, 1996, 144.

12. Rao, A.V., *The Indo-Anglian Novel and the Changing Tradition*, Wesley Press, Mysore, 1972, 144.

13. Silone, Ignazio, *Fontamara*, Jonathan Cape, London, 1934, 16.

14. Niranjan, Shiv, "An Interview with Raja Rao" in *In Writing in English*, ed. K.N. Sinha, New Delhi, 1979, 20.

15. Naik, M.K., *Raja Rao*, New York, 1972, 145.

16. Kumar, Gajendra, *Indo-Anglian Novel Criticism: Tradition and Achievement*, Novelty and Company, Patna. 1999, 58.

17. Verghese, C. Paul, *Problems of the Indian Creative Writer in English*, Somaiya Publication, Bombay, 1971, 146.

7

Myth in Raja Rao's *Kanthapura*

I

A primitive habit of the mind, myths are the life-blood of contemporary literature. They are living parables which the writers of archetypal vision imaginatively indulge in. For Richard Chase, it is "literature and therefore, a matter of aesthetic experience and the imagination, and as such, it has a fictional character which is imaginatively true" ("Foreword," *Quest for Myth*, 1969: vi). Myth is expressive of the total vision of the human situation, human destiny, human inspiration and apprehensions. It is an aesthetic channel to ventilate, explore and re-create the experience of the self in relation to the past, a mode of expression of the labyrinthine interaction of the self and the society. Most of the myths, whatever they may have meant to the ancient or savage man, are to us meaningless and shocking; shocking by their cruelty, obscenity and by their seemingly silliness—almost what seems to be insane and eerie. The great myths like Orpheus, Demeter and Persephone, the Hesperides, Balder and Ragnarok emerge like elms out of this rank and squalid undergrowth. Even certain stories which are not myths in the anthropological sense have "mythical quality." Such are the plots of *Dr. Jekyll and Mr. Hyde*, Well's *The Door in the Wall* or Kafka's *The Castle*. Extra-literary, the aesthetic pleasure of myth depends hardly at all on such usual narrative attractions as suspense or surprise.

*Department of English, Rourkela Municipal College, Rourkela.

Human sympathy in a myth is at a minimum. We do not project ourselves so vigorously into the characters which are like some mysterious shapes moving in another world. The pattern of their movements has a profound significance to our own life, but we do not imaginatively transport ourselves into theirs. The story of Orpheus moves our pity and sympathy. It makes us sad but we are sorry for all men rather than vividly sympathetic with him. Often fantastic, myth deals with impossibles and preternaturals. Whether a sad or a delightful experience, myth is always grave and solemn. The experience is not only grave but also awe-inspiring. We feel as if "something" very grave and profound has been communicated to us. The incessant and recurrent efforts of the mind to conceptualise this "something" are manifested in the untiring and persistent tendency of humanity to provide myths with allegorical elucidations. Myths are contemplated as well as believed. Dissociated from ritual but based on them, myths are held up before the fully awake and conscious imagination of a logical and contemplating mind. Since we define myths by their effect on us, it is plain that the same story may be a myth to one man but a fact to another. The value of myth is not a specifically literary value, nor the appreciation of myth a specifically literary experience. The degree to which any story is a myth depends chiefly on the person who reads or hears it. The same book can be merely an exciting yarn to one whereas it may be something of a myth to another. Harry M. Johnson points out that most myths "have to do with the origins—the origin of the gods, of the world, of culture, of certain features of nature. Others myths have to do with the "stories of exploits of the gods or exploits or miraculous events in the lives of religious leaders" (*Sociology* 1980: 405). By living the myths we are transported from "chronological" or "clock-time" to "sacred" or "primordial" time. We move from a definite and concrete plane of existence to an indefinite and an abstract world, from the real to the seemingly unreal. Culturally sacred precedents for present actions, myths are necessarily and traditionally believed by many. Max Muller feels that mythology is the result of a "disease of language" (Qtd. Chase, *Quest for Myth*: 140) because the mythical language manifests itself in symbols, fantasies, rituals, metaphors, words, indicators and objects. The binary opposition between the form and the expression gives rise to the myth. A narrative resurrection of a primeval reality, myth caters to our deep religious wants, moral cravings, social submissions, even practical requirements. It is a strong preservative of tradition, not a dogma. Myths are "constantly regenerated; every historical change creates its mythology" (Chase, *op. cit.*: 79). Eric Gould maintains; "Myth is a synthesis of values.... It is allegory and tautology, reason and unreason, logic and fantasy, waking thought and dream, atavism and perennial archetype and metaphor, origin and end" (*Mythical Intentions*, 1981: 28). Whereas to Northrop Frye, "a myth ultimately means mythos—a structural organizing principle of literary form" (*Antomy of Criticism*, 1973: 136). Myths apparently derive their universal import from "the way in which they try to reconstitute an original event or explain some fact about human nature and its worldly or cosmic context" (Gould, 1981: 06). "The ancient myths" says Rajesh Pallan, "survive in the modern times with all their problematic intensity as they deal with the numinous and the sacred" (*Myths and Symbols*, 1994: 08). Thus, myths are the mirrors that reflect man's inner self thereby discovering the depths of the Unconscious. Products of creative fantasy, they interpret human life in the modern context and make us aware of our existence.

II

Quite a few modern writers have made a deft integration of myths into the thematic fabric of their works. They have emphasised the efficacy of the integrative mythology. James Joyce in *Ulysses*, T.S. Eliot in *The Waste Land*, Eugene O'Neill in *Mourning Becomes Electra* has dexterously and deliberately woven their contemporary material on the mythic parallel. Writers like Thomas Mann, Kafka, James Joyce, Yeats, and Eliot are some of the major writers who have "deployed mythical/archetypal modes of expression in an age during which man has grown absurd, not quite aware of his identity or destiny and when a transvaluation of all values has become the order of day" (B. Das, *IJES*, Vol. XV; 1974: 162). The mythical mode of narration consists in "manipulating a continuous parallel between contemporaneity and antiquity" (Eliot, 1964: 16). The ancient myths and legends are used by these writers to highlight the similarities and contracts between the past and the present. Through

the mythic mode of narration as well as a thematic dispensation of
it they control, order and give "a shape and significance to the
immense panorama of futility and anarchy, which is contemporary
history" (*Ibid*). Myth can be used for compression as well as for
expansion. Eliot's *The Waste Land* is an instance of the former and
James Joyce's *Ulysses* is an instance of the latter. Use of Myth
helps in telescoping the vast canvas of the theme within a short
space. Eliot uses the myth as an "objective-correlative" which
serves as a mirror reflecting his emotions and ideas. The creative
sensibility expresses reality and subjectivity through the creation of
myths. Hence myth plays a vital role in the elucidation of human
condition and human identity. The modern man reckons a new
meaning and design through his mythical experiences. Jung's
observations in this context are quite relevant:

> Myths have a vital meaning. Not merely do they
> represent, they are the psychic life of the primitive
> tribe, which immediately falls to pieces and decays
> when it loses its mythological heritage, like a man
> who has his soul. A tribe's mythology is its living
> religion whose loss is always and everywhere, even
> among the civilised, a moral catastrophe (*The Modern
> Mind*, 1965: 645).

According to Richard Chase, writers are attracted to myth primarily
because "it is literature itself" (*Quest for Myth*, 1969: vi).

III

The Indian English novelists have nourished their moorings on
their own Indian past. They have dovetailed their mythic experiences
with the experience of the immediate present. The ancient culture
of India has provided the mythic backdrop to their literary
explorations and discoveries. They have harked back to the
mythology of their own culture to carve out significant patterns of
fiction. But one striking feature of these writers is that they hardly
or seldom draw their material from the Graeco-Roman or Judaeo-
Christian mythical frame-work. On the other hand these Indian
English Writers often and with ease, draw on their Indian myths
because, as Meenakshi Mukherjee opines: "The Indian people are
still closer to their mythology than the modern Irish or British

people are to Celtic folk-lore or Greek legends" (*The Twice Born Fiction*, 1974: 131). The people in India still listen to *The Ramayana* and other recitals with zeal and eagerness. The Indian psyche is moulded and transformed by our mythological and legendary tales. It is conditioned by the stories from the *Panchatantra*, *The Ramayana* and *The Mahabharata*. Hence Pandit Nehru has aptly observed:

> I do not know of any books anywhere which have exercised such a continuous and pervasive influence on the mass mind as these two... (*The Ramayana* and *The Mahabharata*)...they are still a living force in the life of the Indian people (*The Discovery of India*, 1974: 99).

Why does the Indian Novelist in English make a liberal and easy use of the myths and legends? Does he do it for thematic purpose or with certain didactic and ethical point of view? Meenakshi Mukherjee has given a lucid and cogent explanation for the abundance of mythic paraphernalia in Indian-English Novel:

> If a world-view is required to make literature meaningful in terms of shared human experience, then the Indian epics offer a widely accepted basis of such common background which permeates the collective unconscious of the whole nation (Mukherjee, *op. cit.*, 131).

The "inexhaustible vitality" (Narayan, *Gods, Demons and Others*, 1979: 15) of our classical mythology has helped the Indian novelists to delve deep into our past experiences and discover a link between it and our contemporary existence. This has also made the delineation of the contemporary reality/absurdity more lucid and more meaningful. Sudhin N. Ghosh holds that the collective psyche or rather the societal psyche/consciousness of any period is reflected in the mythology of those people: "Myths tell us more than bare facts. Men would die for their favourite myths, but not for bare facts and imposing statistics" (*Cradle of the Clouds*, 1951: 90). Myth did not find a much important place in the writings of the earlier Indian English Novelists. It is only with the later Indo-English novelists like Suddhin N. Ghosh, Raja Rao, Mulk Raj Anand, R.K. Narayan and B. Rajan that myth came to form an integral and corporate part of Indian Writing in English. Most modern literature, according to P. Lal is ignorant of the Indian myths. "The only possible revival" of these myths, according to him, "will take place if one's own myth-values and structures are studied and loved and absorbed and used with creative and critical imagination" (*Aspects of Indian Writing in English* [ed.] Naik, 1979: 16). Rajesh Pallan maintains:

> The use of myth is discernible in Indian-English novel on two planes—the digressional and the structural. In most mythological novels, the use of various myths does not offer a scaffold upon which the modern experience has been erected...the myth is simply being used in most cases to offer some kind of looser analogy (*Myth and Symbols in Rao and Narayan*, 1994: 19).

The Indian English Novelists do not merely offer myths as analogies, but make them their central thematic or structural principle. In these novelists, the mythological parallel serves as an analogy (as in Anand's *The Old Women and the Cow*) to the contemporary world which forms the back-drop of the novel and this parallel also forms the thematic motif (as Radha-Krishna motif in Raja Rao's *The Serpent and the Rope*). But Sudhin N. Ghose and Raja Rao make a digressional use of the myths. Their digressional technique is akin to the ancient Indian technique of narration. Their works are replete with (1) Puranic myths, (2) Localised myths which Rao calls "Sthalapurana" and (3) Rites and Rituals. The concept of "matra or the sense of propriety" (Pallan, *op. cit.*, 19) is another recurring feature of Ghose's works. In Raja Rao, there is the mythologisation of the contemporary reality. Each Indian English novelist casts the myth in his work in his own unique way. Narayan (in his *The Man Eater of Malgudi*, 1961) makes a structural use of the myth. In his other novels, he uses it in a digressional manner. B. Rajan makes a rambling and spasmodic use of the myth. Mythical allusions in *The Dark Dancer* (1959) and *Too Long in the West* (1961) are desultory, referential and arbitrary. They hardly integrate into the structural design of the work albeit they do have some but marginal thematic purport. Tagore too (in his *Two Sisters, The Wreck* and *The Garden*), has made a significant, use of the myth (esp. thematically). Mulk Raj Anand makes a structural use of myth (in *The Old Women and the Cow*). His use of the myth is from technical point of view. It is a part of the technique. Writers like Anand do not make an imitative, rather, a slavish use of the myths and legends. On the other hand, they recreate these myths for themselves and make an imaginative and fictional use of them by embodying them with new meanings and values. They remould and recreate these myths and legends to fit into the frame of contemporaneity. In fine, the Indian English novelists have made an explorative and innovative use of the myths and legends, thus giving them a new artistic dimension and value. Hence myths impart a new significance to our contemporary existence and "fill the ontological gap between the events and the meaning" (Pallan, *op. cit.*, 21).

IV

Raja Rao makes a digressional use of myth. Myth meanders through the fabric of his fictional canvas. In the "Foreword" to *Kanthapura*, he observes:

> Episode follows episode, and when our thoughts stop, our breath stops, and we move on to another thought. This was, and still is, the ordinary style of our story-telling. I have tried to follow it myself in this story (*Kanthapura* 1971: 06).

Rao employs three types of myths in his novels: (1) Puranic Myths, (2) Localised Myths and (3) Rites and Rituals. The Puranic myths pertain to the binary opposition of the good and the evil symbolised through the characters of Rama and Ravana. The Rama-Ravana myth appears to be the central thematic motif in *Kanthapura*. The novel is a fictional rendering of a localised myth (such as that of Kenchamma), it is the legendary history of a remote hamlet in the Western Coast of India. In order to create the mythic atmosphere in the novel, Raja Rao has resorted to the depiction of rites and rituals of ploughing, of worship and sacrifice. *Kanthapura* is the legendary history of a place or village—what Rao calls the "sthala-purana." The "rites and rituals," observes Meenakshi Mukherjee, "do not form part of myth but provide a frame of reference" (*Twice Born Fiction*, 1971: 139). For instance, the offerings of coconut and betel

nut at the altar of the deity are frequently found in Rao's *Kanthapura*.
Through the telescoping of the past through myths and legends and
relating it to modern context or contemporaneity, Raja Rao has
presented a viable picture of the Indian reality. He has mythologised
contemporary reality. In *Kanthapura*, we have the use of the myths
which are inextricably and intimately connected with the religious
beliefs and practices of the people and are communicated through
symbols. A novel of political resurgence, *Kanthapura* is strewn
with many myths which have been deftly woven into the fictional
canvas of the story. The Puranic myths have been depicted to
dramatise selfless action as expounded in the *Bhagwad Gita*. Murthy
becomes the symbol of selfless action, symbol of the Mahatma.

It is again the contemporary Indian Reality, the freedom struggle
in a tiny hamlet that becomes the cynosure of the action. Taking
recourse to various myths, Raja Rao conveys vividly and most
lucidly "the whole ethos of Indian villages" (Raizada, *Perspectives
on Raja Rao* [ed.] Sharma, 1980: 197). In the "Foreword" to the
Kanthapura, Raja Rao stresses the topical significance of the myth:

> There is no village in India, however mean, that has
> not a rich *Sthala-Purana*, or a legendary history of
> its own. Some god or god-like hero has passed by
> the village—Rama might have rested under this pipal
> tree. Sita might have dried her clothes, after her
> bath on this yellow stone, or the Mahatma himself,
> on one of his many pilgrimages throughout the
> country, might have slept in this hut... (05).

The village deity Kenchamma has a mythical semblance of the
Puranic tales. Her divine presence smacks of the deities in the
ancient legends and myths presiding over the fate of the human
beings. The Kanthapurians are ardent devotees of Kenchamma.
They chant hosannas to her which reminds one of "Durga Stuti":

> Kenchamma, Kenchamma Goddess, benign and
> bounteous, Mother of earth, blood of life, Harvest
> Queen rain-crowned, Kenchamma, Kenchamma
> Goddess, benign and Bounteous (10).

"The story of Goddess Kenchamma settling in Kanthapura," says
Rajesh Pallan, "finds a mythical parallel in the *Ganga-Purana*"

(*Myths and Symbols in Raja Rao and Narayan*, 1994: 26). Like Goddess Ganga, Kenchamma comes down from the Heavens to rescue the Kanthapurians from the draconian rule of the Whitemen, the *phirangis*:

> Kenchamma is our Goddess, Great and bounteous is she. She killed a demon, ages, ages ago, a demon that had come to ask our young sons as food and our young women as wives. Kenchamma came from the Heavens—it was the sage Tripura who had made penances to bring her down (8).

The fight of Kenchamma with the demon brings to our mind the tale of Goddess Durga killing the brute Mahisasura, as depicted in the *Devi-Purana*. Look at what Achakka says about Goddess Kenchamma:

> And she wages such a battle and she fought so many a night that the blood soaked and soaked into the earth and that is why, the Kenchamma Hill is all red (8).

The Kanthapurians resign all their problems to the will of Goddess Kenchamma, so much so that they invoke her grace and benedictions to destroy the English in India. Hence we find that Raja Rao resorts to the localised myth of Kenchamma to elucidate the conflict between good and evil. Like Chinua Achebe's *Arrow of God* (1962), the divine power of Kenchamma is omnipresent in *Kanthapura* to direct, control and preside over the life of the villagers. Several myths have been associated with the river Himavathy, the daughter of Kenchamma. Like the Mother Ganga, Himavathy sustains us, protects us. Several myths have been woven round this river. People say, "the Goddess of the River plays through the night with the Goddess of the Hill" (08). Range Gowda says: "I drank three handfuls of Himavathy water, and I said, 'Protect us Mother' (258). "Himavathy" is to the Kanthapurians what "Ganga Mata" is to all Indians. A reality as well as a fiction, a myth as well as a fact. The legend runs that the river Himavathy, while "in high spate, stood silently to allow the last rites of the pious Ramakrishnayya to be performed" and after the last rites were over, it carried away "in fury all that remained of the holy Ramakrishnayya in the form of ash and bone" (146). The other legend associated with the river Himavathy is related to the Chandals of the warrior Rajput Clan who lived at Khajuraho. Meenakshi Mukherjee elaborating on the function of legend says, "as soon as the local legend has been narrated and established, its function becomes the same as that of a more well-known myth" (*Twice Born Fiction*, 1971: 135). Raja Rao creates the Sthala-purana in projecting the dedicated and selfless deeds of the local Mahatma, *i.e.* Moorthy. "The impact of Gandhi," observes C.D. Narasimhaiah, "was that of a traditional religion" (*Raja Rao*, 1973: 43). Moorthy is the "Gandhi incarnate" or you may say a "Mini-Gandhi" who instills the fire of revolution among the Kanthapurians. Like Godot in Samuel Beckett's play, *Waiting for Godot*, Gandhiji does not appear as a person but his spiritual presence is pervasive throughout the novel. Moorthy, the village Gandhi, is also all-pervasive in Kanthapura and his character has been mythicized. Like the Mahatma, Moorthy leads the Kanthapurians, the little "soldier-saints" (181) of the village, known as "Satyagrahis" who follow "selfless action" (Niskama Karma) as enunciated in the *Bhagwad Gita*. This galvanization of the dormant and slumbering hamlet into action is to Narsingh Srivastava "the metaphysic of selfless action expressed through Satyagraha" ("Image of India" in *Indian Scholar*: 58). Moorthy's character is idealized in the novel to the extent of being regarded as a local Mahatma because a myth "necessarily deals with an idealised man or a man larger than life" (Mukherjee, *op. cit.*, 141). Moorthy is Jesus Christ to the Kanthapurians. He has come to deliver them from sin and suffering. He is their "Gandhi" (109). They say with exultation, "he is the saint of our village" (135). Range Gowda, the village headman, describes Moorthy as "our Mahatma" (109).

To elucidate and explicate the theme of redemptive suffering in human society, Raja Rao "takes the myth of suffering more directly self-imposed to absorb the evil of others" (Alphonso Karkala, "Myth, Matrix and Meaning in Raja Rao" in K.K. Sharma [ed.] *Perspectives on Raja Rao:* 79). Like the chief characters in myths which are mythicised by exalting and elevating them above the common rung of humanity, Moorthy too is presented as an exalted and dignified character. In mythicising the protagonist, Raja Rao adheres to the classical tradition. Moorthy is not only mythicised but also idealised.

Mulk Raj Anand does not idealise the character of Bakha or Gandhi in *Untouchable* and even in *Gauri*. In spite of parallel resemblances between Gouri and Sita in regard to the theme of passive suffering, Gauri's character is not mythicised in such an ideal manner. Gauri turns down Sita's lot, her stance in life and explores a new way for herself. Anand uses myth for illuminating and exposing a character like Gauri or for elucidating and projecting the contemporary predicament of woman. On the other hand Raja Rao almost substitutes the mythical characters with the contemporary ones in *Kanthapura* in such a dexterous manner that one can hardly discern a difference between myth and reality in the novel. The blending of myth and reality is almost perfect and meticulous in execution. The Rama-Ravana myth has its associations with the 'good' and the 'evil' forces used in the novel in order to portray the struggle for independence from the British Rule. The freedom movement is equated with the *Mahabharata Yudha*. There the divine powers of Lord Krishna regulate the war and here the invisible and redemptive presence of the Mahatma control the actions of the Kanthapurians. The illiterate narrator, Achakka, mingles the fact of subtler thoughts of the Mahatma in the contemporary situation with the legends and the myths as embedded in the *Ramayana* and the *Mahabharata*. *The* legendary heroes are "inextricably mixed, linked up with the historical person" (Rao, *The Fiction of Raja Rao*, 1980: 55). Mahatma Gandhi is thus described as the incarnation of Rama and Krishna, born to liberate Mother India from the draconian rule of the demons, Ravana and Kansa. The Harikatha-man, Jayaramachar, mythically narrates the birth of Mahatma Gandhi on the request of Sage Valmiki to Lord Brahma. Thus Raja Rao harnesses the Puranic style to describe the birth of the Mahatma who was sent to this world by Brahma for destroying evil and restoring good. Prof. Srinivasa Iyengar feels that "the style of narration makes the book more a 'Gandhi Purana' than a piece of mere fiction. Gandhi is the invisible God, Moorthy is the visible avatar" (Iyengar, *Indian Writing in English*, 1984: 291). By mythicising Gandhiji's character, the freedom struggle has also been consciously mythicised.

Gandhi's character in *Kanthapura* has been highly idealized like that of Rama in the *Ramayana*. Like Rama, Gandhi is described as a reincarnation of the Almighty. His psychological presence in the novel lends a mythical aura around his saintly figure. The exploitation of the Indians in the hands of the Britishers was immense. Like Ravana, the British had come to kidnap our "political freedom," *i.e.* our 'Swaraja' (257). Gandhi's visit to England to attend the Round Table Conference in 1931 is described in terms of the Indian mythical tradition. It is like Rama's visit to Lanka to save Sita from the hands of Ravana. Sita is our 'Swaraj' and Ravana 'the British.' The ever-present Indian mythos, at length "absorbs he characters and history it has all along been bathing and overwhelming" (Guzman "The Saint and the Sage," *Virginia Quarterly Review*: 39). Gandhi has further been compared with Lord Shiva. The Kanthapurians invoke the grace of Brahma, the Creator, by apprising him of the tyrannous rule of the Britishers. They beseech Brahma to send them one of his Gods so that he may incarnate on Earth and retrieve India from the demonic grip of the British rulers. Brahma pronounces:

> Siva himself with forthwith go and incarnate on the Earth and free my beloved daughter from her enforced slavery.... The messengers of Heaven shall fly to Kailash and Siva be informed of it (22-23).

Gandhi's idea of Swaraja has been compared with the three eyes of Shiva: "Siva is the three-eyed, and Swaraj too is three-eyed; self-purification, Hindu-Muslim unity, Khaddar (20).

The whole situation and characters in the novel are mythicized where the past mingles with the present and the gods mingle with men. Prof. K. Ayyappa Paniker feels that "the divine or the supernatural is deeply involved in the human and the natural predicament in *Kanthapura*" (*Commonwealth Literature* [ed.] Narasimhaiah, 1981: 109). Gandhi is also compared with Raja Harishchandra. Raja Rao writes:

> Like Harishchandra, before he finished his vow, the gods will come down and dissolve his vow, and the Britishers will leave India, and we shall be free, and we shall pay less taxes and there will be no policemen (172).

Gandhi is compared to Harishchandra because he resisted all worldly and mundane temptations as a means to ahimsa.

The battle between the 'suras' and 'asuras,' is a recurrent motif in the Hindu mythology and in Kanthapura too, we have the fight between the Britishers (asuras) and the Indians (suras). The tussle between the Satyagrahis and the agents of the British Govt. is symbolic of the clash between the suras and the asuras. The Skeffington Coffee Estate is the world of asuras in miniature. The morally corrupt British officials there let loose a reign of terror and Mahatma Gandhi, the 'Sura' comes to save these people. Alone doesn't he come. He comes with his 'Vanar Sena,' the 'Satyagrahis.' Good and Virtue triumphs at the end and the whole freedom struggle culminates into a sort of mythological war between Rama and Ravana, "suras' and 'asuras.'

Through the character of the "Swami," another 'asura,' Raja Rao has sarcastically portrayed the Indian natives joining hands with the British to betray Gandhi's fight against the 'Goras' for attaining freedom. The agents of this Swami act as "agent provocateurs" to subvert the 'Rama-Ravana myth' and exercise their diabolic designs to dissuade the villagers from joining Moorthy's non-co-operation movement. Ironically and almost bathotically, the Swami's agent compares the British Government with Rama and Mahatma Gandhi with Ravana.

Alphonso Karkala rightly opines that Raja Rao's "time module in *Kanthapura* can be easily seen in the life of the living village which, having evolved to Kaliyuga, dissolves towards the end like a Pralaya..." ("Myth, Matrix and Meaning" in Sharma ed. *Perspectives on Raja Rao*, 1980: 78). Things fall apart and centre cannot hold. Indeed things do fall apart in Kanthapura when people like Bhatta, Waterfall Venkamma and the Swami's agent start fomenting chaos by joining hands with the corrupt British rulers. Anarchy is let loose upon the Kanthapurians. The evil influence of Kaliyuga is evidenced in Satamma's words:

> After all, my son, it is the Kaliyuga floods and as
> the sastras say, there will be the confusion of castes
> and the pollution of the progeny. We can't help it,
> perhaps... (43-44).

The end of the novel is like the end of Kaliyuga with the Pralaya engulfing the whole village. All the villagers leave Kanthapura at the end of the novel, to settle down in Kashupuru. Range Gowda finds that "there is neither man nor mosquito in Kanthapura" (258). Like Tiresias in Eliot's *The Waste Land*, Achakka, the narrator in *Kanthapura*, serves as a link between the past and the present. An unlettered woman, she mingles myth and fact in her natural manner of reflection and observation. Achakka reminds us of Shelley's 'West Wind.' Like it, she is a symbol of transformation, of rebirth and resurrection and "the myth becomes so open-ended that dissolving itself continues to live again in another formulation and not definitely concretized" (Karkala, *op. cit.,* 80). In his interview with Shiva Niranjan, Raja Rao states:

> I like to write like a Purana. I like the Puranic conception, in fact, that is the only conception of novel for me. I don't want to write like a foreign novelist. I am very much an Indian and the Indian form is the Puranic form ("Myth as a Creative Mode," *Commonwealth Quarterly*: 50).

The tale of *Kanthapura* is told in the Puranic style embodying myths and legends. It has also "the breathless garrulity of the Puranas without attempting at formal organization" (Rajesh Pallan, *Myth and Symbol in Raja Rao and Narayan*, 1994: 38). Raja Rao's purpose of writing in the Puranic fashion is stated in the "Foreword":

> *The Mahabharata* has 214,778 verses and *The Ramayana* 48,000. *Puranas* there are endless and innumerable. We have neither punctuation nor the treacherous 'ats' and 'ons' to bother us—we tell one interminable tale. Episode follows episode, and when our thoughts stop, our breath stops, and we move on to another thought. This was and still is the ordinary style of our story-telling. I have tried to follow it myself in this story (6).

Besides this, the prose descriptions of nature, surroundings and happenings are also reminiscent of the 'Puranas': "Kenchamma lies curled up like a child on its mother's lap" (191); the dead-body of Ramakrishnayya washed and tied to the bamboo and "behind the jack fruit the sun rose like a camphor...and when the waters were still girdling in the gutters, the procession hurried on" (145-146).

The description of Ramakrishnayya's death is reminiscent of the account of Nature's response to the death of Karna in *The Mahabharata:*

> ...when Karna fell, the rivers stood still.... The earth uttered loud roars.... The mountains with their forests began to tremble and all creatures felt pain [Roy trans. *The Mahabharata*, 1956: 283]

In *Kanthapura*, Ramakrishnayya's death is also described in mythical tones:

> And that night sister, as no other night, no cow would give its milk...and calves pranced about their mothers and groaned.... Lord may such be the path of our outgoing soul (101).

T.S. Eliot uses the mythical technique in *The Waste Land* to interpret and criticise the present-day world but Raja Rao uses this technique to glorify the present, to laud it and impart to it the dignity and grandeur of the 'Puranas.' The novel is replete with rituals especially in relation to the celebration of festivals like 'Sankara-Jayanthi,' 'Rama-festival,' 'Krishna-festival' which lend a mythical halo and fervour to the novel. Achakka says that the festival of lights (Dipavali) is celebrated in the month of Kartik "so that when darkness hangs drooping down the caves, gods may be seen passing by, blue gods and quiet gods and bright-eyed gods" (118).

Long poetic descriptions of nature, evocative and symbolic are a feature of the Puranas, esp. the *Bhagwad Purana*. Kanthapura too has such lyrical and poetic descriptions which are prose-poems. The advent of 'Kartik' is described thus:

> Kartik has come to Kanthapura. Kartik has come with the glow of lights and the unpressed footsteps of the wandering Gods.... Kartik is a month of the gods, and as the gods pass by the Potters' Street and the Weavers' Street, lights are lit to see them pass by (118).

The performance of various rituals lend a mythical frame of allusion to the novel. The Kanthapurians offer goddess Kenchamma 'saree' and 'gold-drink' to ward off the malefic influences. During the ploughing time, the villagers wait for the 'Rohini' star to 'yoke their bulls to the plough' (151). Ploughing is considered to be fruitful only if the omen of the Eagle—the vehicle of Goddess Kenchamma, shows itself. The villagers light bonfires and sing and dance in Kenchamma's honour. When Moorthy is in prison, the Kanthapurians sing 'bhajans' with "cymbal, conch and camphor, clapping hands and droning drums, the perfume of the sandal paste, flowers in the hair and in our eyes, Shiva's eyes" (156). Fasting, as an important ritual is undertaken by the villagers to gain divine grace and appease the gods. Moorthy undergoes fasting several times. The congregational worship ritual for appeasing Kenchamma is another instance of the mythic fashion and style. Ratna offers "ten coconuts and a kumkum worship" (98) to Kenchamma for the recovery of Moorthy. Satamma feels that "it was our Kenchamma, she tore a rag from her saree fringe, and put it into a three piece bit, and a little rice and an areca nut, and hung it securely to the roof" (79). Rice and coconuts are to the Kanthapurians, traditional symbols of fertility, of prosperous marital status of a lady, a shaven head without kumkum, *i.e.* a widow, is considered inauspicious. Besides creating a mythical ambience, rituals in the novel are "a device for concretising the point-of-view" (Meenakshi Mukherjee, *op. cit.,* 142). Deeply steeped in local chores, the narrator, Achakka, assimilates the contemporary reality into a mythical frame of structure.

The time bound dispensation of myth in relation to the contemporary predicament in *Kanthapura* serves as a parallel to the concept of the timeless. The interweaving and dovetailing of the myths, legends and rituals transforms contemporaneity into the eternal histrionics between virtue and vice; good and evil; gods and demons and the time and the timeless. Through Achakka's narrations, Raja Rao achieves a deft and artistic blending of the mythical and the real. As a result, the novel becomes a "glorious myth...as profound as a shastra, and as prolific as a 'purana,' yet in its brevity and verbal economy, it excels in capturing excessive critical imagination" (Alphonso Karkala, *op. cit.,* 82). Prof. Srinivasa Iyengar calls *Kanthapura*, a "Gandhi-Purana," as it echoes the high majesty and grand dignity of the Puranas. Myths and symbols in the novel occur as an artistic and a creative mode of conveying "a meaningful world-view of human reality in terms of shared human experience" (Raizada, *op. cit.*, 196). Thus, there is a perceptible mythical pattern in *Kanthapura*. The use of Indian myth is like *The Ramayana* lend a fairy tale charm, a romantic aura to the novel and stimulate our imagination. These myths transport us to the remote times in the past when gods, demi-gods and superhuman beings played a vital role in our lives, the days when myths regulated our emotional and intellectual actions.

WORK CITED

Alphonso Karkala, John B. "Myth, Matrix and Meaning in Literature and Raja Rao's Novel, *Kanthapura*," *Perspectives on Raja Rao* (ed.), K.K. Sharma, (Ghaziabad: Vimal Prakashan, 1980).

Ayyappa Paniker, K. "Man and God in Indian and African Fiction: A Study Based on *Kanthapura*, *Arrow of God* and *Mookajji's Visions*," *Commonwealth Literature: Problems of Response* (ed.), C.D. Narasimhaiah (Madras: Macmillan, 1981).

Chase, Richard, "Foreword," *Quest for Myth* (New York: Greenwood Press, 1969).

Das, B., "Myth, Criticism and its Value," *The Indian Journal of English Studies*, Vol. XV, 1974.

Eliot, T.S., *The Sacred Wood* (London: Mathuen, 1964).

Frye, Northrop *Anatomy of Criticism: Four Essays*, (Princeton: Princeton University Press, 1971).

Ghose, Sudhin, N., *Cradle of the Clouds* (London: Michael Joseph, 1951).

Gould, Eric, *Mythical Intentions in Modern Literature* (Princeton: Princeton University Press, 1981).

Guzman, Richard R., "The Saint and the Sage: The Fiction of Raja Rao," *The Virginia Quarterly Review.*

Iyengar, K.R. Srinivasa, *Indian Writing in English*, (New Delhi: Sterling Publishers, 1984).

Johnson, Harry M., *Sociology: A Systematic Introduction* (New Delhi: Allied Publishers, 1980).

Jung, C.G., "Archetypes of the Collective Unconscious," *The Modern Mind* (ed.), Ellmann and Feidelson, (London: OUP, 1965).

Lal, P., "Myth and the Indian Writer in English: A Note," *Aspects of Indian Writing in English* (ed.), M.K. Naik, (Delhi: Macmillan, 1979).

Mukherjee, Meenakshi, *The Twice Born Fiction* (New Delhi: Arnold Heinemann, 1974).

Narayan, R.K., *Gods, Demons and Others* (New Delhi: Hind Pocket Books, 1979).

Narasimhaiah, C.D., *Raja Rao* (Delhi: Arnold Heinemann, 1973).

Nehru, Jawaharlal, *The Discovery of India* (New Delhi: OUP, 1974).

Niranjan, Shiva, "Myth as a Creative Mode: A Study of Mythical Parallels in Raja Rao's Novels," *Commonwealth Quarterly*, Vol. 4, No. 13, 1980.

Pallan, Rajesh K., *Myths and Symbols in Raja Rao and R.K. Narayan* (Jalandhar : ABS Publications, 1994).

Raizada, Harish, "Point of View, Myth and Symbolism in Raja Rao's Novels," *Perspectives on Raja Rao* (ed.), K.K. Sharma, (Ghaziabad: Vimal Prakashan, 1980).

Rao, Raja, *Kanthapura* (Delhi: Orient Paperbacks, 1971). (Subsequent references in parentheses in the paper are from this edition of novel).

Roy, P.C. (trans.), *The Mahabharata* (Calcutta, 1956), rev. ed., Vol. VII).

Srivastava, Narsingh, "The Image of India in the Novels of Raja Rao," *Indian Scholar*, Vol. 2, No. 1, 1980.

8

Mythic Narrative in Raja Rao's *Kanthapura*

K. RATNA SHIELA MANI*

Myth is and has always been an integral element of literature. According to Alan W. Watts, "Myth is to be defined as a complex of stories—some no doubt fact, and some fantasy—which, for various reasons, human beings regard as demonstrations of the inner meaning of the universe and of human life."[1] Mark Schorer said that "myth is fundamental, the dramatic representation of our deepest instinctual life, of a primary awareness of man in the universe, ... upon which all particular opinions and attitudes depend."[2] The rediscovery of mythology as an encyclopaedia of psychological types and universal emotions stimulated writers to take a new interest in the old myths, thus, making it essentially a twentieth century phenomenon. One reason why poets and writers have been drawn towards myths and legends is their quality of timelessness. Myths, though they do not correspond to contemporary reality, do have for that particular group of men to whom they are culturally relevant, a kind of fundamental significance.

Myth is seen manifesting itself in two ways in literature, the unconscious and conscious use of myth. There are literary works where the writer may not be aware of using a mythical situation, but critics have discovered them; for example, *Hamlet* which Gilbert Murray traced to a primitive myth connected with the ritual battle of Summer and Winter, of Life and Death. This kind of archetypal

*Assistant Professor, Department of English, Nagarjuna University, Guntur.

criticism claims descent from anthropology and Jung's theory of archetypes and racial memory.

The Conscious use of myth by writers is a literary device and part of a modern method—the method of Eliot in *The Waste Land*, of Joyce in *Ulysses*, of O'Neill in *Mourning Becomes Electra*. The old myths often return touched with a new radiance and immediacy of appeal. T.S. Eliot's *The Family Reunion* is a fresh rendering of the myth of *The Eumenides* of Aeschylus, and *The Cocktail Party* of *The Alcestis* of Euripides. Eliot, Joyce, O'Neill and other differ widely in their techniques and intentions, but there is one element common in their diverse methods: each of them uses mythical (or classical) situations or characters in a modern context, thereby seeking to illuminate the predicament of contemporary man, viewing him a larger perspective of time. Eliot praised Joyce for having invented a 'mythical method' or a 'continuous parallel between contemporaneity and antiquity' which enables a modern writer to give 'a shape and a significance to the immense panorama of futility and anarchy which is contemporary history.'[3]

The Indian people, as a whole, are even today close to their mythology than the modern European people are to their own lores. But in comparison to the European writers, the Indian English writer seems to have made very scant use of myth in his works. It is only in the nineteen fifties that we find any significant use of myth in the Indo-Anglian novel, and that too only in exceptional writers like Sudhin Ghose and Raja Rao. For Sudhin Ghose, the myths are so real that sometimes the line that divides mythical time from historical time is quite blurred. Raja Rao uses the mythical parallel to extend the reader's understanding of the present situation.

Indo-Anglian novelists have realised the inadequacy or inappropriateness of the Western novel form for expressing an Indian ethos and sensibility and have attempted to incorporate traditional forms of narratives in their works. Raja Rao was the first inheritor of this tradition among Indian writers of English fiction. The greatest legacy of India's past are the Puranas. The influence of the Puranic tradition in Raja Rao has been very decisive and strong.

The conscious use of myth in Raja Rao is seen in the digressional method of story-telling of which he is the outstanding exponent. This method is perhaps the oldest device in narrative literature. Weaving in stories within a story, or pausing to narrate a parable to drive home a point are characteristic devices of the *Panchatantra*, the *Vishnu Purana*, the *Mahabharata* and the *Ramayana* as well as the Bible and Greek epics, where episode follows episode in a meandering fashion. Thus, we have Raja Rao claiming in his oft-quoted foreword to *Kanthapura*.

> Episode follows episode and when our thoughts stop our breath stops, and we move on to another thought. This was, and still is, the ordinary style of our story-telling. I have tried to follow it myself in this story.

In the employment of the tradition of mythicizing contemporary events, *Kanthapura* offers a rich and fascinating field for study. It should be understood that this mythicizing is not something unnatural. Mircea Eliade tells us that even today people live unconsciously but demonstrably by the remains of perennial mythologies.[4]

Kanthapura[5] is the story of the impact of Mahatma Gandhi and the Satyagraha movement on a small South Indian village which is the microcosm of rural India. But *Kanthapura* is not merely a political novel; its economic and social concerns and the religious undertones are subsumed into myth and legend. It is "a classic of resurgent India told in a poetic almost mythical style" as stated on the backcover of the Indian edition of the novel.

Raja Rao himself in his foreword to *Kanthapura* suggests that he followed in his style, the tradition of 'sthala-purana':

> There is no village in India, ... that has not a rich 'sthala-purana,' or legendary history, of its own. Some god or godlike hero has passed by the village— Rama might have rested under this peepal-tree, Sita might have dried her clothes, after her bath, on this yellow stone, or the Mahatma himself, on one of his many pilgrimages through the country, might have slept in this hut....

Dr. M.K. Naik describes the technique of the Purana thus,

> The Puranas are a blend of narration and description,
> philosophical reflection, and religious teaching. The
> style is usually simple, flowing, and digressive, and
> exaggeration is the keynote of most accounts of
> happenings and miracles. There is much to
> correspond to this in *Kanthapura*.[6]

It is 'Ithihasa' and 'purana' both unified into a 'kavya.' As 'ithihasa'
it is packed with historical action, while as a 'purana' it is full of
legendary memory and archetypal imagery. But above all, as a
'kavya,' it integrates historical action and racial consciousness in
such a way that its temper is at all levels equal to that of the Indian
life itself, which Raja Rao himself declares to be his main artistic
intention.

There are a number of mythical or puranic devices in
Kanthapura. It is an excellent example of the combination of
puranic and folktale elements. The myth of Kenchamma's descent
to earth to kill a demon is *puranic*; but when the narrator connects
the story with the colour of the Kenchamma hill, the elements of
legend and *purana* get blended together to make the story a 'sthala-
purana.' Though conforming generally to the puranic pattern, Raja
Rao liberally introduces elements of oral tradition of story-telling in
Kanthapura in the character of the grandmother narrator. Even
Sidda's serpent lore full of hyperboles and digressions is of the very
essence of folk narrative (72-74). Further, just as in a myth "some
of the chief characters are gods and other beings larger in power
than humanity,"[7] in this novel, Moorthy and Mahatma Gandhi
(though Gandhi is physically present nowhere) are idealised. Gandhi
is regarded by the village women as the Sahyadri mountain big and
blue, and Moorthy as the small mountain. Range Gowda, the village
headman, thus describes Moorthy: "He is our Gandhi. The state of
Mysore has a Maharaja ... and this Moorthy ... has wisdom in him
and he will be our Mahatma" (109). This pattern of having two
figures larger than life, one beyond the other, can be seen in Raja
Rao's earlier short Stories (*Narsiga* and *The Cow of the Barricades*)
also, where, an idealised local character referred to as 'master'
appears, occupying an all-pervasive god-like position. Regarding
the mythicizing of the characters, Indians, by nature, appear to

discover in their heroes the unmistakable analogies of the mythological heroes who permeate their religious life, especially in the villages. Thus, in *Kanthapura*, Jayaramachar, the Harikathaman raises Gandhi to the level of a god by identifying Gandhi with Prince Rama resisting the demonic rule of Ravana, the 'Red-men,' and again with Krishna engaged in killing Kaliya, the serpent of the foreign rule.

None of these analogies can be systematically followed through to find exact points of correspondence, but they do temporarily illuminate the historical situation of the 'thirties, and give an insight into the unlettered mind of the village people that Raja Rao presents in the novel, the kind of mind in which myth and fact are not clearly distinguishable. Moreover, as Mrs. Mukherjee observes, "for such a mind a fact does not become significant until it can be related to a myth."[8] Thus, the grandmother narrator in *Kanthapura* is a superb raconteur and myth-maker, who combines art and acumen, and the narration accordingly takes a meandering course flowing backwards and forwards 'mixing memory with desire.' Kenchamma is the local goddess 'who protects the village through famine and disease, death and despair.' According to legend, she protected the village from onslaught of a terrific monster 'who asked their songs for food and the young women as wives.' This momentous battle becomes imbedded in the racial unconscious, providing an illuminating and clarifying focal point for every historical experience felt by the community, in trials and tribulations. The Second Round Table Conference is 'invested with puranic dignity,' with the naturalness, ease and spontaneity of folktale: "They say the Mahatma will go to the Redman's country ... he will get us Swarajya ... come back with Sita on his right in a chariot of air" (257). The Satyagrahi in prison is the divine Krishna himself in Kansa's prison. Like the teller of tales in the oral tradition, the narrator is endowed with legitimate imaginative freedom and assumes a reasonable omniscience in presenting some scenes as if she were physically present at the time. Her account of Bhatta's visit to Rangamma (41-45) is only one example of many. As she narrates, the story becomes a stream of her memory. Thus, while using the old technique of the ancient myths and legends, Raja Rao also makes use of innovations in the style of Conrad, Joyce and Virginia

Woolf to suit the narrator's rambling and reminiscing speech. For conveying the tempo of the nightmarish and fast moving episodes, he has evolved a racy rhythmic style with long and interminable sentences connected with numerous 'ands' and few punctuation marks.

Another puranic device is mythicizing the central character. *Kanthapura* has been rightly charactrized as a 'Gandhipurana' too, as an epic of Gandhi's India. Srinivasa Iyengar calls it "a veritable grammar of the Gandhian myth—the myth that is but the poetic translation of the reality. It will always have a central place in Gandhi literature."[9] In the novel, Gandhi is an expanding symbol as against the fixed symbol of Kenchamma, which is another moving force behind the life in Kanthapura. In the title-page, Raja Rao quotes the *Gita*: "Whensoever there is misery and ignorance, I come." This doctrine of Incarnation is central to the Puranas and Gandhi is the new Avatar which is sung by the harikatha-man Jayaramachar. The story of Gandhi's birth also serves to introduce the political theme of the novel. He describes how Valmiki informs Brahma that his beloved daughter Bharata is enslaved by foreigners and how Siva himself is incarnated as Gandhi in Gujarat (21-23). The Inter-war period seems appropriate for Divine Grace and to the believer, it was not too farfetched to think that Gandhi was sent by God for redemption of the Indians. Gandhi is described as 'a wise man and a soft man, and a saint' who preaches Love, Truth and Non-Violence. In the mythological context of a god intervening in the affairs of man, Gandhi's principles and ideals have meaning for the villagers; at the same time the Mahatma is correctly interpreted as someone fulfilling, not overthrowing, the Indian tradition. For instance, the harikatha-man initiates the villagers into Gandhian principles in a religious manner: "Siva is three-eyed and Swaraj too is three-eyed: self-purification, Hindu-Muslim unity and Khaddar" (20).

Raja Rao's understanding of the folk psyche and his talent for rendering this understanding artistically, particularly with reference to the narrator and her concrete mental impression of the characters whose story she is telling comes out very well in the novel. Thus, it is seen that the mythicizing of facts serves a two-fold purpose in *Kanthapura*. The narrator being an old woman, mingling myth and fact would be her natural manner of observation and becomes a device of characterization. Secondly, the allusions to various myths are a part of Raja Rao's rhetoric of fiction. There are allusions to different myths: to Prahlad when Moorthy undertakes a rigid three-day fast in a typical Gandhian spirit; to the archetypal image of Hanuman as a devotee when Moorthy is described as having met the Mahatma in a 'vision' in which he fell at the feet of the Mahatma (53); and to the Shabri-Rama episode when Moorthy, after some hesitation enters the pariah quarters of Rachanna's wife for the first time. There are such allusions to myths and the metaphors representing mythological figures are slightly extended to concur with contemporary figures and situations. "These allusions and extensions of metaphors are the aspects of Raja Rao's rhetoric of fiction. They are not meant to give a scaffold upon which the whole novel is erected; but they offer some kind of loose analogy with the mythological figures and is a matter of strategy of characterisation."[10] The novelist has not tried to super-impose mythological correspondences or mythological prefiguration to suit the plot structure of the novel. The overt parallels between the mythological characters and contemporary figures could have become a blemish in the novel but for the fact that the personality of the narrator is in conformity with the requirements of the novel. The success of *Kanthapura* seems especially related to the convincing rendering of 'point of view' of the narrator who can assimilate diverse experiences and facts of Indian folk life with her vernacular personality.

Myth is like a religious ritual which makes life more meaningful and enriches it by penetrating to its essence. Thus, both myth and ritual are seen renewing the life of the community in *Kanthapura*. Certain rituals are described in the novel like the yoking of bulls to the plough under the Rohini star; the different modes of appeasing goddess Kenchamma; or the Kartik Festival of Lights where folk spirit is elevated to the grand myth oaf seasonal renewal and cyclical return. In the description of Moorthy's fasting (91-94), fiction is raised to the level of ritual. Character becomes symbol, action is ritual, speech is 'mantra.' Surface realism, based on the literalness of factual narration, is subordinated to the mythical narrative: for instance, events may not follow the ordered sequence of the chronometer, and instead follow a cyclical, non-causal order.

The immanence of the spiritual in the mundane is the condition of the novel as myth: it unites man and beast and tree and earth.[11]

The quest for form seems central to Raja Rao's creativity as is his perception of the relationship between fiction and reality. *Kanthapura* is in a sense, a world of realism in fiction. And yet, it is not purely realistic or naturalistic. This is combined with the strains of myth, of gods and goddesses, of blind superstitious beliefs and uncanny insights. One means by which the realistic is made to point to the reality or often made to symbolize it is presenting events as a kind of 'sthala-purna' in which, as Raja Rao says in his foreword, "the past mingles with the present and gods mingle with men." Thus, *Kanthapura*, as also the short stories of Raja Rao proclaim the triumph of the revival of the oral tradition of story-telling enriched by modern devices of the novel like the stream-of-consciousness.

The total effacement of Kanthapura towards the end of the novel ("... there's neither man nor mosquito in Kanthapura ...") is not a terminal cataclysm; rather it is a purgatorial process beyond which rises a renewed life. Kashipura is a phoeniz arising in burnished purity out of the ashes of the old Kanthapura; signifying the permanence of India, as a concept, an idea transcending space and time. India may be conquered, but never vanquished, "destroyed by never defeated." This simple story of Kanthapura becomes by the alchemic touch of Raja Rao not merely a 'Gandhipurana' but an historically authentic sage of the Indian nationalism, invested with the solemn dignity and religiosity of a piece of ancient mythology. Thus, the political revolution is 'assimilated into the racial heritage as myth and legend.' C.D. Narasimhaiah says of *Kanthapura*: "for the first time in modern times in India the novel in Raja Rao's hands has become a mature means of enlarging the frontiers of human consciousness."[12] Raja Rao has made an effective literary transcript of the Gandhian myth by artistically attuning the reality of his tale to the poetry of truth and its myriad miraculous transformations in the prism of historical consciousness.

NOTES AND REFERENCES

1. Alan W. Watts, *Myth and Ritual in Christianity* (Vanguard, 1954), 7.

2. Mark Schorer, *William Blake, The Politics of Vision* (Holt, 1946), 29.

3. Quoted in William Righter, *Myth and Literature* (London and Boston: Routledge and Kegan Paul, 1975), 51.

4. Mircea Eliade, *Myths, Dreams and Mysteries* (London, 1960), 23-38.

5. Raja Rao, *Kanthapura* (Delhi: Orient Paperbacks, 1971). Subsequent references are to this edition.

6. M.K. Naik, *Raja Rao,* (Blackie and Son Publishers Pvt. Ltd., 1982), 63.

7. Northrop Frye, *Fables of Identity, Studies in Poetic Mythology* (New York, 1963), 30.

8. Meenakshi Mukherjee, *The Twice-Born Fiction: Themes and Techniques of the Indian Novel in English* (Delhi: Arnold Heinemann Publishers, 1974), 141.

9. K.R. Srinivasa Iyengar, *Indian Writing in English*, 3rd ed. (Bombay: Asia Publishing House, 1983), 312.

10. V.V. Badve, "The use of Mythology in Raja Rao's *Kanthapura*," *The Journal of Shivaji University*, Vol. 10, No. 16, Kolhapur, 1977, 49.

11. K. Ayyappa Panikker, "Man and God in Indian and African Fiction: A Study Based on *Kanthapura, Arrow of God and Mookajji's Visions*," *Commonwealth Literature: Problems of Response*, ed. C.D. Narasimhaiah, Macmillan India Ltd., 1981, 110.

12. C.D. Narasimhaiah, "*Kanthapura*; An Analysis," *The Literary Criterion*, Vol. 7, No. 2, Summer 1966, 70-77.

9

The Village in Raja Rao's *Kanthapura*

Kanthapura of Raja Rao is the story of a village with that name. There is no central character (other than the village, what happens to it, what it becomes). Village life is certainly more closely at the heart of the novel than of any of the other works, in spite of the fact that Raj Rao describes the movement of the village from solidarity to complete and utter annihilation. Much of the early part of the book is spent developing a sense of the village itself, establishing its ambience. In the first paragraph, Achakka informs us of its geographical location:

> Our village—I don't think you have ever heard about it—Kanthapura is its name, and it is in the Province of Kara.

> High on the Ghats is it, high up the steep mountains that face the cool Arabian seas, up the Malabar coast is it, up Manglore and Puttur and many a centre of cardamom and coffee, rice and sugarcane. Roads, narrow, dusty, rut-covered roads, wind through the forest of teak and of jack, of sandal and of sal, and hanging over bellowing gorges and leaping over elephant-haunted valleys, they turn now to the left and now to the right and being you through the Alambi and Champa and Mena and

---

*Department of English, St. Thomas College, Palai, Kottayam.

> Kola passes into the great granaries of trade. There,
> on the blue waters, they say, our carted cardamoms
> and coffee get into the ships the Red-men bring,
> and, so they say, they go across the seven oceans
> into the countries where our rulers live.[1]

Literary critics have, in recent years, begun to re-evaluate space as a category for analysis is fiction. While Bakhtin's famous "Chronotope" intrinsically linked time with its indispensable correlate, the burden of emphasis ever since has nevertheless fallen for the most part upon the temporal.[2] Looking closely at the above-mentioned paragraph, in page 1, the most notable aspect is its sense of geographical space. The first six lines cover the village's geographical space. The next few lines cover the space which is associated with economic production. Then, it is immediately made clear that this is a very particular type of economy: a colonial economy. "This reference to the colonial economy," says Anshuman Mondal, "will, in due course, be explicitly associated with a familiar nationalist trope, that of the economic 'drain' effect first elucidated by Dadabhai Naoriji in the late nineteenth century, which became an axiomatic idea within nationalist discourse."[3] Raja Rao says:

> Our country is being bled to death by foreigners ...
> (the village weavers) buy foreign yarn, and foreign
> yarn is bought with some money, and all this money
> goes across the oceans.[4]

This sentence prepares us for a nationalist interpretation of Indian space and the colonial exploitation of it.

The story is narrated not directly by the novelist but through an intermediary.

> It may have been told of an evening when as the
> evening dusk falls, and through the sudden quiet,
> lights lit up in house after house, and stretching her
> bedding on the veranda a grandmother might have
> told you, new comer, the sad tale of her village.[5]

The events narrated took place less than two years earlier, and the memory there of was quite fresh in the mind of the grandmother. She herself had been an active participant in those events, yet she had not once emphasised her own role. Raja Rao has kept the personality of the narrator completely in the background, and has given her no identity except "Achakka ... of the Veda Sastra Pravina Krishna Sastri's family."[6]

The paragraph, in page 1, also writes about elaborate networks of road and rail which both facilitate and make possible the colonial economy. The Red-men ("Standard Hindu colloquialism for the British," the author states in his notes), colonialists, who manipulate the villagers from thousands of miles away. The page 1 sets the scene in the colonial India, which is "unsettled, dynamic, disruptive and dislocating."[7]

In the paragraphs that follow, Kenchamma, the village goddess, is first introduced ("She has never us, I assure you, our Kenchamma,").[8] The village itself was neatly divided into Brahmin quarter, Potters' quarter, Weavers' quarter and the Pariah quarter. There was Bhatta, a priest turned moneylender and Zamindar, Postmaster Suryanarayana, Snuff Shastri, Pandit Venkateshia, Old Ramakrishnayya better than whom nobody could read the *Sankara Vijaya*, and Corner-house Moorthy. There was also the University graduate Dore. They were all Brahmins, the dominating section of the society. Then, there were the potters Lingayya, Ramayya, Subbayya and Chandrayya, weavers Chennayya, Rangayya, beadle Thimayya, Pock-marked Sidda, Patwari Nanjundia, Sampanna and Ramanna, Postman Surappa, businessmen Rama Chetty and Subba Chetty, and Patel Range Gowda. This last named was the most powerful man in Kanthapura. "If the Patel says, it, even a coconut-leaf roof will become a gold roof."[9] There is a pervasive veil of caste hierarchy in Kanthapura. Every caste has its own space of living. Of all the castes, Brahmins are the supreme inhabitants of the village. Achakka's Brahmins status as a narrator, at first, poses some problems. She has been taught in her childhood to uphold the caste system. When she describes the outcaste quarter early in the narrative, she comments: "Of course you wouldn't expect me to go to the Pariah quarter ..."[10] When Moorthy returns to Kanthapura and begins to associate with the artisans, Achakka comments, again mirroring the rigid and claustrophobic caste system in the village:

> he even goes to the Potters' quarter and the Weavers'
> quarter and the Sudra quarter, and I closed my ears
> when I heard he went to the Pariah quarter. We said

to ourselves, he is one of these Gandhimen, who say there is neither caste nor clan nor family and yet they pray like us and they live like us. Only they say, too, one should not marry early, one should allow widows to take husbands and a Brahmin might marry a pariah and a pariah a Brahmin. Well, well, let them say it, how does it effect us? We shall be dead before the world is polluted. We shall have closed our eyes.[11]

Raja Rao wants us to Know the feminine point of view in *Kanthapura*, something atypical of most Third World fiction. Therefore, he writes that the village protector is a goddess, Kenchamma, not a god. Her power resides in her past actions, and the origin of the village is attributed to her initial accomplishments :

Kenchamma is our goddess. Great and bounteous is she. She killed a demon ages, ages ago, a demon that had come to demand our young sons as food and our young women as wives. Kenchamma came from the Heavens—it was the sage Tripura who had made penances to bring her down—and she waged such a battle and she fought so many a night that the blood soaked and soaked into the earth, and that is why the Kenchamma Hill is all red. If not, tell me, sister, why should it be red only from the Tippur Stream upwards, for a foot down on the other side of the stream you have mud, black and brown, but never red. Tell me, how could this happen, if it were not for Kenchamma and her battle? Thank heaven, not only did she slay the demon, but she even settled down among us, and this much I shall say, never has she failed us in our grief.[12]

Some old men did die of cholera, but "they would have died one way or the other anyway." Barber Chennav's wife Sankamma too died, "but then it was not for nothing her child was born ten months and four days after he (Chemmav) had died ... such whores, always die untimely. Ramappa and Subbanna, you see, they got it in town and our goddess could do nothing. She is the goddess of Kanthapura, not to Talassana."[13]

Mondal interprets this dependence on Kenchamma as rigid and static and contrasts it with the colonial authority: "Added to this, there are differing locations and principles of authority for each of these matrices. On the one hand, authority is represented by colonial law, the secular principles of empire and capital, and the historical authority of the King Emperor; on the other, authority is divine, represented by the goddess Kenchamma, codified by the *dharmashastras*, and the figure of authority is a religious one, namely the Swami. Whilst modern authority is invested in the urban institution of the court (located in the city of Karwar), the villagers locate their authority in the Kenchamma temple. In addition, each of these matrices is presented at first hand as mutually exclusive to each other, as symbolically illustrated by the adjacent but enclosed spaces of the Coffee plantation and the village. Thus, whilst the Coffee plantation is physically encircled by a fence and gate keeping both the coolies in and others out, the village is represented as closed and exclusive social order keeping the agents of the colonial matrix out. Hence, Bade Khan, the Policeman, as a figure of colonial authority is not offered a home in Kanthapura and instead finds himself quarters in the Coffee Estate."[14]

The coming of rains in Vaisakha is different for Kanthapura and Skeffington Coffee House labourers.

> The rains have come, the fine, first-footing rains
> that skip over the bronze mountains, tiptoe the crags,
> and leaping into the valleys, go splashing and wind-
> swung, a winnowed pour, and the coconuts and the
> betel-nuts and the cardamom plants choke with it
> and hiss back. And there, there comes over the
> Bebbur Hill and the Kanthur Hill and begins to paw
> upon the tiles, and the Cattle come running home,
> their ears stretched back, and the drover lurches
> behind some bel-tree or pipal-tree, and people leave
> their querns and rush to the courtyard, and turning
> towards Kenchamma temple, send forth a prayer,
> saying "There, there, the rains have come,
> Kenchamma; may our house be as white as sliver.[15]

The rains, so welcome to the villagers, appear differently to the labourers of Skeffington Coffee Estate.

> ... When the eyes seek the livid skies across the
> leaves, there is something dark and heavy rising
> from the other side of the hill, something heavy and
> hard and black, and the trees begin suddenly to
> tremble and his ... there is a gurgle and grunt from
> behind the bamboo cluster—and the gurgle and grunt
> soar up and swallow the whole sky. The darkness
> grows thick as sugar in a cauldron, while the bamboo
> creak and sway and whine, and the crows begin to
> wheel round and flutter, and everywhere dogs bark
> and calves moo, and then the wind comes so swift
> and dashing that it takes the autumn leaves with it,
> and they rise into the juggling air, while the trees
> bleat and blubber. Then drops fall.... [16]

P.C. Bhattacharya writes: "The labourers in the Coffee estate were
not of the soil; they were brought from far off Andhra and Tamilnadu,
lured by the prospect of good pay and plenty of food. Their spirits
already broken because of drought, famine, and neglect by the
landlords.... Disillusion was not long to come. First, there were
snakes and then rains, and then malaria."[17] The colonial matrices in
the Coffee estate contrast sharply with Kanthapura, the former
bringing sorrow and the latter joy.

Apart from being an inexhaustible storehouse of beauty, Nature
is also a source of never-ending wonder to the unsophisticated
rustic mind. Pariah Siddayya's long, rambling disquisition on serpent-
lore in which hard fact and footloose fancy are blended together[18]
is a fine example of this M.K. Naik Writes:

> The logic of 'through Nature up to Nature's God' is
> readily acceptable to a mind receptive to the beauty
> and the wonder of Nature. Hence, the promontory
> near the village is an 'abode of Siva'; and the river
> Himavathy is the daughter of Kenchamma, the
> Goddess of the Hill. Animal creation too shares this
> divinity in its own way; the eagle is the 'feature of
> God' and the vehicle of Kenchamma must appear in
> the sky at the ploughing ceremony so that the
> Kanthapurians can be assured that the goddess has
> blessed their first agricultural operations for the year.

Further more, the ceaseless and regular operation of
forces of Nature is itself an external manifestation
of the divine moral law that governs the universe ...
It is precisely because of this noble nexus that there
is perfect empathy between Man and external Nature
including the animal creation."[19]

Ramakrishnayya declares: "There is still many a good heart in the
world else the sun would not rise as he does nor the Himavathy
flow by the Kenchamma Hill."[20] Hence, when his remains are burnt
on the banks of Himavathy, the river pays its homage to him by
rising and sweeping the bones and ashes away; and

that night ... as no other night, no cow would give
its milk, and all the night a steady rain kept pattering
on the tiles and the calves pranced about their
brothers and groaned.[21]

It is again because of this imperishable bond between Man and
Nature that human experiences and attitude are described in terms
of forces of Nature, as and when the narrator describes the sea-
change that has come over Kanthapura as a result of the Gandhian
movement in these terms: "There is something that has entered our
hearts, an abundance like the Himavathy on Gauri's night; when
lights come floating down the Rampur Corner."[22]

Between the Kenchamma temple (as an institution of orthodox
authority) and the law court (colonial authority), stands, in opposition
to both, the "Kanthapuriswari temple" of god Shiva which "did not
exist more than three years ago."[23] In other words, it is clear that
this is the centre and source of the narrative. Esha Day says: "... the
historical action of the novel ... is not connected in any way with
Kenchamma. Kenchamma's traditional sanction plays no part in the
introduction and dissemination of Gandhian thought, nor is it the
scene of crucial happenings."[24] As Esha Dey quite rightly notes, it
is in this temple that Gandhian ideology is introduced, and it is
hence that many of the scenes associated with the Gandhian struggle
are enacted. Thus, the oft-quoted harikatha recited by the famous
Jayaramachar which begins "Siva is three-eyed ... and Swaraj too
is three-eyed: Self-purification, Hindu-Moslem unity, Khaddar[25]
takes place in this temple of Siva. Mondal says:

> "One immediately becomes aware that the novel's
> ideology is clearly affiliated to this matrix and that
> the tripartite structure of matrices constructed within
> the opening chapter is clearly meant to indicate
> certain positions in the field of power: nationalism
> (by which is meant Gandhian nationalism) *versus*
> colonialism on the one hand, and *versus* orthodoxy
> on the other. In this respect it is also significant that
> the temple is dedicated to an all-Indian deity such as
> Siva rather than to the local deity, Kenchamma,
> whose powers if appear have only a limited and
> locally specific purpose ... such a goddess is clearly
> an unsuitable figurehead for the nation."[26]

Both C.D. Narasimhaiah and M.K. Naik have mentioned Ignazio Silone's *Fontamara* in examining *Kanthapura*. In both the narrative the theme is the destruction of a village by the forces of tyranny and oppression in both the stories are told by narrators (In *Fontamara* three—an old peasant, his wife and their son, in *Kathapura* only one—a grandmother), in both the writers speak as native sons fully in tune with the sensibilities of the people of whom they speak, and in both the language but not the idiom used is alien. There are many points of difference also between the two novels. In *Fontamara* the viewpoint of the writer is that of socialist and an anti-fascist, in *Kanthapura* it is that of deeply religious man and an anti-imperialist.

Raja Rao does not idealize the village folk, though he stresses their innate simplicity and sense of devotion. He is also aware of the evil spirits in the village: Venkamma, Advocate Seenappa and Bhatta. The cruel and calculating nature of Bhatt is fully delineated. His coffer is ever full:

> He knows how much there is in it. Something around
> three hundred and fifty rupees. Already a little gone;
> just ten rupees for Rampur Mala. Nuptial ceremony
> of some sort. Six per cent interest, and payable in
> two months.[27]

Sometimes the people are slaves to effete traditions and trite conventions. Dowry System is a bane to the poor:

> And he was telling me how he could find no one

for his last granddaughter. No one. Every fellow
with matric or inter asks, "What dowry do you
offer? How far will you finance my studies?—I
want to have this degree and that degree."[28]

Some oppose Moorthy's campaigns and schemes. The Swami
does not approve of his mixing with the low-caste people and
instantly excommunicates him. Now Bhatta Charges interest upto
eighteen and twenty per cent from congress members. To some, it
is difficult to offend Bhatta or the Government.

The Gandhian movement spreads in Kanthapura and the village
becomes a part of All India Panchayat, a territory to be ruled by a
parallel Government. The inspired women sing:

There is one Government, sister,
There is one Government, sister,
And that is the Government of the Mahatma.[29]

Our villages provides a basic pattern easily discernible all over
India. As Meenakshi Mukherjee observes: "It is, therefore, often in
the rural context that the regional reality and the Indian reality more
or less merge."[30] Kanthapura is thus any village in India, India in
microcosm.

In the concluding chapter, Achakka expresses her beliefs that
what has happened in Kanthapura is to be interpreted as essentially
positive: "They say the Mahatma will go to the Red-man's country
and he will get us Swaraj"[31] that is Independence. Charles
R. Larson says:

The time is propitious, the culture has been renewed,
things will never be as they were. The pessimism
that has for so long been a controlling factor in
Third World fiction has begun to shift towards
optimism. Cultural renewal can only begin within
the culture itself, from within its basic foundations:
the village and the family.[32]

The introduction of Gandhian nationalism upsets the apple-
carts of the Brahmin orthodoxy and the British colonialism. Moorthy,
the central Gandhian character, rejects the colonial symbol by
symbolically dumping his city clothes and adopting *Khadi clothing.*
He rejects the Brahminical orthodoxy by his embracing of the

village untouchables. Sometimes, the Brahminical hierarchy colludes with the British colonial systems in Kanthapura to suppress the deprived and depressed peoples. Bhatta is a symbol of colonial oppression. Brahmins have always been benefices of the orthodox socio-economic system in Kanthapura.

The Gandhian nationalism securalizes the secular space of the nation. Mondal writes:

> The circuit of collusion is, however, shown to be short-circuited by Gandhian nationalism, at first in conflict with orthodoxy and latterly in conflict with colonialism. By this point, the orthodox space of the village has been replaced by an incipient Gandhian space, a process initiated at the moment of the Swami's exposure and additionally signified in two ways: First, the departure of Bhatta and second, the symbolic death of Ramakrishnayya, the village custodian and interpreter of the "Vedic texts which are the texts of orthodox authority... The next chapter opens with a significant alternation in social relations, as, for the first time even the women take it upon themselves to be custodians and interpreters of the sacred texts ... This new era is consummated by the villagers' commitment to Gandhism.... Hence, we now find the village symbolically isolated form the colonial space around it.... In effect, this isolation dissembles the village—lifting it out of its relation to the concrete spaces around it....[33]

NOTES AND REFERENCES

1. Raja Rao, *Kanthapura*, Delhi: Hindi Pocket Books, 1. All references are to this edition.

2. Mikhail Bakhtin, "Forms of Time and of the Chronotope in the novel," in *The Dialogic Imagination*, Austin: University of Texas Press, 1981, 84-258.

3. Anshuman Mondal, "The Ideology of Space in Raja Rao's *Kanthapura*," in *Journal of Commonwealth Literature*, Vol. 34, No. 1, 1999, 103-04.

4. *Kanthapura*, 16.

5. *Ibid.*, Foreward.

6. *Ibid.*, 12.
7. Anshuman Mondal, 104.
8. *Kanthapura*, 2.
9. *Ibid.*, 14.
10. *Ibid.*, 5.
11. *Ibid.*, 9.
12. *Ibid.*, 2.
13. *Ibid.*, 9.
14. Anshuman Mondal, 105.
15. *Kanthapura*, 157.
16. *Ibid.*, 76.
17. P.C. Bhattacharya, *Indo-Anglian Literature and the works of Raja Rao,* Delhi: Atma Ram and Sons, 1983, 252-53.
18. *Kanthapura*, 69-72.
19. M.K. Naik, *Studies in Indian English Literature, New Delhi:* Sterling Publishers Pvt. Ltd., 1987, 36.
20. *Kanthapura*, 131.
21. *Ibid.*, 145.
22. *Ibid.*, 256.
23. *Ibid.*, 7.
24. Esha Dey, *The Novels of Raja Rao*, New Delhi: Prestige Books, 1992, 32.
25. *Kanthapura*, 10.
26. Anshuman Mondal, 106.
27. *Kanthapupra*, 32.
28. *Ibid.*, 37.
29. *Ibid.*, 207.
30. Meenakshi Mukherjee, *The Twice-born Fiction: Themes and Techniques of the Indian Novel in English*, New Delhi: Arnold-Heinemann, 1971, 213.
31. *Kanthapura*, 181.
32. Charles R. Larson, *The Novel in the Third World*, Washington DC: INSCAPE/ Publishers, 1976, 142-43.
33. Anshuman Mondal, 112.

10

Gandhian Ideology: A Study of Raja Rao's *Kanthapura*

UDAY SHANKAR OJHA*

Raja Rao's first novel, *Kanthapura* (1938) depicts the impact of Gandhi who launched the Freedom Movement in the 1920s to liberate India from the slavery of the Britishers. M.K. Naik rightly opines that the novel is predominantly political in inspiration and does not reveal the author's characteristic metaphysical preoccupations, except in a general way.[1] But a deep probe into this novel reflects Rao's perpetual interest in ontological themes. The novelist assiduously explores the Gandhian ideals of loving one's enemies, non-violence and abolition of untouchability. Mulk Raj Anand, R.K. Narayan and K.A. Abbas do not ignore the impact of Gandhian ideology. Mulk Raj Anand refers to the immense popularity of Gandhian thought in *Untouchable*. R.K. Narayan idealizes Gandhi as a great leader in *Waiting for the Mahatma*. K.A. Abbas also depicts the impact of Salt Satyagraha, Jallianwala Bagh Tragedy and Gandhi-Irwin Pact in *Inqilab*. Raja Rao was greatly influenced by the ideology of Gandhi. Rao spent a few days at Gandhi's ashram at Sevagram. At the time of Quite India Movement Raja Rao was "associated with the underground activities of the young socialist leaders."[2]

Raja Rao's confidence in Gandhian thought led him to idealize Mahatma Gandhi as a true saint. In this novel, Rao depicts Mahatma Gandhi as an emblem of divine power. Gandhi is presented as an incarnation of Krishna who will assuage the distress of the Indians.

*Lecturer in English, Jagdam College, Jay Prakash University, Chapra (Bihar).

Gandhi would kill the snake of foreign rule as Krishna had killed the snake Kaliya. As a leader, Gandhi gives advice to spin yarn to the people of India in that if they do it, the money that goes to Britain will be retained in India to feed the hungry and clothe the nude. The novelist elevates the Gandhian movement to a mythological plan. Mother India, "which is the Goddess of sapience and well-being" portrays the enslaved daughter of Brahma and so Seva incarnates Gandhi to liberate Mother India from the bondage of foreigners. Rao illustrates a fine analogy of Ram and Ravana— Ram for Mahatma Gandhi and Ravana for the British Government. In this novel, Mother India or freedom is compared with Sita, Gandhi is presented as Ram and Jawaharlal Nehru is considered to be his brother Bharata. The novelist alludes to Gandhi's exiled existence. To liberate India Gandhi leaves his home, roams the length and breadth of India and passes his banished life. Rao says Gandhi, like Ram, will go to Britain, Lanka, and he will get us freedom, Sita. It is a struggle between the divine and devil K.R.S. Iyenger rightly says:

> The reign of the Red-Man is Asuric rule, and it is raised by the Devas, the Satyagrahis. The characters sharply divide into two camps: The Rulers (and their supporters) on the one hand and the Satyagrahis (and their sympathisers) on the other.[3]

As an apologist to Gandhian ideology, Rao believes that "the future of the world is in Gandhism."[4] Moorthy obtains spiritual power in his very first meeting with Gandhi, who primarily gives instruction to him in his political ideology. Moorthy says: "There is in it something of the silent communion of the ancient books" (52). He is spiritually influenced and states: "There is but one force in life and that is Truth, and there is but one love in life and that is the love of mankind, and there is but one God in life and that is the God of all" (52-53). In essence Moorthy explicates his faith in Gandhism and acquires self-realization after catching a glimpse of the Mahatma. Inspired and influenced by the ideology of Gandhi, Moorthy starts preaching Gandhian philosophy of non-violence, love of mankind and abolition of untouchability. Moorthy sees Seetharamu's willing acceptance of the torture by the British Government and it strengthens his belief in the Gandhian ontology of non-violence. The term non-violence indicates the extirpation of ill-will from one's heart, for it causes enmity and violence. When Range Gowda wants to teach a lesson to Puttayya for unjustly drawing all the canal-water to his fields, Moorthy preaches him the Gandhian principle of non-violence and love for the enemy. Once Range Gowda wishes to settle scores with Bade Khan, the policeman appointed by the British Government to watch over the political activities of the freedom fighters in Kanthapura, Moorthy dissuades him from indulging in any violence.

Gandhi's axiom of non-violence presents an astonishing paradigm for the whole world as it is a "war without violence and battle without hatred."[5] Moorthy holds the Gandhian view that "good ends can be achieved only by good means."[6] Each individual observes the same abiding awareness underlying all jivas, whether friends or foes, hates none. In this novel Jayaramachar articulates the ideology of Gandhi: "Fight, says he, but harm no soul. Love all says he, Hindu, Mohammedan, Christian or Pariah, for all are equal before God. Don't be attached to riches, says he, for riches create passions, and passions create attachment and attachment hides the face of Truth. Truth must you tell, he says, for Truth is God, and verily, it is the only God I know" (22). Jayaramachar continues by saying that Truth is God and, therefore, the countrymen should speak the truth. It has the tone of Bhagavad Gita, which emphasizes truthfulness as a part of human behaviour. Moorthy's opinion that he is just "a pebble among the pebbles of the river, and when the floods come, rock by rock may lie buried under" (100) implies that he is without arrogance. Moorthy's recitation of "Sivoham, Sivoham" is vedantic in spirit. Rangamma inspires the Satyagrahis to face the oppression of the police boldly and preaches that no one can hurt the immortal soul: "No, sister, the sword can split asunder the body, but never the soul" (153). C.D. Narasimhaiah observes that the novel delineates the dynamic power of a living religious convention. He states that "religion seems to sustain the spirits of the people of Kanthapura."[7] The inhabitants of Kanthapura willingly pledge to spin yarn, maintain non-violence (Ahimsa) and speak truth. When Moorthy is arrested the villagers implore goddess Kenchamma to set him free: "The Goddess will never fail us—she will free him from the clutches of the Red-man" (134). The inhabitants of

Kanthapura go to Kenchamma Hill and invoke goddess Kenchamma to protect them from the savage assault of the British Government. Men and women are assaulted and arrested by the police. Most of the male freedom fighters are taken to prison but Moorthy is left out: "But Moorthy they would not take, and God left him still with us" (200). A large number of freedom fighters from other corners of the country come and join the movement in Kanthapura. The Satyagrahis, knowing that the soul is immortal and indestructible, come and jump into the ocean of death sans fear.

During his early years, Rao was influenced by the ideology of Gandhi which is one of the most challenging ideologies of the 20th century. According to Jawaharlal Nehru Gandhi is "like a powerful current of fresh air... like a beam of light that pierced the darkness and removed the scales form our eyes; like a whirlwind that upset many things, but most of all the working of people's minds."[8] Gandhi gave the great weapon of non-violence to the people of India and strengthened it subsequently by the non-cooperation and civil disobedience movements in the thirties. Gandhi, through this movement, not only sought political freedom but also aimed at economic liberty and spiritual regeneration. Gandhi wanted all the people, the opulent and the indigent, to lead a dignified life sans exploitation of any sort. Rao's faith in Gandhian thought led him to idealize Gandhi as a true God. In *Kanthapura* Mahatma Gandhi is depicted as an emblem of divine power as well as a great reality. The theme of the novel, "Gandhi and Our Village" has a mythical significance in that the past blends with the present. The age-old faith of the villagers that gods walk by lighted streets of Kanthapura during the month of Kartik indicates that the myth co-exists with the contemporary reality. As the gods pass by the potters' street and the weavers' street, lights are lit to see them pass by. This reference affirms the peasants' perpetual faith in gods—a faith which is shared by the author with his characters. Rao lays stress on the role of religion in the struggle for Independence. That is why religion and politics are often interwoven in the novel. The importance of independence is delineated in a religious metaphor. The political activity of the inhabitants of Kanthapura gains power from their religious faith. Rao adroitly deals with the conventional mythology which is interlaced with contemporary reality. The recurrent reference to myth adds new dimensions to the struggle for freedom, for the "exaggeration of reality by myth is the necessary way of achieving the eternity in space."[9]

Thus, Raja Rao's maiden novel *Kanthapura* presents the Gandhian ideology of non-violence and the abolition of untouchability. The great importance given to caste, the mythical presentation of Gandhi and mother India and the spiritualization of the Freedom Movement within the parametres of Indian cultural convention imply the tremendous impact of Gandhian ideology in *Kanthapura*.

NOTES

1. Quoted by M.K. Naik in *Raja Rao* (1972; Bombay, 1982) 75.
2. Naik 6.
3. K.R. Srinivasa Iyengar, *Indian Writing in English* (1962; New Delhi: 1983) 391.
4. Ratna Rao Shekhar, "Seventy Six Years of Solitude," *Society* (August 1985): 30.
5. G. Ramchandran, *Promotion of Gandhian Philosophy* (1966; Mysore: 1973) 33.
6. Ramchandran 34.
7. Narsimhaiah 47.
8. Jawaharlal Nehru, *The Discovery of India* (1961; Bombay: 1972) 358.
9. Swami Nityabodhananda, *The Myths and Symbols in Indian Civilization* (Madras: 1980) 7.

11

Kanthapura: A Portrait of Village Gandhi

MALLIKARJUN PATIL*

Nothing in the history of Indian English fiction is as significant as Raja Rao's *Kanthapura* both in plot-construction and use of language. C.D. Narasimhaiah feels *Kanthapura* is the most satisfying of modern Indian novels. The novel has Raja Rao's in-depth understanding of swaraj struggle and its deeper consequences in the Indian citizens. *Kanthapura* is the story of how Gandhi's struggle for independence from the British came to a typical village Kanthapura in Southern India. The dramatic and vivid tale told by the old woman Rangamma evokes the spirit of India's traditional folk-epics and puranas. It is said "the novel is a landmark in the history of Indian fiction in English, as it points to a definite stage in the formation of an Indian style of writing in English."

Mulk Raj Anand is known for his social concern, R.K. Narayan is known for his mythological evocations of social life, while Raja Rao writes about Indian life in a historical perspective. His philosophical viewpoints exposed here and there in *Kanthapura* may not be quite rich as in his later novels, but they do suffice in the historical context. The novel *Kanthapura* reveals us the whole saga of a village in the wake of freedom struggle. There are at least three levels of experience in the novel. The first is the political struggle—a struggle for securing freedom to the country; the second is the religious life—a life that highlights Indian life; and the third social concerns.

*Lecturer, Dept. of English, Gulbarga University, Gulbarga (Karnataka).

Kanthapura deals with Indian independence movement set in a smooth Indian village. The village Kanthapura is like any other villages in India with its own culture and history. Like Malgudi, it has a river Himavathy, many hills like Bebbur Mound, temples like Kenchamma's, Kanthapurishwari's, Ishwars and colonies of Weavers, Potters, Pariahs and Brahmins.

The village is located on the way to Karwar. Maddur, Rampur, Satturu, Maluru, Shantipura and Kashipura and many more are the neighbouring villages. The whole region is located on the Sahyadri mountain range on the western coast of India. Full of woodland terrain, it has a lot of wetland as well as dry lands growing rice as its staple food. In this small village there are people of all castes, crafts and ideologies.

Raja Rao says Moorthy is from the Corner House, and there are Bhatta, Patel Rangegouda, Rangamma, Venkamma, Madanna, Rachanna and many more. There are good lives as well as bad lives and lives that are isolated. If Moorthy, Rangamma, Patel go together, we find people like Venkamma evil-minded, while men like Bhatta remain a dumb spectator to the entire panorama of the village's participation in the freedom struggle.

A University dropout Moorthy comes back home. He is carried away by Gandhi's struggle for the freedom. The latter's doctrines such as truth and non-violence, his concern for the social harmony and untouchables, grips Moorthy. So Moorthy starts following Gandhi in every way. His village reforming acts begin with his desire to bring Kanthapura under the purview of the national issues. So starts Moorthy to convince everyone about the usefulness of Khadi and no wonder, all start it as it helps them to get free cloths and a sense of patriotic belongingness.

In the wake of Khadi spread, Moorthy also being free from caste prejudices, starts eradicating untouchability. So he freely goes to Pariah quarters and even has harijan boys as his friends. Altogether they work at charkha. The traditional brahministic attitude of the Brahmins is hurt. So elderly people like Venkatamma and Bhatt warn Moorthy to stop his Pariah business. But the latter does not budge. He knows what is right and what is wrong. Like Gandhi he understands it is man who created caste and the same, for the human welfare, can be eradicated. So Moorthy's works for improving the lives of harijans' progresses. But none is more afraid of possible excommunication by the authoritative Swami than Moorthy's mother Narasamma. No doubt, she dies within a week when Moorthy does not stop his pariah business.

Moorthy is a man of social concerns. He goes even to the Sheffington Coffee Estate to teach the coolies the art of weaving. Even he teaches them alphabets and grammar and arithmetic and Hindi. Moorthy feels Hindi must be the national language and like Chaucer's clerk he learns it gladly and teaches it to others gladly.

A small event that involves Moorthy to violence at Coffee Estate indirectly, as in the case of Gandhi, makes him repent. Nothing other than a three days fasting makes him happy. When he sits for fasting at the Kenchamma Temple there come all the villagers to stop him. But he does not. Yet success lies in his convincing of others of the importance of fasting. An insult Venkamma showers upon him while meditating since he did not marry her daughter, makes him remember Kabir.

The road to the City of Love is hard, brother,
It's hard,
Take care, take care, as you walk along it (89).

Singing this, Moorthy shines with a rare radiance in his face. He utters truth is God and God is truth just echoing Gandhi.

Come the harsh activities of the police in the village, Moorthy turns more active and does a full time social work. The police Bade Khan's indifferent attitude towards the villagers and the coming of the more police to suppress village freedom activities, strengthen Moorthy's domain of works. Even the Patel Rangegouda, the elders of Potters and Weavers and Pariah Colonies agree with him to undertake religious and social activities in the village to promote national struggle at the same time.

Gandhi's vision of life finds an outlet in *Kanthapura*. People start a Congress Committee in the line of Karwar Congress Committee. Moorthy, Patel Rangegouda, Rangamma, Rachanna and Seenu—all become members of it. No doubt, there is Rangamma a woman and Rachanna an outcaste. The formation of committee and its many fold activities provoke Bhatta who is a pontifical

Brahmin but lately a moneylender. As so he amasses a great wealth. Since he hates Gandhi's view of life specially his social concerns, Bhatta hates Gandhi's followers.

The mere presence of village activities under Moorthy's leadership provokes the British authorities. One day seventeen of the villagers including Moorthy are dragged to the Santur Police Station. Later all except Moorthy are released and he is kept in the Karwar jail.

When Shankar, the Secretary of the Karwar Congress Committee and Advocate Ranganna meet Moorthy to convince him of the futility of an in-depth Satyagraha, Moorthy is not carried away by their shallow politics. He shows he is a real village Gandhi committed to the cause of the nation. This makes people at Kanthapura and outside hymn up in praise of Moorthy and Shankar, Ranganna and Dasappa make speeches about the incorruptible qualities of him. People all alike appreciate this village Gandhi in high terms. They say he will not budge to the aliens' atrocities since he is like a pure gold. Rajamma curses the evil government, which has imprisoned thousands of Moorthies. All are unhappy as Rangegouda got dismissed from his Patelship.

Moorthy is like an orbit influencing all its satellites. It is because of his nobility of heart, authenticity of action, dedication to the nation's cause and social concerns; all people are swept by him. If Rangegouda joined him leaving his Patelship, the advocate Shankar practises his law in Gandhian way. So is his noble impact upon Rangamma and Ratna, both noble savages. Still there are pariahs like Rachanna, Madanna, and a horde of coolies who have come down to the terrain of coffee estate right from the catchment area of Godavari in Andhra Pradesh.

Moorthy's impact upon the villagers is deep-rooted. More of women than men are attracted by his social activities. These women under the leadership of Rangamma who was Moorthy's right-hand in Kanthapura go to toddy groves just to destroy toddy business that worsened people's lives. They sing songs while doing all this brave work in the teeth of British opposition.

At least a toddy pot, sister,
At least a toddy—leaf, sister,

> We'll go to Boranna's Toddy grove,
> We'll go to Boranna's Toddy growth,
> And procession back at least a toddy-leaf, sister (182).

The strikers address the people that toddy is a crooked tree and its milk is poison. They ask them not to drink it at least in the name of the Mahatma. The intelligent people—all destroy many of the toddy trees and risk their lives in police lathi-charges. This brings a great insult to womenfolk and seeing them humiliated by the police, no wonder, all the toddy shopkeepers stop selling toddy. This is a happy and healthy impact of Gandhian struggle for social harmony.

Picketing of toddy either at fields or at shops, burning of foreign cloths, opposing of British laws etc. leads to a national struggle involving all the people of Kanthapura. Moorthy is forced to jail again. So are Rangegouda and many more. Now the satyagraha continues in the village under the leadership of Rangamma and Ratna. Then there comes the issue of paying taxes, which the government has increased deliberately with an intent to punish the rebellions. But the people under Gandhian sway of Civil Disobedience are not prepared to pay taxes. As a result, the rulers decide to auction the lands of those who do not wish to pay taxes. So troubles brew up in Kanthapura as everywhere in the Indian subcontinent. The satyagrahis start their anti-government activities. Look at the following comments:

> But the volunteers go on, 'Yes, sister, yes, the Government is afraid of us, for in Karwar the courts are closed and the banks closed and the Collector Never goes out' (228).

People sing, people dance and they work for the elimination of an alien rule:

> Lift the flag high
> O, lift the flag high,
> Brothers, sisters, friends and mothers,
> This is the flag of the revolution (238).

The slogans, Inquilab Zindabad, Mahatma Gandhi Ki Jai, Vande Mataram are drilled often. Finally the bloody government auctions most of the lands of Kanthapura to the rich people from outside forcing most of the villagers to other villages like Kashipura, Malur and Ramapura. Thus by fate they are forced to sacrifice their lands and assets for the liberation of their mother nation.

12

The Feminine Principle in *The Serpent and The Rope*

Raja Rao is one of the most significant writers of modern India. His works have received high praise all round. The back cover of *The Serpent and The Rope* carries the remark of Lawrence Lurrell; "You not only do India great honour, but you have honoured English literature by writing it in our language." Similarly his *Kanthapura* carries this remark from E.M. Forster "...the finest novel to come out of India in recent years." Santha Rama Rao has called him "...perhaps the most brilliant—and certainly the most interesting—writer of modern India."

Raja Rao has a very high sense of the dignity of his vocation as a writer. He looks to his work in the spirit of dedication. For him literature is *sadhana*—not a profession but a vocation. Explaining his views on literature he remarks:

> So the idea of literature as anything but a spiritual experience or *sadhana*—a much better word—is outside my perspective. I really think that only through dedication to the absolute or metaphysical principle can one be fully creative...........................
>
> ....
>
> Literature as *Sadhana* is the best life for a writer. The Indian tradition which links the word with the absolute (*subdabrahman*) has clearly shown the

*Principal, Dr. Ram Manohar Lohia College, Ranchi.

various ways by which one can approach literature, without the confusions that arise in the mind of the Western writer viewing life as an intellectual adventure. Basically, the Indian outlook follows a deeply satisfying, richly rewarding and profoundly metaphysical path.

All this may sound terribly India, but it is not so really. Valery, Rilke, and Kafka, for instance, are as close to this view as Tagore in looking upon literature as *sadhana*.[1]

According to Raja Rao, a man must be a man first and a writer afterwards. By man he means the metaphysical entity. One can, however, realise one's metaphysical entity only by following the Indian way and seeking the guidance of a "guru." Though Raja Rao is a man of great literary cultures, being equally home in the knowledge of classical Sanskrit and modern European literature, he is basically an India. His whole approach to life and literature has been outlined against the broad perspective of the Indian philosophy and tradition.

Raja Rao believes in the Advaitic truth of "Shivoham, Shivoham; I am Shiva, I am Shiva," as Sankara says. According to him, Shiva is the opposite of *Shava*. Shiva is not a god. He is the absolute Truth and can be realized when a Guru, who is himself a realized being, gives one the *upadesam*. Otherwise Shiva is an empty word. Though born in a Vedantic family, Raja Rao could not realize the full significance of *Vedanta* till he met his Guru, Shri Atmananda, to whom he dedicates *The Serpent and the Rope:*

> *The Serpent and the Rope* came as a result of spiritual fulfilment—that is to say it was born after I had met my Guru.[2]

Raja Rao's metaphysical bent of mind, and deep love for India, have not made his mind oblivious to the superiority of Europe in certain areas. One field in which Europe is definitely superior is systematic thinking and writing. In *Europe and Ourselves* he writes:

> The habit of analysing things accurately, of learning the whole truth by measuring things with each other, is foreign to our people. We think as we please and

we write as we please. These somehow carry their own meaning to the people, and sometimes this meaning is of the greatest importance. But it is difficult to under-stand them line by line. In these countries, on the other hand, whatever the subject might be, they write clearly, with the individual units of meaning. A single reading enables us to grasp it. This is something we have to learn from Europe.[3]

Before undertaking a study of the works of Raja Rao, it is always desirable to keep in mind what he himself has to say about them:

All writers write only autobiography. Certain aspects of my life are emphasised in each book, so they are a fairly accurate statement of my life, though not so far as facts are concerned.[4]

In other words, Raja Rao keeps himself confined to thing within his personal experience. There are no free flights of fancy; nobody would say after reading his work, "Here's God's plenty," but nobody can remain unaffected by his sincerity and authenticity. And nobody can avoid stopping and wondering at his achievements as a literary artist—both in language and treatment of the themes.

Raja Rao's first novel *Kanthapura* (1938), expresses his attitude towards woman. The person who tells the story in *Kanthapura* is not Raja Rao, the omniscient novelist, but a woman named Achakka. He was abandoned his position as story teller, giving it over to his fictive female persons. *Kanthapura* is the story of a village with that name. Much of the early part of the novel is spent developing a sense of the village itself, establishing its ambiance. The communal point of view is established immediately and placed in its colonial context—the red-man ("Standard Hindu colloquialism for the British, "The author states in his note to the novel, 185), the colonial power manipulating the villagers from thousands of miles away.

The most significant of the characteristic is Achakka's Brahmin position and the fact that she is female. Achakka's Brahmin status initially presents some problems for her as a narrator. Flexibility, however, typifies her character, quite early in the story she adopts

Gandhiji's teachings. In the riots that culminate at the end, Achakka is out there, proudly marching with the others—Brahmins and pariahs, potters and weavers, coolies, even Mohammedans.

The female point of view, however, is much more important than her Brahmin status, giving us, something a typical of most Third World Fiction. Much of the novel's power is Raja Rao's determination to keep the viewpoint entirely feminine. For this reason, it is especially important that the village protector is a goddess, Kenchamma, not a god. Her power resides in her past actions, and the origin of the village is attributed to her initial accomplishments.

> Kenchamma is our goddess. Great and bounteous is she. She killed a demon ages, ages ago, a demon that had come to demand our young sons as food and our young women as wives. Kenchamma came from the Heavens—It was the sage Tripura who had made penance to bring her down—and she waged such a battle and she fought so many a night that the blood soaked and soaked into the earth, and that is why the Kenchamma Hill is all red....Thank heaven, not only did she slay the demon, but she even settled down among us, and this much I shall say, never has she failed us in our grief.[5]

Symbolically, Kenchamma's power, incarnated in the women of Kanthapura such as Achakka (engaging in a similar battle), brings about the great social change that radicalizes the village, for Gandhi and Moorthy are only the catalysts, the inspiration for what eventually happens. They become increasingly insignificant as the narrative continues, Moorthy even disappearing from the village itself. The women are the force, they bring about the real revolution, since their husbands have had to hide in the jungles around the village. Without the force of the women, there would not, in fact, have been a revolution in Kanthapura.

It is true that women are subordinated in Kanthapura society, they are not treated with outright contempt. When Rangamma is nominated by the men on the Congress Committee, the reason Moorthy gives is "We need a women in the Committee for the

Congress is for the weak and the lowly."[6] While the hierarchical structure of the Congress and the subordination of women in the family allow them to emerge only as a second rank leadership, the novelist perceives them to be the strength of the movement and of the village too, in a more vital sense. A good example is that of the pariah women's reactions to politics.

When Moorthy visits the pariah quarters, and addresses the women, he wants them to vow that they will spin at least a 100 yards of yarn everyday. They refuse, and Moorthy, feeling desperate, appeals to Rachanna's wife, who replies: "If my husband says 'Spin,' I shall spin learned one."[7] Thus, his direct approach to the women proves fruitless and it is only his approach to the men which works. Moorty asks the men whether the women will participate, "They will do as we do,' said Rachanna."[8]

Clearly, the structure of the husband-wife relationship intervenes between women and the movement. This question, however, does not surface as a conflict except briefly when the men object to the Sevika Sangh, saying that it will interfere with the women's performance of domestic duties. Rangamma's response is not to question the sex-based division of labour but to say, "If we are to help others, we must begin with our husbands."[9] She also tells Satamma to be more regular in cooking. The Choric comment is "...we all say, 'we should do out duty. If not, it is no use belonging to the Gandhi group.'"[10]

Ruth Vanita comments, "This is a faithful reflection of how the Gandhian movement, by and large, envisaged women's role—that of a giver whose giving extends beyond the family but does not exclude it; a mother and sister not to a few individuals but to the country and to the world. Yet the novelist, very subtly, goes on to point out that the self view of the giver, and the way other view her, does change, by the fact of her political activity, even if the assertion of an individual identity, is not their primary goal."[11]

Ruth Vanita comments, "Gandhi often said that he wished he had been born a woman, and would like to be reborn as one. The identification here of Gandhi with a mountain topped by a temple recalls the Kenchamma hill. While the visible leadership may be male, the envisioned goal is non-male. Kenchamma's presence as female protector pervades the book. India is referred to throughout as "The Mother," and these symbols are identified with the heart on whom survival depends."[12]

Towards the end of the novel, when nothing can stop the women from marching against the soldiers sent in by the British, the change has been so complete that the women (in spite of the fact that many of them have been killed) make the voluntary choice to continue their protests. They are driven by an uncontrollable force—not Moorthy, not Gandhi—a new revolutionary consciousness.

...Some strange fever rushed up from the feet, it rushed up and with it our hair stood on end and our ears grew hot and something powerful shook us from head to foot, like Shamoo when the goddess had taken hold of him, and on that beating, bursting day, with the palms and the champaks and the lantana and the silent well about us, such a terror took hold of us, that we put the water jugs on our hips, and we rushed back home, trembling and gasping with the anger of the gods....Moorthy forgive us: Mahatama Forgive us: Kenchamma forgive us: We shall go. Oh, we shall go to the end of the pilgrimage like the two hundred and fifty thousand women of Bombay. We will go like them, we will go....[13]

The women envision a nation-wide women's revolt, liberating all of India. Kanthapura has become insignificant—it is a simply the village where the riots began. That is why these same women decide to burn down what is left of the village, rather than return to it. For them, life can never again be as it was in Kanthapura. The revolution is now self-perpetuating.

In retrospect, this changes from passivity to activity is explained by Achakka as a king of uncontrollable religious possession, growing out of the foundation of the villagers beliefs.

> Kenchamma forgive us, but there is something that has entered our hearts, an abundance like the Himavathy on Gauri's night, when lights come floating down the Rampur corner, lights come floating down from Rampur and Maddur and Tippur, lights lit on the betel leaves, and with flower and Kumkum and song we let them go, and they will go

down the Ghats to the morning of the sea, the lights
on the betel leaves, and the Mahatma will gather it
all he will gather it by the sea, and he will bless
us.[14]

At the end of the story, when Ranga Gowda tells Achakka
"'There's neither man nor mosquito in Kanthapura...,'"[15] it might be
easy to conclude that what has taken place in Kanthapura is
essentially negative. But this is not so. Though the value and the
vision of peaceful, happy co-existence that the women and the
novelist identify with the Mahatama have not been fulfilled today
any more than they were in 1937 when the novel was written or
1947 when independence was attained, their conception remains an
uplifting one, of a day when "Ravana will be slain and Sita freed....
And we shall all be happy."[16] Kanthapura's women perform heroic
deeds like Kamala Devi Chattopadhyaya, Aruna Asaf Ali, Sarojini
Naidu and Hansa Mehta. They are not only good mothers and
sisters but also great freedom-fighters. Neither R.K. Narayan in *The
Dark Room* nor Mulk Raj Anand in *Gauri* could show such heroic
deeds in their women characters.

We come to Raja Rao's *The Serpent and the Rope*. K.R.
Srinivasa Iyengar says "If *Kanthapura* is Raja Rao's *Ramayana*,
then *The Serpent and the Rope* is his *Mahabharata*. If *Kanthapura*
has a recognizable epic equality, *The Serpent and the Rope* is more
than a miniature epic—it is almost encyclopaedia in its scope."[17]
M.K. Naik comments, "If *Kanthapura* is the Indo-Anglian history
as modern Sthalapurana, or legendary history of a place, *The Serpent
and the Rope*—a far more complex work—is the novel as a modern
Indian Mahapurana (major epic legend) in miniature...."[18] The story
moves around Ramaswamy, Madeleine and Savithri.

The hero, Ramaswamy, is a young man of great literary cultures.
He knows Kannada, Sanskrit, English, French and Italian. He is a
vastly read and widely travelled man, "a wanderer on earth" or a
"holy vagabond." He has as much knowledge of Catholicism,
Catharism, Manichaenism, Darwinism, Marxism, Conceptualism,
Existentialism, Surrealism and Dadaism as of Zoroastrianism, Islam,
Taoism, Confucianism, Hinduism, Vedantism, Buddhism, Jainism,
Yoga, Lingayats and Tantrics. He describes Greek, Roman, and
Hindu gods and goddesses and mythology and Christian saints with

the same understanding as he does historical heroes, things, queens, statesmen and politicians of the different countries of the world. He talks with the same authority about Socrates, Plato, Aristotle, Mani, Plotinus, Peter, Abetlard, Neitzsche, Jeremy Bentham, Sigmund Freud, Jaspers, Homer, Dante, Cervantes, Shakespeare, Marlowe, Montaigne, Rousseau, Lamartine, Péguy, Ronsard, Villon, Guizot, Renan, Chateaubriand, Verlaine, Rio Soleil, Saussuet, Cejame, Victor Hugo, Saint Beuve, Balzac, Jane Austen, Wordsworth, Shelley, Goldsmith, Dr. Johnson, Thackeray, Pascal, Zola, Dostoevsky, Paul Valery, Baudelaire, Rilke, Jean D'Arc, Claudel, Gide, Romain Rolland, Taine, Gerald Manley Hopkins, Cuillaume de Montanphyol, Thoreau, Emerson, Whitman, Gerald de Narvel, Sir William Jones and Sir John Woodroffe as he does about Yagnyavalka, Maitreya, Gargi, Sage Madhava, Sri Sankara, Nagarjun, Panini, Bhartrihari, Kalidasa, Roger Ramanujam, Saint Ramananda, Tulsidas, Kabir, Mira, Dayananda, Vivekananda, Ramakrishna, Rabindranath Tagore, Aurobindo, Ananda Coomaraswamy and Damodhara Gupta.

Being a product of many cultures Rama's mind is a seething whirlpool of cultural currents and cross currents. Unlike the simple story-teller in *Kanthapura*, who knew only Indian myths and legends, Rama is familiar with myths and legends of different civilisations and he can discern parallels between them and forge a link between the past and the present by comprehending the essential oneness of history.

The Serpent and the Rope, therefore, contains the myths of Shiva, Parvathi and Nandi (35), Radha, Krishna and Durvasa (380-382), or the legends of Satyakama and Ramadevi, the princess of Avanti (119-121), of Jagannatha Bhatta and Shahjehan's daughter (178), or of Ishwara Bhatta's emphasising to his Brahma Bhatta the importance of retelling of Rama's story every Saturday (250-255), as well as the Chinese fable of Wang-Chu and Chang-fi (125-126), or the classical myths of Demster, Poseidon and Ulysses (37), or the tale of Tristan and Iseult. At some places the legend of one civilization is blended into that of another while at other places the mythical incident is related to the historical one. The love of Iseult for Tristan is analogous to that of Radha for Krishna or of Savitri for Satyavan (363). Holy Grail has its origin in Buddhism and Chalice is the mendicant alms-bowl upturned (67). Karna and Uttara of the *Mahabharata* are no different from Innocent III or Hugue de Noyers, Bishop of Auxerre. "There's always a Karna and an Uttara in every battle, whether their names be changed to Innocent III or Hugue de Noyers, Bishop of Auxerre.... It was the same battle between Pascal and the Jesuit Fathers" (101). "Godse, who killed Mahatama Gandhi, was like Saint Dominic" (171). King George VI who had succeeded to the throne only after his brother Edward had abdicated his claims is equated with Bharata, King of Ayodhya, who merely substituted for a brother for nobler than himself (204).

Madeline, the wife of Ramaswamy, is vividly created and her life too passes through the most breath-taking vicissitudes. Brought up in the Judaic-Graeco tradition, she could be an atheist, a Catholic, a communist and even a Buddhist, because all these beliefs (or lack of belief) are based on dualistic principles. Bhattacharya says: "To her, marriage was like a pair of parallel rails on which runs the life's train. She had accepted Rama, she wanted to possess him wholly, but she could never merge her identity with that of his, she could never become a member of his larger family, accepting his tradition as her own and continuing with that tradition in future; she could never be like the Brahmaputra that merges with the Ganga and conjointly flows to the sea."[19] She became a Buddhist, "The intellectual brilliance of Buddhism has no equal in the world; it's the religion of the modern age...since we could not accept God, we had to invent a mother of God, make her into a Virgin, and then accept her Son and find out how he was born. How simple and beautiful is the birth of the Buddha, in comparison.... Buddha is born, like any others, in the normal psychological way."[20]

L.S.R. Krishna Shastry says, "Savitri too—the Cambridge-returned Rajput princess discovers the full meaning of life through Rama's association. There is mutual attraction between them, and while Rama sees himself in Savitri, Savitri feels he is her Satyavan. He is Tristan and she is Iseult, he Krishna and she Radha. Even the toe-rings given by Little Mother, Rama's second step-mother, seem to fit her. They also marry, in a symbolic way, in England, but soon she returns to India to marry the bridegroom of her parent's choice—Pratap, a jagirdar. Both Rama and Savitri realise ultimately that their 'marriage' is only spiritual and should never be corrupted by physical desire. He reveals to her the true nature of love-rejoicing in the rejoicing of the other. He accepts her as his principle, his Queen Savitri achieves her happiness in life as a true wife."[21]

Dr. S. Nagarajan says, "*The Serpent and the Rope* is Indian in another sense, it makes a central use of certain important Hindu myths and rituals....The particular ritual is the worship of Ramaswami by Savithri. This worship of one human being by another has given offence to many. I think the dissatisfaction arises from some misunderstanding."[22] First, the basic fact in the novel is the peculiar rendering of the characters of both Rama and Savithri which discourages a full-blooded human approach to them; Madeleine, the wife of Rama, compares the impersonality of her husband to "mountain-air, the honeypine of the heights, the smell of incense while the mist rises." Secondly, the episode is insistently mythicized from the very start. Thus Savithri says, "Bring me some Ganges water in this,"[23] and Rama narrates, "I put some plain water in her silver plate."[24] Elsewhere he says that all water is Ganges water—which is incidentally a plain statement of an accepted current mode of reference in Raja Rao's part of the country. The mythicization is self-conscious on the part of the characters. Savithri says:

"This Cambridge undergraduate, who smokes like a chimney and dances to barbarian jazz, she says unto you, I've known you my Lord for a thousand lives, from *Janam* have I known my Krishna...."[25] The reply that Rama makes is also stylized. "And the Lord knows himself because Radha is, else he would have gone into penance and sat on Himalay. The Jumna flows and peacock feathers are on his diadem, because Radha's smiles enchant the creepers and the birds. Radha is the music of the dusk, the red earth, the meaning of night. And this, my love, my spouse," I whispered, Is from my home. "This is coconut, this is betel nut, this is kumkum and these the toe-rings my Mother wore, and left for my bridal."[26]

The myth of Radha and Krishna is well-known as well as the allegorical interpretation of their love. In a passage filled with the sweet longing of the *gopi* for Krishna, of the soul for the divine, Raja Rao describes Savithri's desire for Rama:

A Hindu woman knows how to worship her Krishna, her lord. When the moon shines over the Jumna and lights are lit in the households, and the cows are milked, then it is Janaki's son plays on the banks of the Yamuna in Brindavan...Krishna dances on the red earth. What Gopi, my Lord, would not go to this festival of love? Women lose their shame...for in Brindavan Krishna the Lord dances.[27]

Let us examine Raja Rao's references to Tristan and Isolt. Savithri is to Rama what Isolt of Ireland was to Tristan. In the way that Tristan is unsuccessful in his relationship with Isolt of the White hands, "no warmth came for there was no love in him," so too is Rama unsuccessful with Madeleine when he returns after being with Savithri in London and Cambridge. Savithri understands him and Rama accepts her as a positive force. Some would prefer to think that he forces her into accepting his view of say, woman's function, seen in relation to man. This is exemplified in the plane-radar comparison (368).

It seems more likely, however, that Savithri is in positive agreement with Rama, and not merely a receiver of ideas. Madeleine wrote to Rama from Aix that she liked "to be tortured and to be his slave." But Rama did not want a slave. Rama, somewhat ice-heartedly, excludes Madeleine as a possible companion of pilgrimage. To Madeleine Rama says categorically: "One can never be converted to Hinduism,"[28] one has to be born in India. Annie Walden says:

Tristan refers to Isolt of the White Hands as his 'gentle pain.' Rama echoes this over and over in his attitude to Madeleine. The day he returned from India to discover she had been converted to Buddhism he acknowledges the futility of pretending that they could communicate with each other. 'I was filled with such pain that I was on the point of sobbing my heart hollow.' Much earlier, after Rama's return from a previous trip to India, Madeleine called to him, 'My love' and he replied, 'Mamie, my friend.' Madeleine asked him if she had failed his gods, to which he replied, 'No...you've failed me.'

On Tristan's wedding night, he is filled with remorse as he prepared to go to bed with Isolt of the White Hands, Remembering how tenderly he loves and longs for Queen Isolt, wife of Mark. "Indeed, I am so committed to the Queen that I must not lie with this girl, and am so committed to this girl that I cannot possibly retreat. Compare this passage with Rama's account of his feelings towards both Madeleine and Savithri."[29] S.C. Harrex says, "One can conclude from Walden's comparative approach that the effect of Raja Rao's use of Tristan parallel (and this effect is a strength in the novel) is that the metaphysical issues underlying the personal relationships are put on emotional perspective.... Seem as Tristan, Rama the metaphysician has more credence as Rama the lover, and the human dimensions of the symbolic chronicle can be communicated at the crucial level of understanding through feelings."[30]

Then, there is another ritual, known after Savithri, the legendary heroine who wins her husband back from death after pleading with Yama, the God of Death, who also restores her husband's lost Kingdom to him. Savithri is one of the prototypes of wifely devotion, and Hindu brides even today are blessed with the benediction that they may be like Savithri. There is an exchange of conversation between Rama and Savithri.

"Then you, become me, will be the real Savithri."

"And who's the Satyavan?"

"The Self, the Truth," I said, and heaved a sigh....

> "No, Satyavan cannot die. Man must unto himself
> be himself and his bride. You remember I told you,
> all brides be Benaras born."[31]

Sometimes this ritual is also known as the Disha-Gauri ritual (*vrata*) with a different story to justify its observance by all married women. When the Pandavas, the heroes of the *Mahabharata*, were living in exile in the forest, having been deprived of all their possessions by their unrighteous cousins in a rigged game of dice, Draupadi, the common spouse of the Pandavas, approached Krishna and asked him what she should do that the Pandavas might regain their lost heritage. Krishna advised her to perform this ritual. It was, said Krishna, performed by Queen Damayanti when her husband, King Nala, lost his possessions in somewhat similar circumstances. S. Nagarajan says, "However, in the part of the country where Raja

Rao comes from, the ritual is known as the Jyothisthambha ritual. And the story is different again this time. King Vajrababu of Saurastha lost by sudden death his only son who was as famous for his virtue as for his valour. The king and the queen were plunged into sorrow, and they were even unwilling to part with the dead body. On the contrary, they wished to see their son married as if he were still living. They offered a reward of a lakh of rupees to anyone who would give his daughter in marriage to the dead man. A certain Brahman, living in great poverty, was tempted by the offer and gave away his daughter. The marriage duly took place. The dead body with all the adornments of a bridegroom and the bride were taken to the cremation-field and left there by themselves as if it were their bridal chamber. Night fell and the poor girl saw moving fires and heard the blood-curdling shrieks and howls of ghosts and demons all around her. But she did not want to leave the place because the dead body represented her husband. She prayed to the great god Shiva, who according to still current belief, is fond of haunting cremation and burial grounds (he is the god of dissolution and destruction after all) and to Shiva's consort, Parvati. They were pleased with her devotion to her husband and revived the dead man. In honour of this exemplary spouse, the ritual, we are told, was instituted."[32]

In all these rituals, it will be observed, there are certain common elements, there is a woman who is utterly devoted not unto but even beyond death to her husband. S. Nagarajan explains, "She is a *sati*, as we say in India, through her efforts her husband gets back his lost heritage; in two versions, there is also a revival of a dead husband representing a triumph over death.... There is, to begin with, the duty of the wife to be a *sati* (derived from a Sanskrit root meaning *to be*) who in fact is a *sati*? How can she help her husband to win back his lost heritage—that is, his true identity? How should she bring him back from death—which in the novel is interpreted as a belief in the existence of the object, of the world, *samsara*? What exists, of course, the one without a second, is a self, neither man nor woman nor the world. To think that the world exists is the metaphysical disease; it is *avidya*, the time-born ignorance of the native of reality, of which it is said in Indian philosophy that it is without a beginning but not without an end."[33] Woman is *prakrti*, creation and man is *purusa*, the self. *Prakrti* exists to prove that it has no existence independent of *purusa*. This is the paradox, says Ramaswamy, the mortal paradox of man; and Savithri adds, that the paradox is the fever. The fever is allayed and removed by discipleship to the Guru. Ramaswamy tells Savithri during the worship, "Don't you know that in marriage both the spouse and the espoused become anointed unto godhead? That explains why in Hindu marriages the married couple can only fall at the feet of the Guru and the Guru alone—for the Guru is higher than any god."[34] It is the Guru who brings the lantern and shows us that we saw as the serpent in the dusk of the dying evening and cried out in terror is only a piece of twisted rope. When the wife forgets that the Truth, the realisation of the sole reality of the self, is the aim of marriage, she ceases to be a *sati* and must be regarded as having failed her husband as Madeleine fails Ramaswamy.

Savithri embodies not only the feminine principle as surrender to the masculine but also the hypostatic presence that the protagonist, Rama, has been seeking. Rama's association with Savithri gives him an integral vision and feelings.

"People have asked me—Georges among them—what indeed it was that happened between Savithri and me in Cambridge. Nothing more hand happened, in fact, than if you look deep and long at silence you perceive an orb of centripetal sound which explains why Parvathi is the daughter of Himalay, and Sita born to the furrow of the field. I heard myself say I heard myself. Or I send my eyes see that I saw. She became the awareness behind my awareness, the leap of my understanding. I lost the world and she became it.

For whatever I gave her she accepted, as the Ganges receives the waters of the Himalayas, that go on down to the sea and come again as white flakes of snow, then blue, then very green; and as, when the sun comes northward again, the ice melts and once more the Ganges takes the water to the sea—so we gave love to each other, as though it did not belong to us but to a principle, an other, an impersonal reality, from which we saw gifts emerge in each of us....[35]

K. Venkatachari says, "The union between Rama and Savithri that culminates ultimately in a fantastic ritual wedding symbolises the marriage of Being and Power to Become the Divine (Kameswara and Kameshwari) as a result of which 'Power assumes certain postures—*mudras*—in its stressing to manifest as Universe. The first of such produced stresses is from the *Tattva* aspect, *sadasiva* and from the *mantra aspect*, inchoate sound or movement called, *Nada*. The state is shown by the Hexagon with a crescent moon, the symbol of *Nada*, in its centre.... In the next Mantric stage... the crescent moon enlarges into the full moon—like *Bindu*.... The word *Bindu* also means seed, for it is the seed of the universe as the result of the union of its ultimate principles as Siva and Sakti. The point or *Bindu*, is shown as a circle, so as to display its content and a line divides the point, one half representing the 'I' and the other, the 'this' aspect of experience... the *Mantra* equivalent of the state in which the *Bindu* divides and becomes threefold is the first manifested sound, which is the great Mantra, *Om*. Rama's account of what happened between Savithri and himself suggests the profoundly symbolic character of Raja Rao's work. *The Serpent and the Rope*, since 'the orb of centripetal sound' that he speaks of is *Bindu*, the supreme expression of Shiva Shakti...."[36]

REFERENCES

1. S.V.V., "Raja Rao," *The Illustrated Weekly of India*, 5 January 1964, 44.

2. Raja Rao, 44

3. Quoted from G.S. Amur, "Raja Rao—the Kannada Phase," *Journal of the Karnatak University*, Vol. X, 1966, humanities, 46-47.

4. Elizabeth Wohl, 'Raja Rao on America,' *Span*, Vol. XIV, No. 1, January 1973, 37.

5. Raja Rao, *Kanthapura*, Delhi, 2.

6. Raja Rao, 108.

7. Raja Rao, 104.

8. Raja Rao, 105.

9. Raja Rao, 151.

10. Raja Rao.

11. Ruth Vanita, "Ravana shall be slain and Sita freed...." The Feminine Principle in *Kanthapura, Woman/Image/Text: Feminist Readings of Literary Text*, Ed. Lola Chatterjee, New Delhi: Trianka Publication, 189.

12. *Ibid.*, 190

13. Raja Rao, *Kanthapura*, 161-62.

14. *Ibid.*, 180.

15. *Ibid.*, 182.

16. *Ibid.*, 258.

17. K.R. Srinivasa Iyengar, *Indian Writing in English*, New Delhi, Sterling Publishers Pvt. Ltd., 1993 (Reprint), 397.

18. M.K. Naik, "The Serpent and the Ropes: The Indian Anglian Novel as Epic Legend," *Critical Essays on Indian Writing in English*, 257.

19. P.C. Bhattacharya, Indo-Anglian Literature and the Works of Raja Rao, New Delhi, Atma Ram & Sons, 1985, 292.

20. Raja Rao, *The Serpent and the Rope*, Delhi Orient Paper backs, 1960, 301.

21. D.S.R. Karishna Sastry, "Raja Rao," Calcutta: *The Second Writers Worship Literary Reader*, Ed. P. Lal, 1973, 62.

22. Dr. S. Nagarajan, "A Note on Myth Ritual in *The Serpent and the Rope*." *The Journal of Commonwealth Literature*, Vol. VII, No. 1, June 1972, 45.

23. Raja Rao, *The Serpent and the Rope*, 211.

24. *Ibid.*

25. *Ibid.*, 211-12.

26. *Ibid.*, 212.

27. *Ibid.*, 209.

28. *Ibid.*, 331.

29. Annie Walden quoted in S.C. Harrex's "The Fascination of What's Difficult: Some Student Responses to Raja Rao," *Indo-English Literature*, Ed. K.K. Sharma, Ghaziabad; Vimal Prakashan, 1977, 190.

30. S.C. Harrex, *Ibid.*, 191.

31. Raja Rao, *The Serpent and the Rope*, 360.

32. S. Nagarajan, "A Note on Myth and Ritual in *The Serpent and the Rope*," *The Journal of Commonwealth Literature*, Vol. VII, No. 1, June 1972, 47.

33. *Ibid.*, 47.

34. Raja Rao, *The Serpent and the Rope*, 212.

35. *Ibid.*, 169-170.

36. K. Venkatachari, "The Feminine Principle in Raja Rao's *The Serpent and the Rope*," *Critical Responses: Commonwealth Literature*, Sterling Publishers Pvt. Ltd., New Delhi.

13

The Serpent and the Rope:
A Reappraisal

H.U. KHAN*

I

The Serpent and the Rope (1960) is regarded as the spiritual auto-biography of the great novelist Raja Rao. It was published after a long gap of twentytwo years after the publication of his first great novel, *Kanthapura* in 1938. With the publication of Mulk Raj Anand's *Untouchable* (1935) and *Coolie* (1936), R.K. Narayan's *Swami and Friends* (1935) and *The Dark Room* (1938), and Raja Rao's *Kanthapura* (1938) novels in Indian English had come of age. Raja Rao is a sincere artist with a meagre literary output. He has written only three novels in addition to short stories, essays and sketches. His third novel, *The Cat and Shakespeare* was published in 1965. As a matter of fact Raja Rao wanted to achieve perfection in his literary art, and therefore, he wrote very slowly and revised his literary works perfectly. He was also a philosopher and a religious man. Therefore, his religious and philosophical concerns left him little time for his literary art of writing novels. Raja Rao was not a prolific writer.

Although Raja Rao was a contemporary artist of Mulk Raj Anand and R.K. Narayan, the two great Indian novelists writing in English, he was entirely different in his art as a novelist. He won the Sahitya Akademi Award in 1966 for his great novel, *The*

---

*Prof. and Head, Deptt. of English, Govt. College of Education, Bilaspur.

Serpent and the Rope (1960). The prestigious award of 'Padma Bhusan' was also given to him in 1969 by the President of India. This novel is a meritorious work of art of the novelist's maturity and at once he was hailed as a pioneer in the realm of Indian English fiction. In terms of quality of an epic novel, *Kanthapura* is indeed Raja Rao's Ramayan, his next great novel, *The Serpent and the Rope* may be rightly called as his Mahabharata. Both the novels reflect the novelist's great learning in the realm of philosophy, religion and mythology. This Sahitya Akademi Award-winning novel, *The Serpent and the Rope,* a truly magnificent novel by the great novelist, is one of the best Indian novels ever written. The novel is highly acclaimed by both Press and writers; it portrays the meeting of East and West on the most intimate plane through the story of Ramaswamy, an Indian, and Madeleine, a French girl, who meet at a French University shortly after the World War II. Their union is the central theme of the book. It is in telling this story that Ramaswamy reveals, much more deeply than most writers are able to suggest in their lifetime, the meaning of love. Thus, Raja Rao has founded a new genre of prose fiction and has enlarged the scope of the novel-form through this great novel which has brought him name and fame in the eyes of the world.

II

The story of the novel is narrated by Ramaswamy, the hero-narrator of the novel. He belongs to a South Indian Brahmin family, and their ancestral home is called 'Vishnu Bhawan.' It is a well-to-do orthodox Indian family. The last rites of their ancestors since times immemorial have always been performed at Banaras in Uttar Pradesh. His grandfather Kittanna is a noble heroic person. Nothing was considered impossible by him. There were a number of aunts in the family. One of them was Aunt Lakshaamma, a widow who looked after the orphans in the family. When she died Rama could not believe that she was really dead.

> "The other day—that is, some seven or eight years ago—when we were told that Aunt Lakshamma, elder to my grandfather by many years, had actually died, I did not believe it. For I cannot understand what death means" (*The Serpent and the Rope*).

Ramaswamy or Rama became an orphan at the age of seven when his mother Gauri died. After his mother's death his father married a second time, and then a third time. From his second wife he had three daughters, Kapila, Saroja and Sukumari. From his third wife Vishalakshmi, referred to as Little Mother in the novel, he had one son, Sridhara. He died when the child was hardly eleven months old.

Rama became a lecturer in History after completing his education and took up research work and went to France at the University of Caen, where he first met Madeleine. She was twentysix years old while Rama was only twenty one. They fell in love and studied together in France.

> "Madeleine was altogether unreal. That is why, I think, she had never married anyone—in fact she had never touched anyone. She said that during the Nazi occupation, towards the end of 1943, a German officer had tried to touch her hair; it looked so magical, and it looked the perfect Nordic hair. She said he had brought his hands near her face, and she had only to smile and he could not do anything. He bowed and went away."

> "It was the Brahmin in me, she said, the sense that touch and untouch are so important, which she sensed; and she would let me touch her. Her hair was gold, and her skin for an Indian was like the unearthed marble with which we built our winter palaces."

> *(The Serpent and the Rope,* page 13)

It was love at first sight. They were soon married. A son was born to them. He soon fell ill and died. Madeleine was shocked. She could never get over his death. Soon after the death of the child, Rama was informed that his father was ill. His father wanted him to return to India, and therefore, Rama came to India. Soon after his arrival his father died. So he went to Banares accompanied by the Little Mother. The funeral rites being over, they sailed down the river in a boat. Banares reminds Rama of the rich cultural heritage of India, of her spirituality, traditions and customs. From

Benares they went to Allahabad where they stayed for some time with an old friend of Rama's father. There he met Pratap Singh who was betrothed to Savithri, the young Western educated daughter of the Raja of Surajpur. She did not want to marry Pratap. She came back home from Cambridge for vacations. Rama was fascinated to her. Rama was fascinated by her charm and beauty.

In India Rama had two sisters, Saroja and Sukmari. Saroja was a young and beautiful educated lady but she was dissatisfied with conventional and orthodox life. Sukmari was an ordinary school-going girl contended and happy with her routine life. Rama had to return to France to complete his research work. He expected that he would take one year more to complete his research work. During that time Georges was visiting their residence frequently. Lezo also came there thrice a week to give lessons in Pali to Madeleine in order to help her to study Buddhism. He tried to make love to her but was badly rebuked.

Rama and Madeleine also visited uncle Charles and aunt Zoubie. Then Catherine, the cousin of Madeleine came to stay with them for some time. Georges and Catherine fell in love and later on they were married.

Savithri also visited them on her way to Cambridge from India. Rama also visited Cambridge in connection with his research work. He came in close contact with Savithri. He was passionately in love with her. Savithri also visited him in his apartments. One morning she came with coconut and kumkum and performed aarti and touched his feet and took him to be her master with God as their witness. Rama gave her the toe-rings which Little Mother had given to him for Madeleine. Savithri was ready to elope with him, but he advised her not to do so. Savithri married Pratap Singh. It was hoped that she would be a good wife to her husband.

Rama received letters from Saroja and Litter Mother and was informed of affairs at home. When Saroja's marriage was fixed, he came to India to supervise the arrangements of the marriage as head of the family. During this time Madeleine underwent a Caesarian operation for delivery of a child. Her life was saved but her second child also died. It was the second shock which she received. It changed the whole course of their future life. Rama came back to

Madeleine. He found that there was a great change in her. She gave up all her comforts and became a Buddhist. She spent most of her time in prayer and meditation. They continued to live together.

Rama went to London for his research work. He fell ill and was hospitalised for a long term medical treatment. His lungs was to be taken out. Savithri who was in London frequently visited him. Lakshmi, a young lady whom he had met at Cambridge also visited him. After his medical treatment he came to Paris to complete his research work. He also visited Madeleine and found that she had become a 'Sanyasni.' After a short stay in Paris, he returned to his apartment. It was their last meeting. Divorce proceedings were initiated at Madeleine's instance and they were finally divorced.

Rama was still in France but without a home. Little Mother lived with Saroja and her husband. Sukmari was also married and went to her husband's home. Catherine and Georges lived in Paris. Rama visited them frequently. He was deeply attached to Vera, their only child. Georges completed his research work. After the work was over, he planned to go to Travancore where he hoped to find a 'Guru.' At the end of the novel it was not clear whether Rama would return his home in India or his attachment to Vera kept him back in Paris.

> "How was Vera," said Catherine. "You don't need to go to India for a job, Rama. You look after Vera. Vera loves you: she is so quiet when you are here. And you can write your abstruse theories. I will give you back your small room. And Georges will drink chocolate and translate your clever ideas."

(The Serpent and the Rope, page 405)

III

The title *The Serpent and the Rope* at once captures our attention and indicates its basic theme: the anti-thesis between Appearance and Reality. The serpent stands for Appearance or illusion, unreality, 'May' or this 'Sansar' while the rope stands for Reality or truth or 'Braham' or the Absolute. This world is merely 'Maya,' unreal, an illusion. It is merely the serpent. Due to our ignorance we take it to be the rope *i.e.* Truth or Braham or the Absolute. We can be saved only by the Guru from this illusion or ignorance.

The analogy of the 'Rope' is taken from the non-dualistic philosophy of Indian philosopher Sankaracharya who flourished in the eighth century A.D. He says: "Just as owing to one's ignorance of the rope, the rope appears to be a serpent, the self is regarded as the individual soul, owing to the absence of the true knowledge of the self. At the word of a reliable person, the illusion disappears and what seemed to be a serpent is now seen as a rope. When truth is known we are no longer deluded by the appearance—the snake—appearance vanishes into the reality of the rope, the world vanishes into Braham. This darkness of ignorance is dispelled by the light of wisdom which the Guru brings. It is then that we realise that Braham or the Absolute is the Reality or the rope, and all else is serpent or unreality."[1]

The Serpent and the Rope can be read at various levels and interpreted in different ways as it is a complex work of art which has brought name and fame to the novelist in the eyes of the world. A number of themes and ideas have gone into the making of complex texture of the novel. However, the basic theme of the novel is the quest for self-knowledge or self-fulfilment. It is the hero, Ramaswamy, who calls himself a 'holy vagabond' for he wanders about in search of self-knowledge and self-realisation. He comes to the conclusion that in the spiritual quest for knowledge the role of a 'Guru' is essential. Ramaswamy is an extremely sensitive, imaginative and learned Indian, and the novel may be called his spiritual autobiography, because it is a record of his progress towards self-realisation. Ramaswamy is a close self-portrait of the novelist, the novel is regarded as the spiritual auto-biography of the novelist himself.

Ramaswamy, the hero-narrator of the novel, wanders round the world in the quest of self-knowledge. He calls himself a 'holy vagabond' and a pilgrim. There are two ways of self-realisation. One is the way of the denial of life, of renunciation and asceticism which is chosen by Madeleine. The other way is the way of active involvement in human life and human activity. This is the way chosen by Ramaswamy. He is involved in different kinds of human relationships. He is a son, brother, friend, lover and husband, and through his involvement in these relationships, he seeks to achieve self-knowledge which can be achieved only when the ego is destroyed. Rama rises above self and achieves a higher degree of self-discipline and self-realisation.

Ramaswamy's ideals are worldly enough. He falls in love, marries and hopes to settle down to the comfortable life of a professor in an Indian university. He tells us that once his doctorate was over, he would take Madeleine home, and she would settle with him. When Savithri enters his life, his marriage disintegrates rapidly. His relationship with Savithri acts as a catalyst. He cannot endure her marriage with Pratap and seeks compensation by plunging into an affair with Lakshmi in Bombay. But soon he realised his mistake that he had taken a wrong turn. He recovers his poise and sanity. The story of Gautama renouncing the pleasures of the world in order to seek salvation comes to his mind. The Lakshmi episode is over and Ramaswamy returns to France.

Madeleine has become a Buddhist ascetic. While in London Rama falls seriously ill and has to undergo an operation of lungs. During this time Savithri comes to meet him. He now comes to terms with Savithri's mundane relationship with her husband Pratap. This relationship does not clash with the spiritual bond between himself and Savithri. In the end Rama finds most of his worldly ties cut off. He has to take a divorce from Madeleine who has now renounced the world. He is filled with a strange restlessness. He realizes that he must go to his Guru at Travancore. "The end of Rama's quest at the feet of his Guru is in keeping with the age-old spiritual tradition of India which gives the Guru the highest place in Man's quest for Truth. Rama does not tell us which way is to be his. But it is enough to know that he is on his way to his Guru, that his ship is nearing port."[2]

The hero heard the call of his Guru, the Abode of Truth, and forgot all that he had planned, done or suffered and came to regard it as mere illusion. Spiritual truth is higher than physical truth. It is in this higher sense that Rama is a self-portrait of the novelist and the novel is his spiritual autobiography.

IV

The novel, *The Serpent and the Rope* (1960) also examines the theme of East-West encounter from an entirely new perspective. The East-West conflict is not the result of any political differences but it is a result of cultural, religious and philosophical concerns between India and Europe. India, as depicted in the novel, is not in general terms but from the viewpoint of the hero-narrator, Ramaswamy, who makes his own preference for the Brahmanic Vedantic India based on metaphysical ideas.

Ramaswamy, the hero-narrator, is an Indian Brahmin, broad-minded and liberal by virtue of his learning and his life-long quest for truth and knowledge. He met Madeleine when he went to France in 1946 for higher studies. He fell in love with her at first sight. He was fascinated by her physical charm, but it was a union of minds. The two have their close temperamental affinities. Rama is pagan and sensuous and so is Madeleine. They live together for a pretty long time in France and get married. Being an Indian Brahmin Rama believes in the 'Advaita' philosophy of the Vedanta. Madeleine is also a devout Catholic and there is much that is common in Brahminism and Catholicism. Both religions stress and value of rituals and ceremonies. Through his marriage Rama comes near experiencing man's highest state—that of self-realisation. Spiritualizing of physical union is a step toward realising that as a man he is separate from woman, but as a human being he is one with woman. Here he realizes that as a man he is separate from the animal, but as a being, the man, the woman, the animal, the stone are all one. Through his marriage he understands the attitudes and values of both the countries—India and Europe. He is thus both of the East and West.[3]

When Rama returns to India to perform the last rites of his father, Little Mother, his second step-mother, treats him with love and affection, reposes full confidence in him and treats him as the guardian and head of the family. His step-sister Saroja also loves him and has full confidence in him. He is also loved and admired by Madeleine, Savithri, Lakshmi, Catherine and others. Rama with his step-mother goes to Benares to perform the last rites of his father. He says:

> "I cannot remember anything more about Benares.
> We spent a further two or three days there, and
> while Little Mother went to hear 'parayanams' in a

> private temple I wandered, like a sacred cow, among
> the lanes and temples of the Holy City."
>
> (*The Serpent and the Rope*, 25)

When he was in England, the same emotions are observed:

> "For me, as I have said already, the past was
> necessary to understand the present. I felt England
> in my bones and breath; how I reverenced her"
> (199).

Madeleine is a dutiful good house wife. She takes care of her husband. She always looks to his comforts. Rama always finds her shy and cute like an 'Indian woman.' She even tries to participate in his superstitions in a playful manner. She once expresses:

> "I love you, Rama, with a strange, distant impenitent
> love. I wish I had an assurance of love, that I did
> not love you for your purity,...I can, And therefore I
> await you, you my young love." How Indian
> sometimes I become—I see and I wonder" (40).

We also find that the conflict between Eastern and Western civilization comes on the surface when Rama brings two little toe-rings of his mother for Madeleine. As a matter of fact the toe-rings are the symbol of the continuity of the family tradition.

> "The toe-rings, I thought; what a sweet thought of
> Little Mother's, My mother had them from my
> grandmother, and when my father married Saroja's
> mother, the toe-rings went to her...now they would
> go to her who bore Krishna to me" (53).

But the unfortunate part of the story was that Rama did not give the toe-rings to Madeleine, but presented her to Savithri who accepted Rama as her lord and Master.

In London, Rama put up in a room on the third floor of an old building. He was away from Savithri, but her thoughts were full of her. He remembered all that she had said and done during his stay at Cambridge. According to her promise, she came next morning. He wanted to touch her, but refrained as he felt that there was something strange, mysterious about her. She had come prepared to worship him, her lord to perform 'aarti' and in this way to accept him as her husband. Then she knelt before him. Kneeling again and placing her head on his feet, she stayed there long with her breath breaking into gentle sobs. Then she gently held herself up. Taking the 'kumkum' from the box Rama placed kumkum on her brow, at the parting of her hair. Then he suddenly remembered her mother's toe-rings and brought out from the old box and presented them to Savithri who was highly delighted to receive them.

> "Yes, but it was a preparation made a very long time ago—a long time, Savithri. Not a life, not ten lives, but life upon life...." "Yes, she said, 'This Cambridge undergraduate, who smokes like a chimney and dances to barbarian jazz, she says unto you,' I've known my Lord for a thousand lives, from 'janam to janam' have I known my Krishna..." (211, 212).

The interesting part of the story is that where Madeleine fails, Savithri succeeds. Savithri is absolutely Western in her life-style— she smokes, dances, dates—and understand Rama's deeper yearnings. She readily makes herself the means by which Rama can accomplish his spiritual quest. The relationship which exists between Savithri and Rama is based on the spiritual and cultural ethos. They go through a symbolic marriage where Rama gives her his mother's toe-rings. The novelist has drawn beautifully both the characters— Savithri and Madeleine—in the following words:

> "I think, what is this India we are building? Oh, Rama, it makes me sad, sad! Some want it to become like our neighbour China, and others like their foster-mother white England. And nobody wants India to be India.... With Madeleine everything was explanation. With Savithri it was recognition" (340).

Saroja is the step-sister of Rama from his father's second wife. Rama gives us an account of her fascinating personality. Saroja had grown so lovely. She was tall and fair in the family. She had a deep and a noble wisdom. Saroja was a strange sensation for Rama. Here was a mystery which he had never observed before: the girl becoming woman, and the thousand ways it shows itself; in shyness, in language, in prime presence. He would himself pluck flowers for her hair and take her out on long walks and speak to her of Europe and of Madeleine. Saroja also wanted to come and study in Europe. She said she would be a doctor, and later she would get Little Mother to live with them. Rama was intoxicated with Saroja's presence, like a deer could be before a waterfall, or an elephant before a mountain peak. It is indicated that Rama was in love with Saroja, even though she was his sister. He prays for Saroja and feels that "it was the absence that had become presence again." He realised that, "All brides be Benares born," and he smelled the Ganges and the Jamuna in her. They were mutually attracted.

One evening Savithri went back early to college. Rama dined alone with one of her girl friends Lakshmi. She was just an ordinary girl and she thought that Savithri was a great flirt, for she went out with several youngmen. She told Rama:

> "I cannot understand how Savithri can go about with so many men at the same time. You'll hate me for saying it, but she's flirt. 'I don't mean she does things.' Lakshmi continued, Indians are shocked at this freedom. It comes from going straight to liberty after centuries of 'zenana' life" (168).

Such views were resulted from the complete failure to understand her real character. As Rama told Lakshmi, such freedom was the result of perfect innocence and not of sin. "We shall never have such innocence, Savithri is a saint." For Savithri to be in love, was to be in bondage, and to be in such bondage was to be free in the real sense of the word. She wanted to surrender to Truth—and be free. That is why when Rama taught Savithri the 'Nirvana Shataka' she was very happy and she could sing it with deep emotion.[4]

One evening at Savithri's request, Rama took Lakshmi and Sharifa out to dinner. He told them a great deal about India. They were much amused at his account of Benares, and that Indians in England look like Brahminic kins. Rama talked to them at length about Indian history. As in Vedantic Philosophy, and in Music, there is nothing new, and no going backward and forward, so also in Indian history there is no to and fro movement. He further says:

> "Indian history plays a melody to itself creating and recreating itself, standing not against sound but in

silence. India is apart, that is why she has no history. India is everybody's: India is in every body. It is in that sense, I think, that Mahatma Gandhi said, "When we are free, all will be free." Let us truly be satyagrahis—graspers of the Truth."

Georges is one of the brilliant young Russian intellectuals brought up in the best of European and Orthodox traditions. His father was a well-known critic belonging to a progressive group of thinkers. Georges is deeply religious. He speaks with the noble anguish of the believer with the feeling that if God is not true He must be made true, and that if God could not be made true, then impious man must be made to go through hell fire so that God might be. He seems to have only metaphysical and religious interests. There is nothing sensual about him. He is a frequent visitor, is often found alone with Madeleine, often they have long philosophical discussions and go out together for long walks, but he never tries to make love to Madeleine or seduce her as does Lezo. Madeleine brought him that feminine presence which man seeks in pain—a hand, a look, the gesture to lift a coat or help across a difficult step. Madeleine's hand was ever there, and she seemed to sure of herself; it was Georges who leaned on her.

In later course of his life Georges marries Catherine and is a good and affectionate husband to her. He continues to love her and treat her kindly, even after he knows of her unfaithfulness to him. In the end, we get a glimpse of their happy married life. He corrects Ramaswamy's thesis and provides him with that 'home' and sense of belonging which he urgently needs. Indeed Georges is a true and sincere friend.

Self-indulgence is represented by Lezo. In spite of his philosophy, he is not above making advances to Madeleine, and by Uncle Charles whose occasional visits to Paris lead to sexual affair resulting in bad headache. On the other hand, Ramaswamy does not suffer from any inhibitions in matters of sex. He accepts it for what it is, neither shunning it nor pursuing it. It is, therefore, of no consequence in his relationship with Savithri. Even his brief affair with Lakshmi is only "like eating pickle" for him. He decides to end it. It is not because it is sinful, but because he realizes that it was a blind alley from which he must retreat, if he wished to progress on the road to salvation. Ramaswamy says:

> "I spent a week in Bombay. Not that there was anything important to do. But I smelt something as it were, among the stars. I wanted to be far from home—far from Madeleine, far from everyone. Captain Sham Sunder offered me hospitality. I had met him in London: "When you come to Bombay, do not forget me," he had said. His Colaba flat was just by the sea. He had two very clever children and his wife, Lakshmi, was a fine looking woman—somewhat round, but kind sad and entertaining. Captain Sham Sunder, I think, had other interest; he came home from his club late at night, and every day of the week, it was so. Once he said to me, laughing, "Since my return from Europe I prefer white skin to brown." What a very clever remark to make!" (294)

It was Ramaswamy's belief in the Indian Advaitic principles that stood in the way of his enjoying a happy and enjoying relationship with Madeleine. On the other hand, Madeleine's involvement with Buddhism widened the gap which separated Ramaswamy's Vedantic India from Madeleine's West. She became a Buddhist nun while there is no concept of 'Nun' in Hinduism.[5]

Thus, we find that the theme of East-West encounter is the result of tensions between the two modes of life and cultures as drawn by the novelist. As a matter of fact Raja Rao has a firm belief of the superiority of the East over the West as he has deep faith in the Indian Vedantic philosophy of life. He could not find anything comparable to Vedanta in the West. Therefore, he ruled out the possibility of arriving at a common meeting point between the East and the West. They continue to exist as two separate cultural realities in life.

V

The Serpent and the Rope (1960) is a great work of art of the novelist. Although a number of themes and ideas have been working in the making of its complex texture, it is an Indian novel in the real sense of the term based on the Indian Vedantic philosophy of life and theme of the quest for self-knowledge, self-transcendence or self-fulfilment. The end of Ramaswamy's quest for self-knowledge at the feet of his 'Guru' is in keeping with the age-old spiritual tradition of India which gives the 'Guru' the highest place in Man's quest for Truth.

India as presented in the novel is more a metaphysical concept than a geographical entity. The Indian tradition has been forcefully evoked in the very beginning of the novel. Ramaswamy, the hero-narrator of the novel says:

> "I was born a Brahmin—that is, devoted to Truth and all that. "Brahmin is he who knows Brahman," etc., etc..." (5).

As we know it well that the Indian tradition is metaphysical, vital and living, the novelist has adopted various ways to evoke this vitality, the cultural strength of the Indian tradition and its cultural heritage. India represents the idea of the Absolute, the particular for the Universal, the shadow for the Substance, the rope for the serpent. Only that knowledge is knowledge which makes for this discrimination that the end of all earthly endeavour is the knowledge of the Self. It is the yearning of the human soul for the Absolute. It is this quest which makes us realise the "divine within us," and the Indianness of the novel lies in the recognition of this quest. It is the yearning of the human soul for the Absolute.

The novel reflects Raja Rao's great learning, his mastery over a number of literatures, mythologies, philosophies and religions. It is the work of the artist who has taken all knowledge to be his province. It has been widely acclaimed by critics as well as Press and writers. Denis de Rougemont says: "I know nothing in literature that confronts East and West more tenderly, more rigorously."[6] Another critic Lawrence Durrell observes: "Hurrah for you! You not only do India great honour, but you have honoured English literature by writing it in our language...truly magnificent...packed with the real magic of poetry...a truly contemporary work—one by which an age can measure itself, its values."[7]

Raja Rao, in an interview, published in the *Illustrated Weekly* in January, 1964, said: "For me literature is 'sadhna'—not a profession but a vocation." According to him, one must be a man first, and a writer afterwards. By 'man' he means a metaphysical entity, one who has realised the Absolute Truth. This Truth can be realised only through a 'Guru,' who is himself a realised being. His vision of life is fully expressed in *The Serpent and the Rope*. As he himself tells us, "*The Serpent and the Rope* (1960) came as a result of spiritual fulfilment—that is to say it was born after I had met my Guru."

In *The Serpent and the Rope* Raja Rao has extended the scope of the Western art-form by giving it a new subject-matter, by using it as a vehicle for the quest of metaphysical wisdom or meditations on the nature of existence from the Indian point of view. Raja Rao once remarked: "The Indian novel can only be epic in form and metaphysical in nature. It can only be a story within story to show all stories are parables." Thus, he has given a distinctively Indian character to English novels written in English by Indian novelists. The Indian Vedantic vision has been woven into the fabric of the novel.

REFERENCES

I. Primary Source:

RAO, RAJA, *The Serpent and the Rope* (1960) (1968, Reprint, New Delhi, Orient Paperbacks).

II. Secondary Sources:

1. Ali, Ahmed., 'Illusion and Reality: the Art and Philosophy of Raja Rao,' *Journal of Commonwealth Literature*, No. 5), 16.

2. Amur, G.S., 'Raja Rao: The Kannada Phase,' *Journal of the Karnataka University*, 1966.

3. Mukherjee, Meenakshi, *The Twice Born Fiction: Themes and Techniques of the Indian Novel in English* (New Delhi: Heinemann, 1971), 84-86.

4. Hemenway, Stephen, *The Novel of India* (Calcutta, Writers Workshop, 1975), 60-66.

5. Naik, M.K., Desai, Amur (ed.), *Critical Essays on Indian Writing in English* (Dharwar: Karnataka University, 1968), 216-218.

6. Nagarajan, K., 'An Indian Novel,' *Sewanee Review*, Summer 1964).

7. Naik, M.K. (ed.), *ibid.*, 219-220.

14

Search for Identity: A Study of Raja Rao's *The Serpent and the Rope*

S.P. SWAIN*

Raja Rao's *The Serpent and the Rope* is an intricate medley of philosophy, religious systems and cultural history. Like R.K. Narayan's novels, it is not a realistic and humorously ironical portrayal of Indian reality but a philosophical exposition of Indian way of life. Mystifyingly bewildering, it postulates the intrinsic point of the novelist's thematic preoccupation. The novel is not only an assertion and affirmation of Indian values but an acute and melancholic longing for such affirmation which stems from one's being alienated from the core of one's self. The paper aims at a study of this sense of rootlessness and the consequently identity crisis, that forms the thematic focus of the novel.

The novel opens with a note of deep anguish. At the very outset, Ramaswamy is delineated as a rootless being, awe-struck at his orphaned existence: "...I am an orphan. Am I always going to be an orphan" (10)? It is this quest motif, which leads to his spiritual journey towards the realisation of a genuine Indian identity. Raja Rao is trying to probe the spiritual roots of his motherland through the rootlessness of his protagonist. The quest for the Absolute is portrayed through the psychic and intellectual encounters between an Indian husband and his French wife. Ramaswamy's realisation

*Department of English, Rourkela Municipal College, Rourkela.

of his true Indian identity comes through a triangular pattern of relationship between his French intellectual wife Madeleine and his overt spiritual love for the Hindu princess Savithri. Intellectually and academically committed to an Indian interpretation of history, he has frequent recourse to the Vedantic concept of the Absolute consciousness in order to assert and justify the ruthless extermination of medieval heresies.

Ramaswamy is a brahmin who is "never contemporary" (125). Aware of his privileged stance in the Hindu social hierarchy as a Brahman, he struggles for the assertion of his Brahminhood through a metaphysical exploration into the quintessence of it. His quest for identity starts with—"A Brahmin is he who knows Brahman" (05) and the quest ends with it too. True Brahminhood is that which "commences when you recognise yourself in your eternity" (215). But Ramaswamy's spatio-temporal involvement in the chronicle of life isolates him from the very purport of his quest. Instead of making a journey to Eternity, Ramaswamy, the Brahmin makes a journey to the temporal world of "the historical sciences" (231). He oscillates between two polarised modes—of time and timeless, of history and meta-physics.

By profession, Ramaswamy is a historian but by tradition and nativity, he is a Brahmin, who exists beyond historical time: "There never was time, there never was history, there never was anything but Shivoham, Shivoham, I am Shiva, I am the Absolute" (197). There is no harmony between the academic identity of Rama and his religious identity. He feels ill at ease with his Indian identity because of the infrequent incursions of his historical self, which is rooted in the modern Western mode of Judaeo-Christianity and which fails to synthesise with the Indian timelessness. He is a scholar seeking a balance between his existential involvement with life and an intellectual quest for meaning. He is engaged in an intellectual and spiritual journey to reach out to future destinations. But he fails, since the intellect is out of tune with the spirit and the two seldom compromise. He is torn between the concept of timelessness—his Indian identity and a time-bound historical existence—his other identity, that of the historian. The presence of two opposing forces in his psyche—the historical West and the traditional India—keep on warring within his quagmired self. They never reconcile. Hence, his search for identity.

Ramaswamy could never get over the death of his mother—an irreparable and irretrievable loss. The death of the mother becomes a haunting obsession throughout his life, escalating his anguish and alienation: "When I was twenty-two I sat in a hotel—it was in the Pyrenees—and I sobbed, for I knew I would never see my mother again" (6). His anguish issues out of his being a "Being" in the historicity of human existence and his awareness of the laceration of isolation in conceivable time that death is the end and beyond it lurks nothingness, vacuum. He searingly feels the pangs of death: "There is no pain more acute than a pain unnameable, and all the shine of the world is only a prophecy, a shout that death is, that one loses another—" (133). The Vedantic concept that he so assiduously and avowedly cherishes and which crystallises in his mind with self-realisation, is but an intellectual conviction severed from his existential passions and predicaments.

Ramaswamy's attachment to his step-mother, to his sister Saroja and to Savithri, generate in him an awareness of the different facets of the feminine—mother, sister and concubine and he feels an inner vacuum. He realises the absence of something significant in his affinity with his French wife Madeleine. His encounter with the feminine principle symbolised in his relationship with little mother and his sister Saroja makes him able to reckon all of a sudden the cause of his alienation from Madeleine. The lack of feminine principle in Madeleine is manifested in her emotional incommunication. Madeleine is an individual feminist more concerned with the abstract concepts of individual human rights and the quest for personal independence, dismissing all socially defined roles. On the other hand, Rama is a relational feminist. An advocate of relational feminism, he stresses on women's rights as women in terms of their nurturing capacities in relation to men. Madeleine falteringly responds in love. She abhors contact: "Touch as I have said, was always distasteful to her, so she liked the untouching Cathars, she loved their celibacy.... The bridge, was anyhow there and could not be crossed..." (15). Indeed, Rama could never cross the "bridge" between Madeleine and him. But, does the bridge endure? No, it crumbles and eventually topples, when she turns a Buddhist and assumes asceticism which denies "womanhood a right to exist" (170).

Ramaswamy, in contrast to his wife, is free from her emotional ossification. She is self-centred but he is an extrovert and can step out of the self and participate in the ceremonial ritual of life. He is an articulate and imaginative being. When she asks him, "What is it separates us, Rama,"? he tells her, "India" (331).

Madeleine, the realist is different from Rama the Vedantin. She believes that one cannot transcend the realities one sees and feels. S. Nagarajan aptly affirms that she is a believer in the actual reality of the world and of the human person.[1] Thus, the tryst of Rama-Madeleine is a fusion of two contrary and polarised *weltanschauung* and hence the note of estrangement in their marital life. Madeleine's failure to form harmonious ties with Rama is on account of her dualism, the assertion that purusa and prakrits are two separate entities. She gradually drifts away from Rama's life into a state of asceticism. She moves from social communication to divine communion.

The husband-wife have a friend, an expatriate Russian, Georges, who is beginning to adopt Catholic mysticism. The three of them have prolonged metaphysical and mystical discussions. In the course of their deliberation, Madeleine shows more emotional response to George's feelings than to Ramaswamy's intellectual wanderings. This drives Ramaswamy to the feeling of envy. He feels *de trop*.

Deficient in feeling and sensation, Ramaswamy fails in emotionally communicating with Madeleine. His concern for the other is an organic need. He reflects: "I need the other in order to realise fully all the structure of my being" (190), and in order to realise, he must be free. For him, Savithri is the true woman, since in her there is an absence of freedom of choice: "For a woman to choose, is to betray her biology" and because Madeleine ultimately chooses Buddhism, she is not the right woman for him. She is a centrifugal being whereas he is a "centripetal being" (195). Rama as a man and a husband is incomplete like Narayan's Marco. He is a partial man. This inadequacy of manhood is revealed in his callous attitude to Madeleine's grief over the death of her children. Madeleine's deep love for Ramaswamy goes unheeded and unresponded. He is an emotional stranger to her. The emotional sclerosis of Ramaswamy approximates a state of psychic buoyancy: "I lose you—I know I will lose you. And yet where can I go but to you" (218)? He has no commitments and assurances to offer: "Rama, tell me—tell me, that you love me" (242)? Rama's cold and lackadaisical response indicates his isolation and non-commitment: "I am mine and you Madeleine are a chunk of truth—as the sun, the moon, the space of the stars—(242).

Ramaswamy is caught in the grip of an existential anguish. Orphaned, abandoned and impotent, his identity is for ever lacerated and the gulf between "the Brahmin and I" (135) is never bridged. Rootless and homeless, he leads a hermetically cocooned existence of timelessness, outside historicity. Through time, he seeks the timeless and through timeless, the unattainable. Thrown away into the flux of time, he is irrevocably carried away from his native ethos by the stream of existential history. His quest is a means to transcend his own mundane limitations and is an exploration of the essence of traditional values that can be assimilated into the self of an individual to forge a new identity. His obsessive concern for numbers is also an indication of his search for identity. At the end of his encounter with his other identity, he wails out: "There is nobody to go now: no home, no temple, no city, no climate, no age" (402). The pangs of rootlessness strikes him with such finality because of his existential anguish in an intrinsic and fundamental alienation from his native heritage. Time has impinged upon his eternal brahmanic self. It has transformed him imperceptibly into a new being, a new entity, that is eternally isolated from the archaic ethos. Som P. Ranchan attributes Rama's alienation from his wife to his anima possession,[2] but to me it is due to his intellectual hubris.

The phenomenal reality of India is lost to Ramaswamy. Time has incarcerated him. An alien, even to his nativity he avers: "I was born an exile and could continue to be one" (376). Yet the Brahmin desperately struggles to cling to his Brahmanical tradition. Severed from the archaic Hindu way of life, he expounds his philosophy, typically Indian, not in the context of the Upanishads but in relation to Plato and Nietzsche. His withdrawal from the traditional Brahmin life suggests a fundamental polarisation. He is stirred by an inscrutable and mysterious force, stronger than the concerted strength of an ancient tradition. A hypostatic call urges him in his quest. He says: "Mother mine, I will go" (149). Drawn into the vortex of existence by historical time, Ramaswamy longs for the Infinite and hence his quest for the Absolute, and the Ultimate Reality. He disowns Madeleine's 'dualistic' Buddhism, since it is anti-Indian, the non-dual affirms the truth" (41). To Rama, "there is no world" (336). For him the only reality is the Absolute. Raja Rao himself has maintained that the meaning of life reveals when the duality resolves into non-duality. But this resolution does not occur in Ramaswamy's encounter with either Madeleine or Savithri. With both of them his affinity is marked by temporal isolation. Rama is the symbol of a mortal paradox. Though he himself declares: "...the meaning of life, play" (205), yet he remains forever groping for a meaning, a value: "There must be something that exalts and explains why we are here and what is it we seek" (399).

In him there is a desperately dire need to effect dissociation since he never cherishes the feeling of a rapport between him and the world. He wants to run away, to withdraw from the mainstream of a mundane existence: "Man is a stranger to this earth" (136). "I must leave this world, I must leave, leave this world" (399). Cut off from eternity, Rama the Brahmin is captivatingly entangled in the anguish of time, which he seeks to annihilate. Turned away from his wife, he has an initial feeling of rootlessness but finally sets out on a spiritual odyssey to 'know thyself,' to find his lost self. The painful realisation of his own spatio-temporal isolation weighs heavily on his soul. He feels dejected and vacant: "There is nobody to go now: no home, no temple, no climate, no age" (402). His agonising sense of alienation reduces him to a mere nothing, a cipher. He becomes a prey to incertitude and anxiety. The traumatic memories of the past crystal-lisingly creep into his sense and intensify his affliction. Truth prevails over him and on one dreadful night, he leaves for Travancore, searching for a Spiritual Guru, a paraclete: "No, not a God but a Guru is what I need" (402).

Prof. K.R. Rao observes: "The theme of alienation effects a change of focus in the novel's total design. The deepening of Rama-Madeleine estrangement can be read as symbolic because it illustrates the unbridgeable disparity that exists between the two cultures to the East and the West. Both Rama and Madeleine succumb to the characteristic determinisms of their individual cultures."[3] Despite their efforts to transcend their own cultural limitations and attain a harmony in mutual personal understanding, they fail. Madeleine declines to involve herself in Rama's sense of values, his intuitive world of introspection. She dwells on an intellectual plane and wants to flee from his life. What is real for Rama, is but a travesty of the real for her. Her love and fascination for India borders on false romanticism. Madeleine is torn by the conflicting demands of Hinduism, Buddhism and her own Christianity. Without a firm base, she drifts from one self to another. It aggravates her self-alienation, since Rama is a part of her feminine self. Recognizably, a relic of the Western predicament of identity-crisis and isolation, she is a fiasco in achieving a fusion of cultural and ethical values. Her attachment to India is only an infatuation, a snobbery. It is the dramatisation of her neurotic pride. Through the technique of juxtaposition and polarisation, Raja Rao has dramatically portrayed the Rama-Madeleine story of alienation, especially the latter's psychological and spiritual isolation. Madeleine's quest for identity drags her to the fringe of intellectual abstraction and her severance of her ties with Rama, symbolises her withdrawal from Reality, which completes her self-isolation. She realises the utter incompatibility of her views and concerns with Rama's vedantic values and rituals and gradually moves away from him. She even snaps all ties with him to emancipate herself from the bondage of an earthly life. She attains self-identification by equating her Catholicism with Buddhism. *The Serpent and the Rope* is indeed a quest for the Absolute. It can be considered as a novel of pilgrimage of a picaresque saint, Ramaswamy. The pilgrimage culminates in a symbolic and mystical marriage in London. Savithri becomes a "hypostatic presence." She serves as a catalyst to Rama's entry into a transcendental existence. Rama's realisation of his nativity becomes a reality and his search for a Guru becomes a spiritual need.

Ramaswamy, the pilgrim, participates in his metaphysical journeys both at the symbolic and literal plane. He is drawn to a focal point whereform he sets out to assert his identity. Member of a specific religio-cultural ethos, he could perceive birth of a new being from his incarcerated self. His spiritual quest is structured around palpable and metaphysically perceptible socio-psychic movements and his inner predicament assumes the form of an internal struggle between antithetical forces and unresolved conflicts. His quest, though without any apocalyptic moment, is nevertheless real. It is self-affirmative and it crystallizes in the need of a Guru and a retreat from the world of illusion to the world of reality, from the serpent to the rope.

Madeleine tries to be other than herself and her world and hence her identity crisis. The genuine 'otherness' in her remains latent. She fails to realise: "We can only offer others what is ours" (123). It is her pseudo otherness which carries her away. She begins to identify more and more with her anti-self. But, Rama is never carried away. He is far from being impervious to the subtler savour of an alien culture. "Otherness" alienates Madeleine but in Rama, it gives vent to forces working towards understanding and assimilation. It makes Rama identify, together with a note of detachment which enables him to see more than "the other" can usually see itself. The Brahmin can be at home in the full-bodied reality of an English pub. Not as one of the crowd but also bringing with him a perspective the crowd has no share in. Rama's is a rootlessness having roots; It is a detachment, which is also an involvement and attachment, that is aware of the Thames flowing with the bear and human warmth and festivity. Hence, the clauses— "While the Thames flowed"—brings home to him the realisation of the diverse identities at the pub, in perpetual fission and fusion, strife and strain. His utlimate identification with the cosmic self of a Guru is metaphysically spiritual. Since his real identity lay in his mother—*i.e.* Mother India, from whom he has alienated himself. Alienated from the archaic Hindu existence, he expounds his philosophy not in the context of the Upanishads but in relation to Plato and Nietzsche.

Ramaswamy's quest for identity forms the thematic motif of the novel. His rootlessness leads to the search for identity which to Raja Rao is a "quest for the absolute,"[4]—the Guru Deva, Guru Brahma and Guru Maheswara. His quest for identity is a means to arrive at a value system. It is an assay to forge a new identity to suit his inner urges and drives in a socio-psychically transformed milieu.

Besides mirroring an East-West dichotomy, Rama's search for identity symbolises his desire to establish psycho-emotional certainties in psycho-emotionally disturbed milieu. It is a quest to bring about coherence and unit to his socio-historical vision and to assert his time-bound historical self in a metaphysically timeless existence. The inter-cultural nature of Ramaswamy's being leads to the quest for identity, a leitmotiv in Indo-Anglian fiction. In delineating Ramaswamy's search for identity, Raja Rao lacks sufficient tenacity to push the quest to its natural finale. His quest to strike roots ends in an existential awareness of his spiritual urge manifesting in a symbolic surrender before the paraclete.

REFERENCES

1. Nagarajan, S. "An Indian Novel," Considerations (ed.) Meenakshi Mukherjee (New Delhi: Allied Publishers, 1977), 85.

2. Ranchan, Som. P. "Ramaswamy's Dilemma: An Analytical Interpretation of *The Serpent and the Rope*," Explorations in Modern Indo-English Fiction (ed.) R.K. Dhawan, (New Delhi: Bahri Publications, 1982), 102.

3. Rao, K.R. The Fiction of Raja Rao (Aurangabad: Parimala Prakashan, 1980), 71-72.

4. Kaushik, Asha. "Meeting Raja Rao," The Literary Criterion, XVIII, No. 3, Dhvanyaloka, Mysore, 1983, 36.

   Rao, Raja. *The Serpent and the Rope* (New Delhi: Orient Paperbacks, 1968).

   (All page numbers in parentheses within the text of the paper are from this edition of the novel).

15

The Serpent and the Rope: A Critical Inquiry

R.S. TIWARI*

(A)

The award of a Prize by the Sahitya Akademy to *The Serpent and the Rope* in 1963 as the best novel for the preceding three years by an Indian writer in English made Raja Rao, in the words of Professor Narsimhaiah, "part of the establishment." The observation ill affords to be controverted inasmuch as the novel blazed a new trail in the domain of Indian Fiction in English, attracting the attention of the scholars by the significant title.

The title is evidently an English rendering of the famous "Vedāntic" logic, "*The Sarpa-rajju-nyāya*." The logic is employed to illustrate the Absolute Reality of the "Brahman" as against the Un-reality of the visible universe. Even as a rope is mistaken for a serpent in darkness, so also the phenomenal universe, which is false, is regarded as Real for lack of accurate knowledge: "*Brahma satyam jaganmithyā.*" That is, "Brahman" is the Single Reality and the visible world is an Illusion which fact is denied to our perception because of our psyche being enveloped in "Avidyā" or "Ajnāna."

Ramaswamy, the Protagonist, bethinks himself of being born a "Brāhmana" who is devoted to "truth and all that" and of his hoary lineage, traceable to Yājnyavalkya, the renowned "Rishi" of the Upanishad. He is internally harassed by incertitude (born of his

---

*Ex-Principal, Saket Postgraduate, College, Ayodhya (U.P.).

Upanishadic knowledge as to the immortality of the soul) whether his ancestors died or did not die. Their death was a material reality, but spiritually they had survived death as the famous Geeta declares that the Soul simply relinquishes the tattered physical frame, opting for a new, even as one changes the torn raiments and puts on a new apparel.

From such a title to the plot, it will be quite natural and legitimate to believe that the conflict between Reality and Unreality will occupy the seminal attention of the author.

(B)

To begin with, let us quote the much cited following passage:

"The world is either real or unreal...the serpent or the rope. There is no in-between-the-two...and all that's in-between is poetry, is sainthood. You might go on saying all the time, 'no, no,' it's the rope, and stand in the serpent. And looking at the rope, from the serpent is to see the paradise, saints, avatars, gods, heroes, universe. For wheresoever you go, you see only with the serpent's eyes. Whether you call it duality or for modified duality. You invent a belvedere to heaven, you look at the rope from the posture of the serpent, you feel that you are the serpent...you are...the rope is. But in true fact, with whatever eyes you see, there is no serpent, there never was a serpent. You gave your own eyes to the falling evening and cried, 'Ayo ! Oh It's a serpent.' You run and roll and lament, and have compassion for fear of pain, others' or your own. You see the serpent and in fear, you feel you are at it, the serpent, the saint. One...the Guru...the Guru brings the lantern; the road is seen, the long, white road, going with the statutory stars. 'It's only the rope' He shows it to you and you touch your eyes and know there never was the serpent. Where was it, where, I ask you. The poet who saw the rope as serpent, became the serpent, and so a saint. Now saint is shown that the sainthood was identification,

not realisation. The actual, the real has no name.
The rope is no rope to itself."[1]

The above lengthy utterance by Ramaswamy, a "holy vagabond,"
researching in the Albignansian heresy in France, to Madeleine, a
French lady teacher, whom he has married and who is gradually
turning a Buddhist. On her asking "Then what is it?," Ramaswamy
replies, "The rope.... Not as opposed to the serpent, but the rope just
'is...'and therefore is no world." Madeleine argues, "But there can
be a Beatrice." 'Yes,' Rama says after a long while. 'Yes, where I
am not. When, I can love the self in Maitreyi, I can be
Yājnyavalkya."[2]

Evidently, Madeleine is opposing her own self by naming
Beatrice to Rama's enunciations, being his sweet-heart as Beatrice
was to the famous Italian Poet, Dante. This argument, apparently
irrefutable, sets Ramaswamy thinking for some time after which he
counters her by alluding to the celebrated pious couple, Yājnyavalkya
and Maitreyi, and here the "battle of wits" has ended, Madeleine
seemingly vanquished.[3]

Now we shall invite the careful reader to bestow a little reflection
on the above tortuous utterance. Raja Rao is shrouding the famous
Vedāntic formulation in an unnecessary rigmarole of seemingly
metaphysical verbiage. The "Advaita Vedānta" clearly suggests the
only existence of the Absolute "Brahman," symbolised by the
Rope, and the non-existence of the Snake which simply appears to
"be" for lack of light, a result of ignorance. Hence the Serpent is
the symbol of Un-reality or Illusion. The opening sentence in the
above lengthy quotation, quite understandably, runs counter to the
thrust inherent in the "Sarpa-rajju-nyāya": "The world is either real
or unreal...the serpent or the rope." There is little room for
equivocation in the Vedāntic pronouncement as to the Absolute
Reality of the "Brahman" and the Fundamental Unreality of the
visible world. The author, however, has made a mess of the whole
truth. That the rope is no rope to itself is tantamount to suggesting
the actual unreality of the "Brahman" itself. ("Brahman" is Neuter
gender in Sanskrit). Raja Rao may be right in stating that the Real
has no name in the sense that the Real, that is, "Brahman" cannot
be described in words: "Neti, neti" as the Vedas have declared.
Nonetheless, it is difficult to concur with Professor Narsimhaiah

when he calls the above passage as "a popular myth, most artistically articulated." Let us comment that the learned Professor cannot be supported when he equates a celebrated axiom of the "Advaita" with a popular myth, to say nothing about Raja Rao's artistic articulation. Art does not confound, it allures and attracts. Raja Rao has here assumed the role of the Greek Sophists.

Ramaswamy has silenced Madeleine by alluding to the renowned Upanishadic couple. Yājnayalkya and Maitreyi: "When I can love the self in Maitreyi, I can be Yājnyavalkya." We are constrained to observe that Raja Rao simply confounds his French wife by indulging tortuous statements in his solicitude to impress the readers as well with his knowledge of Philosophy. It will be worthwhile in this context to quote the relevant passage from the Upanishadic text. The dialogue between the Sage and his spouse occurs in the Fourth 'Brāhmana' of the Second Chapter of the 'Brihadāranyaka' Upanishad. On his wife's asking about the way to Immortality, Yājnyavalkya replies:

> "The husband is dear to the wife not for the sake of the husband, but for her own sake. The wife is dear to the husband not for the sake of the wife, but for his own sake. The sons are dear to the father not for the sake of the sons, but for his own sake. Riches are dear not for the sake of the riches, but for one's own sake... O Maitreyi ! the 'Ātman' is worthy of seeing, hearing and contemplating, and all this is inwardly brought home on acquiring Jnāna (Knowledge). Accordingly, all apparent perceptions are begotten of 'Ajnāna' (Ignorance)." ("Brāhmana" here suggests a sub-section of a chapter.)[4]

Now a careful perusal of the above Upanishadic text evinces that Raja Rao has conveniently forgotten that there is no question of the wife being dear to a husband because of the "Self" in her, but because of her material utility to a husband. Clearly, the riches are devoid of any Soul, yet they are loved by us. The real meaning of Yājnyavalkaya's argument is that all these material relations or possessions should serve as benefactors to an individual in his way of Self-realisation instead of entailing him into their alluring meshes and obstruct the path to Self-realisation.

It will be unfair, however, to suggest that Raja Rao does not understand the fundamental formulations of the "Advaita" Philosophy. The only trouble with him is that he often exercises his knack of mystification after the manner of the Sophists and thereby creating confusion.... Ramaswamy, the narrator, is his mouthpiece and the latter glories in confusing his French consort, and resultantly also confounds the readers.

Ramaswamy alludes to duality of attitudes towards life. "There can be only two attitudes to life. Either you believe the world exists and so you. There is no compromise possible.... The first is the Vedāntist's position—the second is the Marxist's—and they are irreconcilable." And on Madeleine's asking what is in-between, he makes the same reply. "And in-between are many poetic systems: monism, tempered monism, non-dualistic modified monism, God ad Paradise, Islam, etc., etc...."[5]

Now the Vedāntic position can be certified to have been correctly defined, though following a novel line in conformity with some western philosophers, but when the author, with one sweep of the broom, as it were, designates all things in-between, including God, Islam etc., as creations of the "Poetic system," he oversteps the normal periphery of logical discipline. At the root, however, lies Raja Rao's concern to let the readership realise that he is fully conversant with the diverse systems of Indian Philosophy. The conflict between the Vedāntist and the Marxist's positions boils down ultimately to a dichotomy between Spirit and Matter. And it was due to this apparent gulf between Spirit and Matter that the 'Vaishnava' Schools of Indian Philosophy came into existence. To clarify the point a little (full elucidation will require a separate article), we would like to observe that the Hindu Theory of Incarnation ("Avatāravād") symbolises an oblique attempt at merging spirit and matter into a harmonious integration, thereby providing a new blaze of thought that it will be through suffering the vicissitudes, the glamours and glooms, incidental to human life, that man will ultimately attain Divine Companionship. Raja Rao recognises only two attitudes to life, both being "extremist," and forgets that life is essentially a *system of compromises*. Anthropomorphism, that is, Humanisation of The Supreme Reality, should be acclaimed as the boldest product of Indian philosophical thought.

Ramaswamy, manifestly carries on his back a cumbrous load of "Brāhmanic" tradition, promising to become the principal exponent of Indian sensibility. On the philosophic level, he endeavours to make out that "Brahman" is the Ultimate Reality and the visible universe is false, unreal. On the plane of social structure, he upholds the agelong tradition of thought and behaviour, betraying no impact upon his mind of his protracted ramblings on the Continent. He has remained a vegetarian throughout, holding fast to ancient ideals and norms, albeit he has married a French lady, Madeleine. It is a happy coincidence that despite a brief amatory propensity towards Georges, a Russian colleague of hers in the college, Madeleine has preserved her inner sanctity of thought and feeling. And, that, too, has contributed to Ramaswamy's adherence to Indian moorings. He defines "Brahman" as one who knows the "Brahman" or Truth[6] and remains all the while conscious of his hoary lineage. It is conspicuous that his engagement with his researches has found no prominent mention in the novel. Sages like Yājnyavalkya, Shankara and Mādhava are recognised to constitute a significant portion of Indian consciousness which he seldom forgets to articulate.

"My thoughts are very Indian,"[7] Rama states when he opens a letter from Madeleine. Truly, his thoughts have remained "very Indian" throughout. He defines the traditional Indian consciousness on getting a letter from his step-sister Saroja thus: "In the recesses of our being, there are great tracts of the unknown, pastures of the invisible, in which we are familiar, the sons of the family go driving our cattle.... Civilisation is nothing but the familiarity with which we go into this inner property, cultivated and manured from age to age."[8]

Now this definition of Civilisation is begotten of Rama's ever-present consciousness of the long line of Sages and Seers who have composed and fashioned the Indian Ethos as we have inherited today. The Brāhmanas being descendants of the ancient Seekers of Truth, India is virtually to be identified with the Brāhmanic tradition. Ramaswamy explains to Savitri: "The Brahmana is never contemporary—He looks backwards and forwards in time and so has a Sage to begin the genealogical tree, and a Guru to end the cycle of birth and death."[9] Hence, the Brāhmana is Timeless, a part of Eternity; and so is India. When estrangement has begun to show itself between Rama and Madeleine, the latter asks him what has separated them. Rama instantly replies, "India." When she reminds him that she has embraced Buddhism which is Indian, Ramaswamy controverts her and proclaims that India is "the Guru of the world," having no history, as we understand the term today. "History, if anything," Rama explains, "is the acceptance of human sincerity. But Truth transcends sincerity. Truth is 'in' sincerity and 'in insincerity'—beyond both. And that is again India."[10]

This definition of India, to copy Raja Rao's own manner (or mannerism), is both acceptable and nonacceptable. India does have a History as a Seeker of Truth. He, however, in his solicitude to strike the readers with his impenetrable acumen, identifies History with the "acceptance of human sincerity." Understandably, Raja Rao seems to suggest that History is a record of human adjustment with the changing conditions through the roll of centuries. That he regards Truth as a component of "human sincerity" cannot be confuted. Accordingly, Truth can be regarded as an ingredient of History. But Raja Rao (how far he is himself sincere in advancing this logic is open to question) broadens the bournes of Truth when he includes "insincerity" as well in it. Truth cannot be said to lie in "insincerity." And, therefore, seeing that he regards the ancient Sages as Seekers of Truth, his reasoning leads one to conclude that these Sages or "Brāhmanas" also welcomed "insincerity" in their pursuit of Truth. Did Raja Rao visualise the weakness of his logic? Truth and Insincerity cannot co-exist. Although he pronounces Truth to lie beyond both, Sincerity and Insincerity, yet he leaves ample room to us to think that in his psychic spectrum of perceptions. Truth cannot afford to co-exist with Undiluted Sincerity. And, accordingly, the definition of India, in the eventual analysis here, is Un-acceptable. Our Sages had been always true and sincere in their intuitional perception of Truth. We have nowhere, in our perusal of the novel, come across Raja Rao's allusion to the famous prayer of the Indian "Rishis": "O Lord! lead us from non-Truth to Truth; from darkness into light; from death unto immortality."

India does have a glorious History of sincere researches into Truth; and when Raja Rao talks of Truth residing beyond both, sincerity and insincerity, he attempts at imitating the Upanishadic style of defining "Brahman" as being beyond the capacity of Words: "*Neti, neti, neti.*"

How a good intention, however, becomes acutely damaged by a writer's ungovernable impulse to capture the readers' imagination by fantastic utterances is available in the novelist's continuance in the same context that India is a "nation of gamblers"[11] which expression he, no doubt, dilutes by alluding to Indians being "brave," roping together, by way of illustration, Shri Rama, Dharmarāj, Harishchandra and Mahatma Gandhi. The present writer considers this habit of mystification on the part of the novelist as "supremely" undesirable, to say the least. His pre-occupation, however, with identifying Truth with "Brāhmanism" and also with India at large, strikes us frequently. Earlier, in this very context, the novelist has identified Civilisation, no matter, obliquely, with spiritual attainment which has distinguished Indian Ethos in world history. He again speaks of Civilisation thus: "The perfect civilisation, then, is where the world is not, but where there is nothing but the 'I'."[12] This "I" is evidently inspired by the Vedāntic formulation: "*Aham brahmāsmi,*" that is, "I am Brahman." That inner realisation over-rules all other corpus of perceptions which is the famous enunciation of Advaitism. Now, the final conclusion to be reached is: *Brāhmanism, Truth, India. Absolute "Brahman," Unity of Ātman and Paramātman, and Civilisation—all these are synonymous.* The novelist's boldness is to be appreciated.

Alluding to Buddhism—remember Ramaswamy is addressing this elaborate explanation to Madeleine, who is turning a Buddhist …he comments that although Buddhism believes in the evanescence of perceptions, "*Sarvameva kshanikam*" (all is momentary),[13] yet it basically believes in the Truth of Perception which is why it was exorcised from its homeland. Students of Indian History are fully cognisant of the factors responsible for the virtual banishment of Buddhism from its native soil and it will transgress the bounds of this paper if we choose to go into them. Let us candidly affirm Raja Rao little cares for historical accuracy in his pronouncements, both social and philosophical. He purposes to glorify India on the metaphysical and philosophical plane and to that end, he has taken recourse to "*Advaitavād,*" but we are constrained to comment that he has resorted to the technique of mystification which pushes him into the ranks of the Greek Sophists. In the context of Buddhistic "*Kshanavād*," he has spoken of India as "*Jnānam*," Pure Knowledge, leaving ample room for polemics: Is not "Kshanika" perception "Jnānam" (momentary)? Any attempt at elucidation will embroil us into the labyrinth of the diverse systems of Indian Philosophy.

Ramaswamy has defined India more explicitly a little later: "India is not a country like France or like England; India is an 'Idea....' The Ganges was an inner truth to me, an assurance, the origin and end of my Brāhmanic tradition. I would go back to India...."[14] Raja Rao's guiding concern to glorify India is commendable and simultaneously to identify India with Brāhmanism cannot be said to be very far from truth. Years of sojourn in France have not diminished Ramaswamy's passion for India and his desire to return to India. "I would go back to India," he declares. His reference to the holy Ganga as "an inner truth" to him is deserving of special notice inasmuch as the Ganga here symbolises the entire "*Bhārat-bhūmi*" which, by its special geographical or physical attributes has moulded and crystallised what we call "Indian Culture." Raja Rao declares his final conviction, as it were, through the protagonist: "India would never be made by our politicians and professors of political science, but by these isolate existences of India, in which India is remembered, 'experienced,' and communicated; beyond history as tradition, as Truth.... But this India of Coomaraswamy, who will take it away, I ask you, who? Not Tamerlane, or even Joseph Stalin."[15]

We are full of admiration for this amalgam of sentiment, logic, language and poetry, and also patriotism for Raja Rao who has waxed almost lyrical in this exclamation, forgetting his usual habit of mystification. Ramaswamy, in his veiled desire to overwhelm his French wife with a sense of his superior mental acumen, has, willy-nilly, also tried to overwhelm the commonalty of readership.

The close of the novel, however, is disappointing. Ramaswamy has given the go-by to all his earlier protestations about India which has shone till now as a refulgent spot in "the bright book of life," and has decided on going back to Travancore, his actual town of birth. He proclaims towards the end: I have no Benares now, no Ganges, no Jumna; Travancore is my country, Travancore my name. Lord, accept me, vouch that I be where I should...."[16]

A minute perusal of the novel displays that the novelist has promoted a subtle feeling that Ramaswamy will eventually discard his broader Indian obsession and will reconcile himself, like all common men, to settling down in his actual place of birth. All the same, we were not psychologically prepared to accept this "fall from the sublime to the ridiculous," as it were, on the part of Ramaswamy, who has till now always talked of "India." It may be argued in favour of the novelist that he does not recognise any distinction between India and Travancore since the latter is a constituent part of India. Nevertheless, how to account for Ramaswamy's utterance: "I have no Benares now, no Ganges, no Jumna...."? Negation of Benares and the Ganga will be considered as an artistic "Faux pah."

(D)

The thrust in the novel can be said to have been portrayal of Indian sensibility. The European impact is manifested only in Ramaswamy marrying a French lady, who, too is devoted to the study of Buddhism, a religion born on the Indian soil. The inter-action between Indian and European cultures can reasonably be expected, but that has not been manifest in the novel. It will be a moot point to decide whether Madeleine's proclivity to Buddhism has contributed any materially to their being joined in wedlock. Modeleine has felt a little irritated when Rama has remarked that Buddhism was absorbed ultimately in Hinduism.

The novelist has portrayed Indian sensibility in almost all available contexts. Ramaswamy is fully aware of Buddhistic teachings. We explains life as "a passage between life and death, and birth and death again, and what an accumulation of pain man has to bear. Is it then a wonder that the Buddha, with palaces and queens, with a kingdom and an heir, left his home to find that from which there is no returning?"[17]

In the same context, Rama states that "Life is made for woman.... Man is a stranger to this earth. We are all Bodhisattvas, and one night, we, too, will leave the wife lying by the new-born one...."[18]

This observation obliquely suggest the superiority of man over woman which cannot be accepted without a grain of salt, however.

The Upanishadic text clearly certifies that Maitreyi, Yājnyavalkya's wife, patently negates worldly pleasures and pomps, laying store by Immortality. States she in response to the Sage's proposal to divide the family wealth between her and Gārgi, the co-wife: "What shall I do with that possession which fails to render me immune to mortality?"

Ramaswamy is expected to be cognizant of this dismissal of mundane acquisitions by Maitreyi. Hence, it little behoves him to comment that life is made for women while men are immune to such temporal possessions. We are constrained to observe that Raja Rao makes comments according to situations as they are come across, without caring for facts or consistency. As a matter of fact, Indian sensibility is a complex structure, manifesting itself in diverse ways in diverse situations. Accordingly, there appears a dichotomy between the pure philosophical and the actual pragmatic. It is the latter which makes Savitri comment: "To be a woman is to be abandoned by a man." But such a man must exist."[19] "The masculine principle" amounts to Truth, and "surrender to Truth" means to be "free" which is liberation from "sorrow" which abounds in life. Now, this Truth, leading to liberation, dawns upon you only when you discard any instinct to "possess." It is "self-possession" which is necessary to unburdened psychic life.

Life is a pilgrimage—this is emphasised by Ramaswamy more than once. Getting a letter from Madeleine, Rama comments that man is a "pilgrim to knowledge." In his accustomed cryptic style, he says: "You should know a woman and not understand her, then you can never be a pilgrim to knowledge. Women, all women speak poetry, whether they are talking of houses, or aluminium vessels.... Understanding a woman is understanding her inward soul which is yearning for love, understandably love on the fleshly plane. They always speak poetry, designed to ensnare man and that will, of necessity, shut you from internal vision of reality."[20]

Now how far Rama's conception of love accords with Indian sensibility is worth considering. Let us state here clearly that love is mainly personal, a pattern of relationship between two heterosexuals. "What does one know of love at nineteen?"[21] This comment suggests that the "elevating" aspect of love desiderates advance in age which becomes coincident with experience. It is only then that one becomes immune to attractions of "lips" or "limbs." Rama goes on: "Love demands nothing, it says nothing, it knows nothing; it lives for itself.... Who can take away love, who can give it, who receive?"[22]

This mystic outburst of Ramaswamy does not partake of Indian sensibility. (Not even human sensibility.) It is Rama's own outlook to love, not traditionally Indian. There have been religious sects in India which have utilised sex as a means to attainment of the Communion with the Divine. Further, there is the '*Kāmasūtra*' of Vātsyāyana, a celebrated treatise on sexology. Clothing love in a pall of "airy nothing" amounts simply to demonstrative sophistication. Rama's subsequent statement that he is writing his life's chronicle with the "objectivity, the discipline of the historical sciences" gives the lie to his claim since he has just a while ago concealed himself in some ethereal altitudes like Shelley's Skylark....

Melancholy being ingrained in his nature, Rama remains mostly pensive and depressed. His marriage with Madeleine also has not altered the basic composition of his temperament: "Madeleine married me, and this is the sad part of the story." He believes that fear of death causes you to marry and "The fear of extinction is the source of copulation." This is frankly fantastic while the second part of the statement is distortion of a reality, reminding us of some sonnets of Shakespeare's Rama is right when he states that a Hindu wants a son to be born to "light our funeral pyre." The "*Pitrri-rina*" (debt owed to father) is paid off only when a son is born who will help perpetuation the race.

The way, however, Rama approaches the question of love and marriage is neither spiritual nor artistic. Further more "Nobody goes to fight for a Helen in India; rather does Rama send his wife Sita into exile simply to protect his impersonal kingship from any shadow falling on it."[23] This utterance is made by the French Professor who is Rama's supervisor of research. But Ramaswamy takes it complacently, without betraying any sign of disagreement. The novelist should have remembered in this context the fact that an attempt at disrobing Draupadi by Duryodhana in the assembly of Elders triggered off the famous Mahābhārat War. Further, if Rama sent his devoted consort into exile at the remarks of a washerman, he was much too "personal." He is acutely sensitive to the thought as to the ultimate image the people will form of him—the king being held as the upholder of virtue.

The novelist is perfectly right, however, when Rama states that "When the Ego is dead, is marriage true."[24] That means that real matrimonial happiness is an ensuent of the complete merging of individual identities. From the Indian angle, this proposition is all the more necessary inasmuch as marriage amongst us is a religious sacrament to last for life.

Nevertheless, we fail to concur with the novelist when Rama pronounces to Madeleine that "All women are perfect women for they have the feminine principle in them, the 'Yin,' the 'Prakriti,'" adding that men are "perfect when they turn inward, and know that the ultimate is man's destiny."[25] As a matter of fact, Raja Rao seems not cognizant of the entire spectrum of Indian Philosophy. He picks up a key-word or two from Indian or Chinese Philosophy, mixes it with his own perceptions and builds up a philosophy. His skill in effecting such an amalgam in 'The Serpent and the Rope,' especially the title of novel, quite naturally took the world of Indian English writing by storm—not undeservedly. Let us clarify our position. In the 'Sānkhya Darshan,' "Prakriti" and "Purusha," the Feminine and the Masculine Principles are both equally important—"Purusha" setting in motion when in contact with the "Prakriti." The 'Shatapatha Brāhmana' clearly states that the Absolute Brahman, getting bored with solitude, was actuated with a desire to "enjoy" ("Riramsā"), and divided itself into two, man and woman and betook itself to enjoyment. This is manifestly suggestive of the essential cooperation between the masculine and the feminine principles on an equal footing from which the Creation came into being. Only then the extinction of the Ego on both sides would be true and meaningful. Rama's rhapsodical utterance about women: "Woman is the world..."[26] in the background of the impending coronation of Queen Victoria however, enshrines a tribute to woman.

(E)

It has to be noted that Indian sensibility is to be explored in the novel on a twain of planes: philosophical and pragmatical. It is a truth that tradition is best preserved in rites and rituals. When Rama's father has died, naturally Benaras gains importance along with the holy Ganga. The "Pinda-dāna," offering of the rice-balls, in obedience to the directions of the 'Pandas' at the Ghāta, and related procedures are depicted minutely. The Little Mother, Rama's third mother, represents the typical sensibility in her attitude to Benares. She believes that in Benares one does not die: "In Benares, one knows death is as illusory as the mist in the morning."[27] As for Ramaswamy, he mystifies, in keeping with his usual custom, the situation, stating: "Benares is eternal. There the dead do not die nor the living live."[28] This habit of mystification of confounding things, at times exasperates the reader who knows something about Indian culture or the Upanishadic teachings. That Rama takes a handful of Ganga water and pours it back into the stream for the sake of Pierre, his dead child from Madeleine, suggests that Rama has not lost his Indian moorings. Although he does not believe in all that governs the popular mind as to the dead ones reaching their "lunar destination" by catching a Cow's or Bull's tail, yet he respects the popular faith. That the traditional Indian sticks to his inherited psyche, despite his European sojourns, illustrates how deeply the tradition has sunk down into Rama's unconscious. At the time of leaving for India to participate in Saroja's marriage ceremony, Ramaswamy refrains from giving Madeleine a departing kiss or from taking her arm in public as that seemed to him a "desecration," Rama boards the plane, and landing at Santa Cruz, chants the "Gāyatri Mantra." The newly born Republic of India had no meaning for him; it was only the India of "Brahmā" or "Prajāpati"; or "Varuna," "Mithra," "Āryaman etc., that mattered and that made India "a continuity not in time, but in space...."[28] Let us comment that continuity in "Space" is the novelist's special perception, too obtuse for clear elucidation.

(F)

What strikes our special notice, the novelist does not portray any conflict spectacular. This applies not only to Indian *versus* European culture, but also to the relations between the characters belonging to the same ethnic group since Tradition silences all voice of dissent. Accordingly, a universal Culture of Discipline and Subdual of Defiant Individual permeates the entire structure of the novel. This facet we propose to explore with respect to only one or two major characters in the following paragraphs.

As suggested above, the Little Mother is the very embodiment of Tradition. We shall be content only with alluding to a single episode. Rama arriving home from Europe, she would not touch him because of her being in "sacred clothes," engaged in worship. The day being a Saturday, she tells him the story of Shri Rama and recites instances where telling and hearing the story of Rama and Sita every Saturday has worked wonders and failure to do so has created disasters to the families, his own family included. This reminds us in the North of the episodes, figuring in the "Satyanārāyana kathā." True it is that even the educated section of society harbours such a Faith, at any rate, unconsciously. Thus, there is a validity in the novelist's observation that the "crust" of modernity among us is such a "superficiality" that "you can remove it even with a babul-thorn."[29]

Ramaswamy's family at home is quite harmonious, by and large. Everybody, including Rama, head of the family, is ultimately subordinate, rather deferential to the Little Mother's wishes. It is a replica of the ideal joint-family system. Saroja and Sukumari find in Rama an ideal brother albeit they are his step-sisters...the Little Mother being a step-mother to all of them and even quite young in years, but behaving in the fashion of a true Elderly Mother. Saroja, unwilling to marry Subramaniyum Sastry in the beginning, eventually decides to marry him out of regard for the family's honour, especially attaching to Brāhmana family. Her comment is significant: "We know how to bear children. We are just like a motor car or a bank account...." "Between a funeral and a marriage, there is not much to choose," she remarks. She has yet surrendered to tradition which is so precisely defined by the Little Mother: "A woman has to marry a man whether he be blind, deaf, mute or tuberculous. We cannot choose our men...."

In the Indian group of characters, Savitri is the only the lovable and sparkling character though mysteriously drawn. A real Princess by birth, and Cambridge-educated, she has developed interest in a Muslim boy; is yet in deep love with Rama; lives in a world of fantasy; is essentially opposed to Pratap in the Political Service while plans are afoot to marry her to him. She, yet, overcoming her inner conflict, ultimately decides to marry Pratap, yielding to parental wishes. A Hindu woman has to obey her Krishna, her lord.[30] ...this is her final decision. Let us observe that these two girls are happy in their wedlock.

(G)

Coming to the European group of characters, we find almost the same principle of tolerance and accommodation. The spirit of eventual surrender to elders' wishes in the matter of matrimony in accordance with tradition governs them all. Madeleine is the sole exception who has married an Indian scholar, though herself a French by birth. There has surfaced no ostensible conflict in her marital relationship—the estrangement between her and Rama being the offspring of her innate propensity to Buddhism, her obsession with the tears and sorrows that attend upon human existence, and also her knowledge of Ramaswamy's inner drive to return to India. Nevertheless, violent bitterness of any complexion has never marred their conjugal life. Each one goes his or her way...the ultimate divorce being a peaceful affair. Madeleine has been exceedingly conscious of Rama's sensitivity. The baby born is christened "Krishna" by Rama, but the boy falling ill, Madeleine changes his name to Pierre inasmuch as she has nursed an apprehension that Rama has angered the "gods of India" by marrying a European lady and feels that their anger has been added to by naming the child "Krishna," a holy name for the Indians.[31] It is worth noting that Madeleine never calls Rama by his name after the manner of a Hindu wife. Rama has also been constantly circumspect as to Madeleine's feelings and sentiments. Yet, clear the estrangement has taken place, culminating into divorce. No clear explanation is available in the plot as to how such an apparently happy relationship has ended in divorce. All the same, becoming a mother, when Madeleine charging Rama in a letter, with to total ignorance of a mother's sentiments in his "Indian aloneness": "It is the birth of the god in a chalice, the Holy Grail" echoing the Bible[32] articulates her deep sense of loneliness, a faint ray of light is vouchsafed to us to imagine that all was not going well with the couple beneath the surface of tranquil happiness. The paper has assumed, willy-nilly, a length not intended. Let us wind up our assessment of Madeleine's character by commenting that Madeleine is the most lovable, endearing and self-effacing character in the novel before whom

Ramaswamy pales into a shadow. That she has turned a Buddhist Nun in the end, believing in the "Four Āryan Truths," as preached by Buddha, surrounds her with a perennial halo of a Hindu woman.[33]

We deliberately refrain from discussing other European characters and content ourselves with observing that absence of any tangible conflict, inner or outer, and surrender to elders' wishes, as already stated, characterises their responses to situations. We feel, further, inclined to comment that the artist in the novelist is temperamentally not attuned to depicting conflicts and inter-actions.

(H)

Raja Rao's extreme self-confidence, as it were, has led him to take liberties with the rendering into English of Upanishadic texts although he comes to touch the point in his own way. Sample the following famous text:

"हिरण्मयेन पात्रेण सत्यस्यापिहितं मुखम् ।

तत्त्वं पूषन्नपाण्हषु सत्यधर्माय दृष्टये ।।" (ईशोपनिषद्)

"O Pūshan (sun-god)! The face of Truth is hidden in a golden pitcher; remove it so that Seekers of Truth might gain a clear glimpse (of Truth)."

Raja Rao's translation is as follows:

"Om, O face of Truth with a disc of gold, remove the mist (of ignorance) that I may see you face to face" (246—he does not name the actual source).

No elucidation is called for. The error is self-evident. Further he becomes sometimes extremely colloquial in the use of the language: "We are so serious, *deadly serious*, about everything..." (332). "Deadly" here jars upon the ears. One last example of mystification is pointed out here: "The Sage knows the world is but perception; he is King, he, Krishna, the King of Kings. The one cannot be many, but the many can be one, and the one thus transcended to its non-dual source, the 'ekam advayam,' the one-not-two is Truth (In between is the moralist, the Republican of Ferney.... Brother, my brother, the world is not beautiful—you are beauty. Be beauty and we see not the beautiful, my Parsifal" (383).

Raja Rao conveniently forgets the Vedic text which says

"*Ekoham bahusyam,*" meaning "The One I become many." No basic damage accrues in one becoming many. The "non-dualist" source remains even when branches shoot forth from the same tree-trunk. "The world is not beautiful—you are beauty"—this is simply mystifying sophistication added to by "Be beauty and see not the beautiful, my Parsifal." In the above-quoted Upanishadic text, the "*Hiranmaya pātra,*" to wit, "Golden pitcher," is the World which is an Illusion, not the Truth. But, the world cannot be said to be "not beautiful." The Dawn is decidedly beautiful which conceals the Truth of the Sun for a while. The Dawn is symbolical of the world which is attractive and bewitching. We have no space here to dwell upon this axiom. Raja Rao's allusion to Beatrice becoming "an impossible tyrant" in showing the way to Paradise to Dante and calling it "the inversion of Truth" by further roping in the birth of "Tantra" and thereby obliquely denigrating womanhood cannot be said to agree with the episode of Maitreyi and Yājynavalkya, quoted by the author earlier (379). His general attitude as reflected in the novel towards women is "Male-oriented."

Raja Rao's habit of generalisation "ad libitum" is best exemplified in the following passage:

"But life is so much more intelligent than we care to understand. Marxism, Hinduism, Christianity, Islam, Hitlerism, the British Commonwealth, the Republic of the United States of America: all are so many names for some unknown principle, which we feel but cannot name. For all the roads, as the Gita says, lead but to the Absolute" (90). This *pot-purri*— let us assert—of so many disparate things culminating into one Final Reality, sounds fantastic.

Raja Rao seldom cares about consistency. How can one reconcile the above-quoted allusion to the rise of "Tantra" in Buddhism with the observation that "Buddhism died in India because it became ascetic, and so denied womanhood its right to exist"? (170).

Lest we should incur the wrong impression that we have been unfair to Raja Rao in the foregoing sections, let us confess that while perusing the work, having won distinction in the heavy corpus of Indian creative writing in English, one cannot but be impressed with Raja Rao's wide range of learning—History (Indian, European), religion (Hinduism, Buddhism, Christianity), philosophy (Indian, European), literature (Sanskrit, French, English), psychology, mythology, contemporary politics like Communism, metaphysics, *et cetera*—and also with his handling of the English language, moulding it to expression of Indian sentiment and situations. He seems no where laboured or artificial. Furthermore, the fact of allusions being galore, coupled with the sweep of language, demonstrates Raja Rao's special creative genius. His description of Saroja's marriage and the marriage preparations *et cetera* furnishes a fine specimen of his vivid and vivifying skill of portrayal. Furthermore, there are certain expressions worth memorising, *e.g.*, "Destiny, I think, is nothing but a series of psychic knots that we tie with our own tears" (215). "A woman must grumble—it's her biological defence against the strength of man" (260). "This vestment of eighteen aggregates must have fevers and suffer" (313). "For your love is not a system—a canalisation of emotion, an idea. For your love is, an immediate experience, like an intuition" (176). "Truth is the fact of existence. That is, Truth is the essence of fact: and as such, truth and existence are one and the same" (170).

In the Preface to '*Kanthapurā*,' Raja Rao has pointed out the difficulty of an Indian writer in English in the matter of his medium, to wit, the English language. He has been only too true. Creative writing poses linguistic difficulties more than critical writing—this is our personal experience. However, Raja Rao should have been a little more alert while framing such sentences as: "Duty should be defined...which gives man the maximum of happiness and *incurs* the least pain to others" (237). Here "*incurs*" should have been replaced by "*causes*."

In the over-all estimate, we shall comment, with apology to his admirers, that Raja Rao's extreme solicitude to assume the dignified role of an Interpreter of the classical Vedantic Philosophy, coupled with his attempt at integrating all his knowledge and learning into the texture of the novel, has landed him into a sort of creative chaos.

REFERENCES

N.B. The Edition used is published by Orient Paperbacks, Madarasa Road, Kashmere Gate, Delhi-110 006.

1. *The Serpent and the Rope,* 335.
2. *Ibid.,* 336.
3. *Ibid.,* 336.
4. 'Brihadaranyaka,' published by Geeta Press, Gorakhpur.
5. *The Serpent and the Rope,* 333.
6. *Ibid.,* 406, 5.
7. *Ibid.,* 36.
8. *Ibid.,* 90.
9. *Ibid.,* 125.
10. *Ibid.,* 332.
11. *Ibid.,* 332.
12. *Ibid.,* 334.
13. *Ibid.,* 334.
14. *Ibid.,* 376.
15. *Ibid.,* 352.
16. *Ibid.,* 405.
17. *Ibid.,* 135.
18. *Ibid.,* 136.
19. *Ibid.,* 187.
20. *Ibid.,* 219.
21. *Ibid.,* 229.
22. *Ibid.,* 229.
23. *Ibid.,* 221.
24. *Ibid.,* 293.
25. *Ibid.,* 311.
26. *Ibid.,* 353.
27. *Ibid.,* 11.
28. *Ibid.,* 246.
29. *Ibid.,* 273.
30. *Ibid.,* 259.
31. *Ibid.,* 14.
32. *Ibid.,* 36.
33. *Ibid.,* 32. *These Truths are not mentioned.* They are, however, (I) There is *Sorrow* in life. (II) There is *Cause for Sorrow.* (III) *Sorrow can be ended,* and

(IV) There is a *Way for the End of Sorrow*. Buddha enunciates the existence of *"Trishnā,"* Excessive Desire for Mundane Enjoyments, as the Root Cause of Sorrow. Here "Āryan Truths" suggests *"Supreme Truths."* It may be easily understood why Buddhism is often characterised as being *"Anātmavādin,"* that philosophy which negates the existence of the Soul which is the Supreme Truth in Vedānta.

16

In Between *The Serpent and the Rope*

PIER PAOLO PICIUCCO*

Almost forty years after it was first published, *The Serpent and the Rope* has been gaining a central position in the whole fictional production of its author and also in the wider landscape of Indian literature in English. It is interesting to note that, leaving aside those first positive comments which constitute the milestones of literary criticism of the most recent literature in India—I am obviously referring to the works of C.D. Narasimhaiah, M.K. Naik and Meenakshi Mukherjee—, a new generation of very talented scholars has re-evaluated Raja Rao's fiction in the last two decades considering the whole subject under the perspective of the new trends of' modern criticism, this time evidencing the pros and the cons.[1] *The Serpent and the Rope*, in particular, has been the most privileged target of the critics who have adopted, among other positions gender-analysis, indicating, nonetheless, that it remains a novel nobody can afford to ignore, despite all the oppositions to it. Moreover, the writer himself seems to have been fatally attracted by his previous effort to the extent that in *The Chessmaster and His Moves* we can notice the reproposal of the architectural frame of *The Serpent and the Rope*.

The Serpent and the Rope indeed is a cardinal point in the fictional corpus of Raja Rao. After *Kanthapura*, a novel of similar relevance though diametrically opposed to it, it stands as a turning

---

*University of Turin, Italy.

point towards philosophy, spirituality and abstractionism, ingredients which will alternatively flavour all his novels to come. Politics and social realism, that had constituted a crucial characteristic of *Kanthapura*, will finally appear only on the condition that they will be represented from the standpoint of the new dominant perspective. The present paper aims at analysing the modes and the peculiarities of this "revolutionary" moment.

To begin with, it will be necessary to stress that, as far as Raja Rao's novels are concerned, philosophical debate, aesthetic principles and mystic drive are so closely connected to each other that it is not always possible to discuss them separately. A proud disciple of Vedanta, Raja Rao posits the existence of a neutral area, equally far from reality and unreality. The distinction materializes in that both reality and unreality are of this world while the neutral area does not belong to it; the writer concludes that we need a guru—a symbol of the divine—in order to acknowledge it. Its two fundamental characteristics are that it represents the means that connects the two ends yet, at the same time, revealing its full, autonomous identity. The in-between—this is how Raja Rao names this concept—gives a meaning to the two opposites and, at that precise moment, it becomes the most important, the ultimate element, able to contain within itself not only the real and the unreal but the All. Raja Rao's rich symbology abounds in such cases. The most immediate, needless to say, is the bridge. Of all the passages which may be relevant, there is one which seemed particularly meaningful to me. The narrator, Little Mother and Sridara are leaving from Varanasi after the cremation of Rama's father. The whole scene takes place inside a train compartment.

> Suddenly without a reason, Little Mother shook with sobs. She shook and shook with such violent sobs that I sat there, hands on my knees, with no understanding. Long after the bridge had passed it was that I guessed: perhaps for the first time she realized, Little Mother realized, that Father was really dead.[2]

Strange as it may seem, the bridge is the fulcrum of the whole passage. Before the train has passed it, the reader is the witness of Rama's and Little Mother's deep grief, so rooted inside their souls that it is not possible for Rama to trace its origin, or simply to react to it ("with no understanding"). After the bridge has passed, they gradually come to terms with their sorrow and accept their destiny ("Little Mother realized"). The opposition "with no understanding"/ "Little Mother realized" is, therefore, made possible by "the bridge" which is in-between them. Yet, at the same time, the bridge also fictionally materializes suffering which elevates man and allows him to overcome obstacles.

Another essential topic Raja Rao deals with in the novel is love. Love "connects" man and woman: Rama's father and Little Mother, Rama and Madeleine, Rama and Savithri, Oncle Charles and Tante Zoubie, Catherine and Georges, to list but the few that are more specifically described, are all happy or sad protagonists of love stories. These relationships constitute the very structure of the plot of the novel Raja Rao makes it eminently clear how important it is for him to find the element of connection between the two opposites. Writing about Catherine and Georges, he thus comments: "Georges's dominion is the Heaven and Catherine's the earth. All that one needs is a ladder, a golden ladder."[3] As a result, love not only bridges Georges and Catherine? man and woman, male and female principles but also Heaven and earth. As far as the relationship Rama-Madeleine is concerned, love is symbolized by Pierre (or Krishna, as he was called at the beginning), their first son, who, emblematically enough, will die very young. In a very poetic passage we have the chance to see how the boundaries between the two ends become more and more blurred but how clear and definite the in-between appears to us: "Madeleine was like the Palace of Amber seen in moonlight. There is such a luminous mystery—the deeper you go, the more you know yourself. So Krishna was born."[4] It is in Krishna, in fact, that both Madeleine and Rama dissolve to give life to love. Love, like any in-between, is dissolution itself—or *sunya*, to say it in Raja Rao's words—, does not belong to the world and this is why Pierre-Krishna appears so ethereal, his death so symbolical and not the reason for sorrow for his father. In-between, therefore, live in that they are not. "Love demands nothing, it says nothing, it knows nothing; it lives for itself,"[5] and further "Love is not a feeling: it is, as you might say, a stateless state, the whole condition of oneself."[6]

The process of re-shaping what is concrete in terms of the abstract seems to be a major preoccupation for the writer. History opposes the present to the past: the past must be explained according to the present and the present is nothing but the natural result of the past, a sort of mathematical equation. This is why "Benares is eternal. There the dead do not die nor the living live,"[7] or for the same matter, "India has no history, for Truth cannot have history."[8] Eternity (or Benares, or India, or the Ganges), therefore, becomes an in-between. It is opposed to history but, curiously enough, it contains history. And this is the reason why Rama is a historian who goes beyond history: he becomes the guru of the situation as he looks history from eternity (to say it in Raja Rao's way), while Dr. Robin-Bessaignac still cannot do so. While the professor admits that Rama's research is extremely interesting, nevertheless he blue-pencils some passages. In the entries of the protagonist's diary we read:

> One in particular, in my preface, made him laugh. "History is not a straight line, it is not even a curved line," I had written. "History is a straight line turned into a round circle. It has no beginning, it has no end—it is movement without itself moving. History is an act to deny fact. History, truly speaking, is seminal."[9]

Metaphorically speaking, Rama stresses that his vision contemplates a 'circle,' the perfect geometrical figure rather than "a straight line," or better, a circle containing a straight line within itself, a sound paradox which Raja Rao is eager to reiterate very soon: "it is movement without itself moving." But, once more, in-betweens do not belong to this world and, as a consequence, we should not examine them rationally. They go beyond mere reason, they are poetry or sainthood which, albeit for different reasons, are not rational. This seems to be the motivation that drove the narrator to idealize certain peculiar literary figures connotated as rebels, fools or crazy who lived "outside" or at the margins of the society either in voluntary exile or because "banned." I am obviously referring to Hamlet, "who knows his madness is intelligent, while others only see ghosts,"[10] or Dostoevsky, who refuses to surrender to "the tyranny of two and two making four."[11]

Among the many examples of in-betweens, there is one more, at least, which it would be interesting to focus our attention on. Homogeneously scattered along the plot, it is possible to trace images of some kind of magic, which appear to us as in-betweens amidst the possible and the impossible. At the beginning of the novel we come across Grandfather Kittanna, a character of astonishing impact, soon introduced to the reader as "heroic." In the story related to outline his character, we find him performing incredible *exploits* with his horse Sundar in a tale outside time. Rama himself, who has openly declared he has been strongly influenced by this figure, can not find an explanation to what happened but, all the same, insists on the credibility of his grandfather's legendary deeds. It is true, however, that Madeleine is the character who most frequently exhibits such "unnatural" potentialities. She knows perfectly well that she will lose her child and, moreover, she has a clear premonition of the exact period of his death. She incredibly foresees the arrival of a letter to a woman who feared she had lost her husband in war, she heals sick children and, quite curiously, she is described as a fairy performing her magic on a Nazi officer at the time of the French occupation. What is striking, is not much the power she uses and develops in order to defend himself but, rather, the naturalness of the entire description so that the reader accepts it as a matter of fact. In the passage which follows, Madeleine tells the narrator what happened to her in that circumstance:

> She said that during the Nazi occupation, toward the end of 1943, a German officer had tried to touch her hair; it looked so magical and it looked the perfect Nordic hair. She said he had brought his hand near her face, and *she had only to smile and he could not do anything.* He bowed and went away [italics mine].[12]

The Serpent and the Rope abounds in in-betweens. Other examples which we will simply list are the Holy Grail (the subject of Rama's research for his doctorate), an in-between amidst Buddhism and Christianity, the Ganges, an in-between amidst the Himalayas and the Ocean, Savithri, whom is described as an in-between amidst presence/absence and sound/silence and many others.

The relevance of neutral images is testified to, in addition, by the insistence on creating two poles and their in-between. I am now going to list some passages which give evidence of such urgency:

> Madeleine had such a joy on her face, seated between her uncle and her aunt.[13]

> Existence [...] is a passage between life and death, and birth and death again, and what an accumulation of pain man has to bear.[14]

> In between day and night is the space of dusk, that beat of an eyelash which is the light of Brahman.[15]

> Love becomes divided against itself, just as Avignon is split into Petit Avignon and Avignon des Papes. In between is the Rhône and the broken bridge of Saint-Bénézet.[16]

Finally, *The Serpent and the Rope* itself is an in-between. It materializes the neutral position amidst a puranic tale and a modernist novel, it is the perfect compromise between the West and the East, it represents the balance between fictional narration and poetry, spirituality and the domain of the flesh. It contains everything: dialogues, poetry, diary entries, legends and tales, quotations from literary texts, argumentations on philosophical or historical subjects. The particular use of the language, which at the same time is not British English nor Indian English, mirrors that aim. The large quantity of neologisms, such as unself-consciously,[17] Indiahood,[18] un-at-home,[19] whereness,[20] or the peculiar use of "in-between" as a noun and not as a preposition or an adverb, constitute further exemplifications of this tendency. To conclude, curious as it may seem, in *The Serpent and the Rope* Raja Rao makes indirect reference to all the works of his literary career, further novels included. If we consider that this was just the second novel he wrote and the last one he has published came out twenty-eight years later, this is nothing short of astonishing. He in fact makes allusion to Kanthapura,[21] to the cat and the kittens,[22] to the Ganga ghats,[23] to Communism,[24] and to the game of chess.[25]

REFERENCES

1. Curiously enough, critics have not yet discussed the subject of "in-betweenness" in Raja Rao's fiction, though only in a passing way. In particular, in my research I have made use of the following critical instruments:

   M.K. Naik, *Raja Rao* (New York: Twaine, 1972).

   C.D. Narasimhayah, *Raja Rao* (New Delhi: Arnold Heinemann, 1973).

   Shyamala A. Narayan, *Raja Rao: Man and His Works* (New Delhi: Sterling Publishers, 1988).

   Shiva Niranjan, *Raja Rao: Novelists as Sadhaka* (Ghaziabad: Vimal Prakashan, 1985).

   Alastair Niven, *Truth within Fiction:* a Study of Raja Rao's *The Serpent and the Rope* (Culcutta: Writers Workshop, 1979).

   K.R. Rao, *The Fiction of Raja Rao* (Aurangabad: Parimal Prakashan, 1980).

   K.K. Sharma, ed. *Perspective on Raja Rao: an Anthology of Critical Essays* (Ghaziabad: Vimal Prakashan, 1980).

   Paul Sharrad, *Raja Rao and Cultural Tradition* (New Delhi: Sterling Publishers, 1987).

   Narsingh Srivastva, *The Mind and Art of Raja Rao* (Bareilly: Prakash Book Depot, 1980).

2. Raja Rao, *The Serpent and the Rope* (New Delhi: Orient Paperbacks, 1995) 33. Subsequent references pertain to this edition.

3. *S&R* 148.

4. *S&R* 14.

5. *S&R* 229.

6. *S&R* 331.

7. *S&R* 22.

8. *S&R* 102.

9. *S&R* 401.

10. *S&R* 340.

11. *S&R* 99.

12. *S&R* 15.

13. *S&R* 93.

14. *S&R* 135.

15. *S&R* 293.

16. *S&R* 377.

17. *S&R* 136.

18. *S&R* 137.

19. *S&R* 188.

20. *S&R* 303.
21. *S&R* 278.
22. *S&R* 307.
23. *S&R* 10.
24. *S&R* 204.
25. *S&R* 146.

17

The Theme of Marriage in Raja Rao's *The Serpent and the Rope*

S.P. SWAIN*

One of most significant, dominant and sacred institutions, marriage occupies a crucial place in Indian society. It plays a decisive role in human relationships. Portrayal of marriage in Indian English novels is a recurrent feature and it is this element in Indian Writing in English which gives it a typical Indian sensibility. In this connection Meenakshi Mukherjee observes: "Among some hundred and fifty novels published in the last thirty years, one finds hardly two dozen books where a marriage ceremony has not been described" (*Quest*: 38). In *The Serpent and the Rope*, marriage has been presented as a pervasive social institution. C.D. Narasimhaiah maintains:

> No earthly institution can involve man in the world to the extent that marriage does. Hence the centrality of marriage in the novel. The novelist has drawn our attention pointedly to the pervasiveness of this social institution in the manner he presents human relationships (*Raja Rao:* 110).

Madeleine marries Ramaswamy because she has a desire to understand India, to know India through her identification with the protagonist. Ramaswamy says:

> She loved me partly because she felt India had been wronged by the British, and because she would, in

---

*Department of English, Rourkela Municipal College, Rourkela.

marrying me know and identify herself with a great people (18).

The failure of the Rama-Madeleine marriage is on account of their temperamental incompatibility. It is also attributable to Madeleine's successive failures in her life. Shattered by these failures, she takes to Buddhism, its compassion and commiseration casting a powerful spell on her. She finds solace in her self-imposed penance of isolation and subsequently solicits Rama for divorce "in order to free herself from the entanglements that hinder the progress of her spiritual pilgrimage" (70). She writes to Catherine:

> It is all a ghost story—Rama, India ... and the world. Contemplation is the only truth one has (394).

Ramaswamy's socio-cultural values exist on the intuitive rather than the intellectual plane but Madeleine's is a self-endorsed world of intellectualism. She fails to extricate herself from her 'bourgeois virtue, and her circumscribing and stifling intellectual life-style. She declines to be involved in Rama's sense of values, in his intuitive life and hence she fails to participate meaningfully in the rituals through which he (Ramaswamy) seeks to assert his self. Madeleine says:

> Sometimes Rama, I want to run away from you, run far away from you, just to listen to the stupid innocent laughter, like Tante Zoubies; or go to a circus and see the clown make everyone laugh (135).

She declines to come to India with Rama. Even she turns down the bride's toe-rings—a sacrilegious attitude in the Indian cultural context. Madeleine is self-centred, a centripetal being whereas Ramaswamy is a man of the world, and can step out of the self to participate in the sacramental ritual of life. Madeleine fails to achieve consonance with the Indian spirit symbolised by Ramaswamy. K.R. Rao holds that "as against Madeleine's escape into the self-denying Buddhist religion, Rama encounters the Vedantic self-expression and affirmation of the world as celebration. In the Rama-Madeleine relationship, Raja Rao sees fissures in the state of matrimony.

Madeleine fails to accept marriage as a sacrament. She even regards mere 'touch' as unholy. She devalues herself by her pseudo-philosophical attitude to sex. She is psychologically and spiritually alienated from Ramaswamy. Such polarisation leads to the failure of her marriage. A typical Westerner, she associates sex with sin and concupiscence.

According to Havelock Ellis, "Marriage in the biological sense is a sexual relationship entered into with the intention of making it permanent, even apart from whether or not it has received sanction of law or the church" (*Sex and Marriage in India:* 3).

Considering this statement of Ellis we can safely conclude that Ramaswamy's sexual relationship with Madeleine is never complete; it hardly attains consummation. Hence Rama's turning to Savithri for love. She fulfils that which Madeleine could not. An amplification of the feminine mystique, in the legendary tradition of Mira Bai, she at length emerges as the veritable heroine of the novel. The Savithri-Rama relationship forms the crux of the story. It is the pivot on which the action of the story rotates. It deals with the feminine principle which is the very ideal and base of a harmonious marital relationship. Raja Rao says:

> Thus marriage as history (Rama-Madeleine) fails, but love as Savithri-Rama succeeds, for in one Madeleine seeks her own God but Savithri her Rama (through whom she sees the whole experience and beyond).... The true woman of Rama, therefore, is Savithri, even though she is married to his Friend, Pratap... (*Raja Rao:* 84).

Ramaswamy's quest for the self culminates in his mystical marriage in London. Savithri thus becomes a "hypostatic presence" which he had been looking for. She becomes a channel of Rama's entry into a state where he transcends the dimensions of the ego-idea, and annihilates time and space. Love with Savithri gives a new dimension to Rama's life. It gives new meaning to his otherwise ruffled marital existence with Madeleine.

Walker believes that "marriage is essential to the well-being of human society" (*Woman:* 78). He further observes:

> The advantage resulting from the states of marriage are that the two sexes may reciprocally satisfy the natural desires which are felt equally by each ... that

they may equally assist each other throughout life
by reciprocal affection and cares... (*Raja Rao*: 80).

"Marriage and family" according to Cooley, "are the means
used by society to control promiscuous sex and dissipation of
man's energy" (*Hindu Social Organisation*: 238). But in *The Serpent
and the Rope* do Madeleine and Ramaswamy maintain fidelity in
their conjugal life? Does marriage, in any way, help them in "coming
together"? These are the questions which all Rao readers should
answer for themselves. Simon de Beauvoir maintains that "the
tragedy of marriage is not that it fails to assure woman the promised
happiness but that it mutilates her; it dooms her (*The Second Sex*:
496). Madeleine too is mutilated and doomed. She is ruined because
of the duplicity of her husband, Rama, "who takes pleasure in his
role of a Krishna, a mentor and guide." For Rama, the act of love
becomes a sacred orgy. Marriage in the novel often becomes a
crisis for both Rama and Madeleine. Ramaswamy remains a "holy
vagabond" at heart. Hence the evanescent nature of his passion for
Madeleine.

In the novel we have two wholly Western marriages, a "West-
East Marriage," symbolised by the Rama-Madeleine tryst and Hindu
marriages based on the concept of 'Jati' (Caste) which says that the
individual should marry within his 'Jati,' a social situation prevailing
in our contemporary society, though now it is gradually disappearing.
But endogamy still continues to be the prevailing custom among
the Hindus. Thus endogamy (kinship marriage), implies the existence
of a caste or kinship area within which one is supposed to look for
spouse. In the novel this is illustrated by Subramanya, Little Mother's
own causin's son's marriage with Saroja. In this connection G.N.
Ramu observes:

> Gotra (group of people within the caste)
> considerations played an important role in the
> marriages of both Brahmins and Vaisyas consistent
> with the traditional practice. On the contrary
> Kshatriyas did not regard 'gotra' considerations as
> important in marriage negotiations... (*Family and
> Caste in Urban India*: 36).

In the portrayal of Kshatriya marriages in the novel, Raja Rao maintains strict fidelity to facts of contemporary Indian practice by mirroring the proclivity of the Kshatriyas to seek prospective spouses across their caste lines. This is exemplified by the marriage of Savitri to Pratap Singh and on the basis of caste considerations, Jagirdars like Pratap's family members cannot be equal with the Royal family of Raja Rathubir Singh, Savitri's father.

On the other hand, we also find that Savitri's sister (a Kshatriya girl) marries a rich 'banya' (Vaisya) a very reputed politician whose prospects and chance of being a minister was the sole stimulus behind this intercaste marriage.

Occupational status is a deciding factor in the marriage market of the post-Independent India. P.C. Swain aptly maintains:

> Raja Rao's awareness of this recent social trend is amply demonstrated in *The Serpent and the Pope* firstly when the narrator Ramaswamy says, "an Assistant Resident was still a highly respected party in the marriage-market of North India" and secondly when Savitri writes to Ramaswamy that "A Delhi diplomat today is worth two private secretaries to an Indian Governor" (*The Mahanadi Review*: 37).

Further the remarriage of Hindu widows was looked upon with contempt in the pre-Independent India. But widower-marriages are now a very common practice. This aspect of the marriage institution is reflected in Raja Rao's novel, in the lives of Rama's father who marries for the third time and Vikram, a Delhiite, who marries for the fourth time a girl of only eighteen.

Marriages in India were, and are still celebrated, with pomp and show. Raja Rao illustrates this realistic aspect of Indian marriage ceremonies by citing the case of Savitri's official engagement with Pratap which is celebrated with great splendour and fanfare, with a lot of jubilation. Raja Rao says, "Altogether it was a splendid occasion for all concerned" (*The Serpent and the Pope*: 30). Rama's sister, Saroja's marriage with Subramanya Shastri is also a grand celebration. The protagonist, Rama says: "I found joy in the notes of the serpent-clarionet" (262). He further continues, "The music started, on the other street gunfire went off; the vulgar brass band started playing some military march, with Indian style music being piped amidst... (264).

Marriage is now almost a dying institution. It is hardly a success when girls are now sold in the dowry-market. This once sacred institution has now badly degenerated. The overall impact that Rao makes on us about the institution of marriage is one of despair and gloom. It is not basically bilateral and there are a lot of deceptions and beguilements in the marital life of the couples. For instance, Georges is cuckolded by his wife Catherine, Tante Zubie has pre-marital sex with Oncle Charles, Little Mother languishes as a widow and takes refuge in her clandestine love for her stepson Rama. Savithri fornicates before her marriage with Pratap. Mrs. Shamsunder (Lakshmi) has a secret liaison with Rama. Raja Rao presents these married women with all their natural follies and foibles. Hence, it would not be erroneous to say that there is hardly a holy and sacred marriage in *The Serpent and The Rope*.

WORKS CITED

Beauvior, Simon De. *The Second Sex*. London: Pan Books, 1988.

Cooley, Charles. *Social Consciousness* 368. Quoted in Pandharinath H. Prabhu, *Hindu Social Organisation: A Study in Socio-psychological and Ideological Foundations*. Bombay: Popular, 1958.

Mukherjee, Meenakshi. "Awareness of Audience in Indo-Anglian Fiction." *Quest* (Winter, 1967).

Narasimhaiah, C.D. *Raja Rao*. New Delhi: Arnold-Heinemann, n.d.

Ramu, G.N. *Family and Caste in Urban India: A Case Study*. New Delhi: Vikas, 1977.

Rao, Raja. *The Serpent and the Rope*. 1960; New Delhi: Orient Paperbacks 1968. All citations of the novel are from this edition of the text.

Sur, A.K. *Sex and Marriage in India; An Ethno-Historical Survey*. Bombay: Allied, 1973.

Swain, P.C. Contemporary Reality in the Indian Marriages in Raja Rao's *The Serpent and the Rope*. *The Mahanadi Review*. 4.2 (April 1985—June 1986).

Walker, Alexander. *Women: Physiologically Considered as to Mind, Morals, Marriages, Matrimonial Slavery, Infidelity and Divorce*. New Delhi: Mittal, 1987.

18

The Role of Caste in Raja Rao's *Cat and Shakespeare*

RAGINI RAMACHANDRA

If caste has played much havoc in Indian life over the years, it seems to have done no less in Indian Writing, for so often has it been the bane of both. But there have been fortunate exceptions.

While caste is more often than not used as a means to rouse the social conscience of the reader by the contemporary Indian writer whether in English or our regional languages often deteriorating into propaganda, it is used at least by Raja Rao in *The Cat and Shakespeare* as a means of exploration of the higher laws of being. This is not to imply that Raja Rao himself has not wielded this potent weapon to espouse a social cause; to decry an anachronism that is unworthy of a great and humane society. "Javni," one of his most touching short stories is a case in point. In his first novel *Kanthapura*. The very fabric of village life is woven into a complex structure by various castes represented in the brahmin quarter, the pariah quarter, the weavers' quarter, the potters' quarter and the sudra quarter and within this framework the novelist works out the destinies of his characters against a politically charged background. *The Serpent and the Rope* however, seems to transcend many of these social concerns in its preoccupation with man's metaphysical quest. All caste considerations are simply brushed aside in the opening sentence of the novel with its pregnant truth:

"Brahmin is he who knows Brahman."

The idea is carried forward in *The Cat* where significantly it is neither Ramakrishna Pai, a Saraswath brahmin who with a strong predilection for the spiritual, "lived in many, many worlds" (57) himself, nor Bhoothalinga Iyer with "a hair knot on his head, namam on his face and a Ramayana on his lap" (41) that recognizes the supremacy of the Feminine Principle, but the betel-chewing, smoking, non-brahmin Govindan Nair! And that is because as Pai the narrator puts it quite bluntly:

> Only a Nair can see right. Look at the boss, Bhoothalinga Iyer. He can no more understand truth than the buffalo can see a straight line (42).

It is in this sense that *The Cat* is a logical sequel to *The Serpent and the Rope*. Scholars have perceived connections between Ramaswamy's final resolve to retire to Travancore (his 'real home,' is Benaras) and Travancore itself serving as the setting for *The Cat* with the narrator's categorical assertion, "Malabar is Truth." By way of elaboration we might recall how *The Serpent and the Rope* concludes with Rama's anguished soul longing not for a "God" but a "Guru" who could vouchsafe to him the "vision of truth." When he reappears as Ramakrishna Pai in *The Cat*, he has the good fortune of meeting his guru in Govindan Nair, a fact generously acknowledged by Pai himself:

> Govindan Nair is my guide (64).

> Truly to speak, if Govindan Nair had not come... I should never have gone beyond my *Malayalarajyam* and the Government Secretariat, with *The Hindu* for the evening tea (115).

The second and the more important point of relationship between the two novels is while the conception of brahminhood at the beginning of *The Serpent and the Rope* does not go beyond a mere definition, and the hero's query as to how many of his ancestors since the excellent Yagnavalkya have really known the Truth, the entire novel, *The Cat and Shakespeare* is a vindication of the novelist's supreme faith in the view that one's caste is determined by one's propensities often taking the form of plain assertions, backed however by the weight of knowing and feeling:

> He who gives is a Prince
> or
> Brahmin is he who knows Brahman.

And Govindan Nair is both, for he gives as well as knows. Not merely does he give money to Ramakrishna Pai to buy a house for his daughter, Usha, but also explain the Brahman to the Brahmin! In a tone which smacks not of conceit but suggestive of superb self-confidence, he claims:

> Ruling princes taught sadhus the Truth in the Upani-shadic times. Now Nairs alone can teach the Truth in the world (38).

Far from disputing his claim Ramakrishna Pai expresses his implicit faith in Govindan Nair in unequivocal language:

> I knew at once he was right. He was right. He is right. He will ever be right (38).

Yet Bhoothalinga Iyer in his ignorance used to say; 'all Nairs have enough Brahmin blood to be clever...but not enough to understand the truth; truth is the privilege of the Brahmins (74).

Paradoxically however, it is Govindan Nair who topples this make-believe world of Bhoothalinga Iyer; pierces the veil with a mere pen-knife of his and endeavours to build the "Palace of Truth." In fact, it is Govindan Nair who carries the Vedic tradition in his bones; recites verse after verse in beautiful Sanskrit from the *Astavakra Samhita* to the amazement of Ramakrishna Pai who remarks that though a brahmin he "knew less Sanskrit" than Govindan Nair and "understood even less" (37). Indeed Govindan Nair "knew everything for he was so concerned with everything" (71).

> Once he talked so much on manure that an agricultural expert asked if he was Professor at the local college. Just the same way he talked of the twenty-three types of Enfield guns. Or for that matter of boils (17).

Govindan Nair could not merely meet the brahmin on equal terms, but even go beyond him and that not in matters of the Spirit only but even in Intellect. "Important in thought," he could take one through "fearful twists and trysts and imponderables to some majesty" (14). So robust an intelligence could settle for nothing less than apprehending the Absolute. He might well have been an enigma even to Ramakrishna Pai who confesses:

I never could understand all that he meant (33).

The versatility of his mind and the far-ranging nature of his interests implied in his knowledge of Malayalam, Latin, Law, Poetry and Philosophy remind one of the sages of yore who trafficked freely with the cosmos. If adventures come to those who are adventurous, knowledge comes to those who thirst for it. "When one is curious one can know anything" was Govindan Nair's own philosophy of life. His curious mind could indeed traverse through the whole gamut of life, uniting heaven and earth and articulate too his exploits with trenchant logic. Incidentally, he was a law student and was known to be a "grand speaker" even as a youth. "If stars govern me," he would say, "then I must know the stars. If the Travancore Police Manual governs all police officers (and the public), then we must know it too" (57).

It is his remarkable capacity for fusing all these varied and dissimilar experiences into one coherent whole that is indeed Govindan Nair's supreme strength—the reason why he can mediate effortlessly between the two worlds—the temporal and the spiritual, ignoring the claims of neither, splendidly crystallized in his constant gestures of jumping over the "wall," the wall that obscures one's vision and also in the easy transition he achieves between the newspapers and the scriptures. His fondness for playing with children is no less than his fondness for delving into the mysteries of the Abstract.

Yet, his knowledge notwithstanding, he is a man with a "big heart," so big, "it builds a wall lest it run away with everything" (10), a fact admitted not merely by his friend Ramakrishna Pai, but even his boss, Bhoothalinga Iyer. Was it his "big heart" then which enabled him to "love" even Bhoothalinga Iyer and "weep" over his death? Everybody came to "console" him "as if he had lost something" (90) and needed "condolence." In a beautiful gesture of salutation Pai eulogizes him as Bhima who went in search of the flower of paradise so as to become "half-brother to mankind." That this is not mere idealization is authenticated by his little acts of kindness and love. He would slip in two and five rupees through windows where a child cried; make way for ladies when a bus was overcrowded; issue ration cards to widows as if their husbands were still alive. With his faith in the unity of all creation, the whole world for him was "one living organism" (17). "He must speak to tree and mongoose as if they were under his authority" (112). This Rajarshi who could almost command the river Parrar to turn and become a Coromandel river had in him elements of the Brahmarshi too amply borne out by the quality of his thought and the texture of his being. Whenever Ramakrishna Pai "needed" him but never asked for him, there would be Govindan Nair. Whenever Pai was besieged by a creeping sense of inadequacy and cried in anguish over his predicament:

> I am not even a hunter that in his nervousness lets down bilva leaves. Lord, what hope is there for me? (63)

Govindan Nair would always appear at such a moment as though to minister to his soul. It was he who not merely strengthened Pai's longing to "build a big house" but gave a definite shape to his longing by encouraging him to build "a house of three stories," a "secret pact" he makes with Pai. Such is his faith in the realization of this dream, that he transforms the idea into a palpable, tangible reality—and enacts it too, to the reader through the sheer urgency and immediacy of his language:

> ... God will build you a house of three stories— note, please, I say three stories—here, just where you sit. It's already there. You've just to look and see, look deep and see (12).

Little wonder if the idea of building a house of three stories assumes the form of an obsession for Ramakrishna Pai. His dreams are further nourished by Nair's friendly gestures of offering to build him in brick and stone and gold. That this is not an empty bravado is seen in the novelist's remark; Govindan Nair indeed looked as if he had "plowed" the seas to build Ramakrishna Pai "a house in ice" (55). And he was the kind of man who could build in dreams too, the only permanent building that man could ever raise.

The quintessence of Govindan Nair's personality however, is his unconditional faith in the Mother Principle which finds an admirable concrete equivalent in the cat. He always talks of a mother cat which carries the kitten by the scruff of its neck. He says, "Learn the way of the kitten. Then you're saved. Allow the mother cat, Sir, to carry you,"... "The kitten is the safest thing in the world, the kitten held in the mouth of the mother cat" (12).

One day John, his colleague in the ration office plays a trick on him by bringing a beautiful Persian cat in a rat-trap and placing it on his table. For the ardently idealistic Govindan Nair it turns out to be in actuality a good deed in a naughty world! While he addresses it in Malayalam as *Poochi, Poochi*, with utmost tenderness, Boothalinga Iyer who hated cats tries to chase it away with *chee, chee*! The caste factor seems to play an important role in Iyer's prejudice against cats, for as the novelist says:

> Boothalinga Iyer was a Brahmin. For him a cat, a *marjaram*, was a pariah animal. It was sly, unclean, unfaithful. It was evil to see a cat first thing in the morning ... (74).

In fact, "for Boothalinga Iyer rats existed and not cats" (74). Ration shops had rats and that alone was "true" for him. He did not know as Nair did that "what is real ever is" (100). Whether one perceives it or not. On the other hand he would summon his empirical knowledge to argue authoritatively:

> A rat was the vehicle of Lord Ganesha himself... But the cat, which god ever rode a cat? Nobody did—so it was improper, unholy, beyond thought, what is beyond thought cannot be thought out—it is evil to the temple street (75).

Hence, he always used the Sanskrit word *marjaram* ("which carried its own condemnation") and uttered even that "with only the tip of his tongue" (89) as if its very utterance defiled him. He was also sure that for a Persian cat, there was no word in ancient Sanskrit. The cat to him meant "meow-meow business" which was utter "nonsense" and even spelt a "disaster" whereas it came naturally to Govindan Nair to say "meow-meow." "All my language can be reduced to that—meow, meow" (34), he says proudly, a language that is incomprehensible to Bhoothalinga Iyer, "like sound heard and not the word understood."

It is ironical that John who brought "a very God" to this "poor ration office" cannot however be the "priest" himself. The cat is a "feline being" for him which can only evoke his "resentful laughter." Syed Sahib might look upon it as the "purest animal in the world" (87) but Govindan Nair who knows "better" can correct him on his Muslim theology and tell him that it is not "sacred" in Islam as it is in Egypt where it is called "Bastet." For the insult John has done in stuffing a cat into a rat cage, there is sufficient nemesis when Govindan Nair makes him kneel down and kiss the cat not once, but twice as though to reaffirm his submission, which the whole office witnesses in "one noumenal silence" (88). Bhoothalinga Iyer wanted to shout "Get out! Get away! But his tongue would not say it" (89) and Raja Rao seizes the opportunity to bring home to us a profound truth with consummate ease that marks his writing throughout the novel.

"How can you say with what is not what is?" (89). But destiny chooses its exact moment for redemption, not punishment as one might have expected under the circumstances, for when the cat jumped over Bhoothalinga Iyer's head, he opened his eyes wide, uttered the words Shiva, Shiva and died. That is how he who was handcuffed to illusion all the while and was like a "kitten sans cat" was finally released from all bonds of earthly life.

Raja Rao has undoubtedly dared to do something most unconventional in this novel in not merely making the cat, which is in popular imagination a 'pariah' animal a symbol but in making a Nair, an 'outcaste' as far as Bhoothalinga Iyer is concerned the spokesman for man's spiritual aspirations and the expounder of great truth. It is this man who celebrated life in gay abandon, savoured its joys and sorrows with perfect equanimity that extended a lucid invitation to others to live and to create in the very midst of a famine (for there is a famine in the human as well as the rodent worlds). In doing so Raja Rao is not encouraging the view that either virtue or wisdom is the prerogative of Nairs only, because all Nairs even in the novel are not all good nor all Brahmins, for that matter as sordid as Bhoothalinga Iyer, for there is Ramakrishna Pai himself with a strong penchant for the other world. So there is the scheming Velayudhan Nair, the opposite of Govindan Nair, who is "one with the one and other with the other," and who manipulates ration cards with a facility that makes everybody wonder whether he learned street jugglery" (42). His wife had an "array of gold bangles" on her hands; other non-Brahmins like Kunni Krishna Menon and his wife ran huge estates and "amassed a fortune" (39). John had built a "modest little" house as he put it, with questionable means and thought he was "infallible" just because he had some money in the Imperial Bank, the Seth Sahib, a grain merchant from the north wanted to build a spire for the Lord at Jagannath Puri to expiate his sins and so on and so forth.

Raja Rao's intentions in this novel are not by any means to evoke communal feelings and get the reader entrenched in them but rather to *liberate* him from them in showing how a man with a *samskara* can transcend his caste and attain enlightenment, evident in the way the image of the hunter with his bilva tree is made central to the novel. It is important for us to recognize that Govindan Nair's aspirations are different from those of any average man placed in his position. Though a second divisional clerk on Rs. 45 a month, he is concerned not with his economic or financial status, but man's orphaned existence on earth or to use that much-used phrase, the 'human condition' in spiritual terms. For him "to live is not difficult," even to yield to the flesh does not pose any problems, but "A kitten sans cat, that is the question" (82), the truth of which is brought home in secular terms: "can you imagine a state without a govt?" (63). In his magnanimity he makes Abraham, a Syrian Christian the Chief after his boss's death while he himself prefers to be a clerk. Yet Raja Rao's distinction lies in not making his spiritual hero overtly didactic or anything like that, as though to keep dogma and spirituality apart. For instance Govindan Nair would say:

> You no more find the truth in the Himalayas than
> you find it in the Indian Law Register. You may
> find it on your garden wall and not know it was it.
> You must have eyes to see (108-109).

His role in the novel has been to give "eyes" to those who have the potential to see truth right on their garden wall but knew not "it was it." Bhoothlinga Iyer who, despite his Brahminic birth lived like a rat and believed in the reality of rats only, all the while spurning the Mother Cat and Govindan Nair, a non-Brahmin who did not tire of teaching the ways of the kitten have their analogues in Saroja and Shantha, one a wife and another more than a wife to Ramakrishna Pai. Even in the portrayal of these two women the novelist lets us understand that their essential differences stem from the caste factor, for Saroja, a true Brahmin "knows how to take" (23). But Shantha is a Nair. "Her giving is complete" (23). While "Shantha's silence has all that logic cannot compute" (30), "Saroja wants two and two to make four" which provokes her husband to ask desperately.

> When you have Saroja's logic,
> what can you do? (30)

Also "Shantha is always mysterious. Just as Saroja was always clear" (93). While Shantha remains near Ramakrishna Pai helping him to understand himself and believe in the reality of his own existence, Saroja, though a wedded wife lives away from him "busy inspecting the rope making" (31). A "tremendous worker," for her "fact is that which yields" (31). She lives on an island attending to boat repairs and inspecting boats that carried not the kernel, but the "coconut shells." Like Bhoothalinga Iyer who deluded himself when his myopic vision did not allow him to see beyond rats, Saroja also seems to be hugging a life of illusions, so effectively brought out in those innocuous looking words 'rope' and 'shells.' Raja Rao's handling of the two women is a reiteration of the main theme that Truth is his who seeks it as a kitten seeks the Mother Cat and not just anybody's by the accidents of birth.

It is significant therefore that the novel should end with Ramakrishna Pai's desire to buy one of those "lovely dilapidated structures" in the Brahmin streets near the temple and "build it anew" (118). By implication the novelist means to say, what Brahminism has had to offer in the past was "lovely" but in its practice and observance, it has today been reduced to a "dilapidated" condition. To restore these crumbling structures to their original splendour and build the "city of gods" Devanagari should be as Ananda Coomaraswamy puts it, the constant task of civilization.

In the final analysis, here is a novel which cannot easily be compared with any other coming from either the British or the American traditions. For class conflicts, which for instance in

Lawrence confirm and perpetuate the ego (Mrs. Morel is a glaring example) and racial discriminations in Black American Fiction which highlight the need to make the "invisible man" visible cannot be equated with caste distinctions as handled by Raja Rao, for in ridding caste of its social implications and concentrating on transcending the egocentric pre-dicament, he is investing it with a metaphysical dimension. The overmastering question here is not whether a poor clerk from a backward caste will get a rise in his salary, a promotion in his career, be treated as an equal with his boss, succeed in marrying off his son to a girl from the higher caste, etc., but speculation about man's ultimate destiny which is as legitimate a concern for the novelist as other concerns like whether the low-caste would be allowed to draw water from the caste Hindu's well or whether a black man can sit on benches meant for whites only.

The irony however lies in the fact that while most writers are exercised about ensuring social equality and justice to their deprived and oppressed characters and conferring upon them an identity, here is Raja Rao who makes his low-born hero strive for a state of non-identity. "There is mantra even when he speaks" which makes Pai hold his breath. The novel is unique in the subtle twist Raja Rao introduces into his theme. While other works with caste preoccupations are concerned with safeguarding the economic and social well-being of the underdog, *The Cat and Shakespeare* seems to be concerned with the spiritual well-being of not the low-born so much as that of the caste Hindu! All deeply entrenched roles are reversed; the teacher becomes the taught and the disciple the teacher, the educator of people's minds and sensibilities. The ugly duckling has indeed turned into a swan! In throwing all social hierarchies overboard the novelist seems to be shaking the iron-clad citadel of traditions and certainties to its very foundations.

Caste seems to be performing a dual function in this novel. On the one hand it appears to be conferring a distinct individuality upon a character who inherits certain characteristics peculiar to that caste into which he is born and thereby *imprison* him with an identity. On the other it also *releases* a man by granting him sufficient freedom to go outside his own caste and imbibe the best features of another which in turn might help him to go beyond all caste and achieve a state of non-identity. In this sense is the novel a unique experiment, unique in so far as caste is put to a totally different use, different from anything one had hitherto come across in Indian fiction.

19

Raja Rao's *The Cat and Shakespeare*: A Western View

CLAUDIO GORLIER*

Raja Rao's *The Cat and Shakespeare* has been extensively investigated in a variety of critical scrutinies, with an almost constant and appropriate emphasis out on its Indian specificity, enhanced by the subtitle of the book, *A Tale of Modern India*. In one instance, it has been even stressed that without taking into account "Hindu thought,...the story will make little sense." Granted that *The Cat and Shakespeare* brings forth, in many respects, an actual narrative conceptualization of Indian speculative paradigms and categories (Meenakshi Mukherjee points to the pervasive influence of a number of "Sanskrit philosophic" texts), its far-reaching dimension and the complexity of the message it imparts, its universal significance, all seem to call for a critical approach that, while it does not delegitimate such an Indian specificity, yet justifies the recourse to further and not necessarily antagonistic perspectives. I intend to meet this challenge and concentrate on a few crucial aspects of the book, trying, as much as possible, to avoid the pitfalls of overly stringent definitions. Needless to say, I do not assert that my perspective leads to eschewing the Indian specificity. Rather, it implies a study of correspondences and at the same time of diversities.[1]

Let us establish preliminarily some relevant functions that exact our critical attention: time, space, characters, history and actuality,

* Centro per Lo Studio Delle Letterature, E. Delle Culture, Delle Aree Emergenti Universita degli studi di Torino, via Sant Ottavio, 20-10124, Torino, Italy.

symbols, and finally the structure of discourse. The first two are strictly interrelated, and in this respect Mikhail Bakthin's notion of *chronotopos* (borrowed from the language of science and notably from Einstein), the relationship between time and place in a single unit, could be profitably put to use, without necessarily appropriating all its complex underpinnings, conducive to the formulation of the *chronotopos* as a genre. Notice how Rao has his first person narrator declare them in the second paragraph: "Trivandrum, two years ago." To start with, and before uttering the main locale, the narrator has already supplied the reader with an only apparently incidental and factual information: "I have a small house here." In point of fact, this information constitutes a decisive, genetic element to articulate the *chronotopos*, as far as the place is concerned. Then, the time, which completes it. "Two years ago" sets the story in the actuality, in the Modern India of the subtitle, but the present time, reflected in the present tense of the verb, quickly gives way to a reminiscence of the past, when, "some two hundred years ago," the Dutch landed in Kerala, forcing "all the bodied men to fight (or to become Christian)." To operate this time shift, the narrator depends on his wife's recollections. We come across quite a characteristic procedure, reiterated throughout the book, and which substantially questions the notion of linear time. We are compelled to challenge the principle itself of "modern," in that the story literally unfolds, rooted in a present that we would be tempted to consider accidental, or at least circumstantial, *vis-a-vis* the permanence of timeless, perennial India, where time denies any concrete historical, religious, philosophical boundary. The procedure discounts whatever sort of reading based on the paraphernalia of a strictly Western-oriented historicism.

The present is largely referential, to the effect that numerous cultural factors, which display the legacy and consequently the wisdom of an uninterrupted ancestral tradition, also by means of a somewhat intertextual recourse to different, non-English key words, qualify the mind, the behaviour, the speculations of the main characters. They substantiate the narrative texture and, in the long run, the whole discourse.

Furthermore, locality acquires the singularity of an ordinary and possibly banal place, simultaneously propitiating the idea of a microcosm, a cell inscribed in a wider world, in the globality of India and even beyond India. The first person narrator remains initially unnamed, although we are already familiar with the place and with his age, thirty-three, a magically perfect number, multiple of three, having possessed this feature since ancient Greece. He discloses his name only indirectly ("People usually introduce me in the office saying 'This is Mr. Ramakrishna Pai, cousin of Srinivasa Pai of Chalai Bazaar,' as if I belonged to some royal lineage"), indulging in a both naive and ironic exercise in vanity. The task of showing the central character par excellence is upto Pai himself, and he performs the introduction in action: "Just at that moment, Govindan Nair looks up from the leaves and says...." Nair's presentation conforms to a peculiarly modernistic paradigm, being consciously situational; we will meet him, see him physically, only later, but his appearance resolves itself primarily in his way of speaking. His mind coincides with his language, and *vice versa*. Nair is "a mixture of *The Vicar of Wakefield* and *Shakespeare*," and his choice of words and phrases sounds "clumsy" to Pai; on the other hand, "he must twist a thing into its essence and spread it out, a quality well his own."

The factual development notwithstanding, the relationship between essence and words, the search for Truth, the elucidation of Truth, will be endlessly pursued with language and in language, will be sanctioned by language, the absolute talisman. Pai's progressive initiation by Nair, the Sage, the *guru*, will be ingrained in language, in *verbum*. It will take place insofar as he will be able to master his multivalent role as a disciple, as a teller of the fable (Rao's mouthpiece, as underscored by C.D. Narasimhaiah), and simultaneously as an actor in the fable.

The binary strategy, since the story proceeds mainly through the communion between Nair and Pai, constitutes one of the most intriguing features of *The Cat and Shakespeare*. This strategy can be easily traced back to the rhetoric of classical epics (Achilles and Hector in Homer's *Iliad*) but here we wish to single out three typical instances. The first takes us quite naturally to Shakespeare. As the obviously discernible Shakespearian reference in the book bears on *Hamlet*, the specular relationship between Hamlet and Horatio clearly substantiates the binary strategy, and it should be borne in mind that the dying Prince of Denmark entrusts to his friend the task of the narrator: "So tell him, with occurents, more and less (Which have solicited"). But the binary strategy reaches its most consistent fulfilment in *Othello*, where "honest" Iago captivates Othello's confidence and, availing himself of the instruments of a lucid reasoning finalized to a vicious project, makes him subservient and pushes him to his own annihilation. Let us now consider two instances in contemporary literature: F.S. Fitzgerald's *The Great Gatsby* and D.H. Lawrence's *Women in Love*. In both novels, the close relationship between two male characters dominates the narrative structure; in Fitzgerald's book, one of the two characters also operates as the teller of the story. At the end of the novels, neither Tom nor Birkin remain the same as they had entered the stage, and they have acquired, or are in the process of acquiring, a new awareness. Nevertheless, and similarly to *Othello*, the denouement occurs at the cost of catastrophe, enacted in the tragic death of one of the two friends. In other words, the association between the two is truncated, and, far from annulling the duality, confirms it and makes it irredeemable. The contrary is true of *The Cat and Shakespeare*, to the effect that Pai's awareness, his itinerary towards self-fulfilment, toward a both existential and metaphysical truth, stem from his link with Nair, to an extent that any notion of duality becomes untenable and inconceivable.

The binary strategy encompasses Pai's individual experience and the message that he imparts to the reader in his capacity as narrator. With the reader he has established another relationship, the writer-reader relationship expounded in a number of recent theories, and which culminates in the notion of the "death of the author," systematized, for one, by Jacques Lacan. The narrator often provokes the reader "mon semblable, mon frere" (Baudelaire), virtually his accomplice. The reader should take the story upon himself, and somehow complete it, in close co-operation with the writer. Pai's down to earth world view benefits from Nair's metaphysical mastery.

In his seminal book *Mimesis*, Eric Auerbach impeccably demonstrated the realistic valency of symbol and allegory in European literature of the Middle Ages. Medieval bestiaries are both symbolic and realistic; the three wild beasts that confront and threaten Dante in the Dark Wood of *Inferno*, of hell (the she-wolf, the she-leopard and lion) are portrayed with sheer realism while ostensibly carrying a symbolic meaning that each reader can easily decode; on the contrary, the divorce between reality and symbol or the ambiguity of symbol in contemporary literature often confuse or undermine the reader's ability to penetrate the hidden meaning of the symbol (a notable exception could be found in Kafka's *Metamorfosis*, where the transformation of the man into a hideous and huge insect deploys a symbolic pattern, with a multiplicity of interpretations).

Literature, as Raja Rao warns us at the beginning of *On the Ganga Ghats*, is never *real*, but *true*. Truth is liable to present itself in different versions, but its various facets should never decry the potential ability to decode them. Says Nair: "Life is a riddle that can be solved with a riddle.... Thus the world is connected.... The unknown alone *resolves* the unknown" (35, Emphasis mine).

The first concrete symbol to emerge in the book is clearly Pai's house. It is worth stressing that in modern novel, at least since Balzac, the house has represented the abode only at face value; actually, it tends to expand into a status symbol, an ideal stage where the characters play their roles, and the various components (this especially apparent in Henry James) may denote the minds, the attitudes, the inclinations, the inner soul, of those who inhabit the house; all in all, a bourgeois replica of the temple or of the royal palace. Pai's project to build or re-build his house embodies a material, existential scope, no less than a metaphysical goal, a search for perfection. The ambition to build a three storey house (again the magic number) is tantamount to an effort toward spiritual perfection, whose frequent connotation implies verticality; suffice it to recall, a western perspective, the medieval principle of the ascent to the deity, often symbolized by the staircase (*itinorarium mentis in Deum*) or, as in George Herbert's *Prayer*, with its mystic leap to Heaven, from the earth to the "milky ways," where something is finally "understood" (the apprehension of Truth). The diversity here should rather be identified in the fact that the metaphysical perfection does not necessarily require transcendence, ascent to Heaven, but can and must be accomplished in this world, where deities incarnate. In this context, a reference to Rao's *The Serpent and the Rope* is paramount from the very title. If Pai fails to complete the house, Rao has taught us that the two stories carry a concrete meaning, the third storey being simply "the storey behind."

The wall which separates Pai's and Nair's houses provides another stringent symbol. Until the final stage of the book, when Nair performs his peculiar exercise of literally leaping across it, the wall links the two men at the same time that it marks their specular diversity. Leaping across the wall amounts for Nair to effecting a familiar and benign ritual, by which he communicates his teaching to his friend. So far, Pai has not yet been admitted into the garden beyond the wall, a privilege bestowed on him only at the end, when the garden, an earthly paradise and a site of pleasure (a further, transparent symbol that constitutes a universally literary mainstream) sanctions a final phase of recognition and attainment.

The Ration Shop provides a microcosm in the microcosm. It stands for daily work and routine, for bureaucracy, for dubious compromise and corruption, for arrogance, for a hybrid of beliefs and allegiances, for the imprint of colonial rule, at least "other," remote from a pervasive, omnipresent Britain: a travesty and yet an epitome of modern India. Once more, it provides the proper stage for a comedy, serious and grotesque, not only for the men who perform it, but the most suitable scene for the epiphany and for its main agent, the cat. Ultimately, we come to learn that "life is a ration shop."

Britain is spatially remote but casts its shadow on India. In the first phase of the book, Nair shows measure of conditioning British influence, and betrays it in his linguistic mixture of Goldsmith and Shakespeare. C.D. Narasimhaiah convincingly observes that Nair's language, for all its clumsiness, is not simply subaltern, but profound, because he forces the borrowing to become his own. I would argue that his abnormal English somehow outsmarts the original English and reshapes it. In his "running," as Pai cogently says, Nair undergoes a sloughing off of the British influence, and progressively acquires the conscious role of the resolute prophet of a genuine disfranchisement, of a militant advocate for India's independent coming of age.[2]

"Let's drive the British out, "Nair proclaims, but his declaration does not derive from any abstract stance; for him, Pai reminds us, "the whole world was one living organism." Definitely organic is Pai's sickness which triggers Nair's crusade. Pai's British boils, again in the disturbing reality, literally burst up in the terms of an organic signpost of British suffocating, contagious rule. They can be effectively treated only by an Indian doctor who depends on Indian natural medicine, a cure definitely upsetting and even disgusting but infallibly healing. "To fight evil you must use evil," Nair peremptorily states. Here lies the heart of the matter, of the historical matter; in point of fact, the war still raging in Europe does not really impinge on India. Churchill, Hitler, the Russians, the contradictory and almost fabulous ups and downs of the conflict, are merely indirect. The centrality of the cat regards on the one hand the fact that the animal carries several levels of truth, of understanding, of communication and, on the other hand, its belonging to different civilizations which correspond to different ways of naming it. The cat incarnates divine wisdom and love, as Rao himself suggested.

Nair propitiates the cat's entrance on the scene. The cat is the agent, instrumental in reaching the climax of the story, end effecting the epiphany.

In *Alice in Wonderland*, the Cheshire cat results from Alice's vision of a reversed, dream-like reality; here, the cat is coherently real, even when he performs a factual, but symbolic, ritual action, jumping on Boothaling Iyer's head and officiating, as it were, his astounding death in the reiterated name of Shiva, the destroyer.

The feminine principle manifests another quality embodied by the cat, a principle that governs the world, and whose apprehension by Pai, in his affair with Shanta, validates a *Junghian* reading of *The Cat and Shakespeare*. In that Pai is attracted to women, "loves woman," he verifies the *Junghian* paradigm of the male, whose "anima" benefits, in a love relationship, from the woman's "animus," to the point that the feminine "animus" possesses a divine omnipotence.

"Wonderful is man," Shanta says, "he needs to be told he is." Quite appropriately, at the end Pai reaches a state of illumination hearing the music of marriage. In the case of the death of Nair's son, the feminine principle, represented by Pai's daughter, acts in a specular way, but not in a contradictory one. Consequently, death loses any tragic connotation. It then registers the importance of dreams and of dreaming in the book ("the definition of truth is simple—you wake up and you are in front of Truth," says Pai after the sickness) (18). Jung's ideas become largely applicable. "In the dream the whole is real" (75) sound perfectly Junghian; nevertheless, this is only one of the several components of an extremely complex and coherent mosaic. The world—convincingly argues Esha Dey— intended as dream can be recognized "only through meditation and renunciation," following "the great Sankara." The cat symbol and the dream symbol concur in a non-dualistic view of the world, and the path of Ultimate Reality, as Rajesh K. Pallan underscores, leads to Pai realizing that the Truth is the Truth of the Mother Cat (*Marjara Nyaya*), this is the Cat-kitten philosophy. Dey maintains that the adoption of the cat symbol according to *Marjara Nyaya* "is a means to adsorb the ethical essence of Christianity," for "many Indian philosophers trace in this particular subgenre a recognizable impact of Christianity," adding that "the whole background of *The Cat and Shakespeare* is homogeneous only in so far as it is Western." Incidentally, the cat, "a very god" in Nair's words, Bastet, have been brought by John, a Christian.[3] But the same Nair, before proclaiming the cat's divine prerogative ("Bastet, you are sacred"), has already provided an irresistible overview of its sanctity that goes far beyond a mere Christian reference. Bastet, for one, is the sacred cat of the Egyptian tradition; the cat is sacred "in Muslim theology"; "*Felinus Persiana* would be a Persian cat." In conclusion, "a cat is the purest animal in the world" (78-80). The cat becomes the central, decisive figure, the necessary springboard in the most climactic stage of the book, welding together India, the East and the West throughout a timeless history.

Shakespeare's presence in the book must be seen as functional to the narrative more than to its conceptual structure, and it is no wonder that it did not appear in the title of the first version. Given that Shakespeare is "the great Sage," who knew everything of the ration shop, *i.e.* of life (a tribute to the universal significance of his theatre) he makes possible the shift to a dramatic development, and consequently bears on the articulation of Rao's discourse. Rao only apparently borrows from *Hamlet;* rather, he deftly cannibalizes *Hamlet* and subsumes it into his own comedy; he deconstructs it and reconstructs it to his own purpose. He produces an extremely ingenious linguistic texture that avails itself of a series of flashing inventions. Intertextuality brilliantly emerges, for instance, in Nair's dissertation on the nature of cat, even depending on Latin expressions. The intertextual manipulation on *Hamlet* almost verges on a sort of astute parody. Occasionally, the logic or pseudo logic of Pai confronting Nair's "Socratic" logic, is liable to express a mosaic of combinations, based on the rhetoric of premises and deductions, which amounts, to sheer nonsense, as in the long paragraph beginning "Like a pirate on the high seas and ending "The seas meet in Antarctica. Lord, help me build a house" (50).

Sudden references take the reader to diverse territories, geographically and historically: "If Lavoisier...divided oxygen and hydrogen after years of experimentation, our Govindan Nair born in France would only have had to stand and say: 'Water, show thyself to me!'.... And he would not have lost his head at the Revolution" (71). The same applies to the numerous digressions and/or the proverb-like utterances: "Life is a riddle that can be solved with a riddle" (35); "The specialness is that it is not special" (83). "Seeing is sleep" (104).

In the interrelation of these different levels of language, and correspondingly of different levels of meaning; in the seeming recourse to undecidability, Rao came very close to what Jean-Francois Lyotard has defined "paralogic," the unifying factor of "post-modern sublime." Moreover, in *The Cat and Shakespeare* we can easily identify an instance of the *Petit recit*, again theorized by Lyotard, alongside with Umberto Eco's notion of "open work." Rao's paralogic discourse is both narrative and cognitive, and the legitimacy of what I provisionally define a western reading or western view of the book validates its uniqueness.

REFERENCES

All quotations from *The Cat and Shakespeare* refer to the Orient Paperbacks edition. (New Delhi-Bombay, 1971, reprinted 1992).

1. Paul Sharrad, *Raja Rao and Cultural Tradition* (New Delhi: Sterling Publishers, 1987), 2.

Meenakshi Mukherjee, *The Twice-Born Fiction*. (Heinemann: New Delhi-London, 1971), *passim*.

2. C.D. Narasimhaiah, *Raja Rao* (New Delhi-London: Arnold-Heinemann, India, 1973), 130-168.

3. Esha Dey, *The Novels of Raja Rao* (New Delhi: Prestige Books, 1992), 151-4.

Rajesh K. Pallan, *Myths and Symbols in Raja Rao and R.K. Narayan* (Jalandhar: ABS Publications, 1994), 72.

20

Quest for Truth—A Study of Ontology in Raja Rao's *The Chessmaster and His Moves*: *A Saga of Love*

RAMESH KUMAR GUPTA*

Raja Rao's portrayal of quest for truth in his major novel "The Chessmaster and His Moves: A Saga of Love" reveals his deep interest in Indian Metaphysics. The publication of this book has won Rao world-wide fame as a novelist. He has been awarded the tenth Neustadt International Prize for literature. His earnest desire to know the reality discloses that he has an ontological awareness. His announcement that "I have abandoned literature for good and gone over to metaphysics"[1] indicates his quest for truth. He tries to be a metaphysician in outlook and experience when he perceives that he sees "but metaphysical propositions everywhere."[2] Once he himself said, "I would like to be completely nameless and just be that reality which is beyond all of us who hear me—that reality which evokes in me you, and I in each one listening to me this evening, that there be no one there but light. And it is of that reality the sages have spoken."[3] The novelist's quest for truth has presented a metaphysical aura to his writing. The novel "The Chessmaster and His Moves" delineates Sivaram Sastri's metaphysical quest for truth.

'The Chessmaster and His Moves' is primarily a saga of love between Sivaram Sastri, an Indian mathematician and Jayalakshmi,

*Research Scholar, Department of English, Jai Prakash University, Chapra (Bihar).

a Rajput princess, married to Raja Surrendar Singh. It depicts Siva's quest for truth as well as his interest in Buddhist, Vedantic and Tantric ontologies. The novel has a dramatic presentation. The narrator-protagonist Siva is haunted by the echoes of love and its anecdote reveals the flash-back technique. The novel portrays the frustration and the non-fulfilment of love between Siva and Jaya and it contains ontological deliberations on love, God, time, truth and death.

Sivaram Sastri meets Jayalakshmi for the first time in childhood in a temple at Chidambaram when Siva, having lost his mother at the age of eight or nine, goes there on a pilgrimage with his father. They hastily develop their infatuation for each other. But Siva leaves India for his scholarship and joins the Institute International de Mathematique Pure at Paris as a mathematician. Sivaram feels isolated in France and he sees Suzanne Chantereux and becomes infatuated by her bodily beauty. In a short time his fascination for Suzanne takes a new direction and he considers that Suzanne appears holy and "untouched" and "knows no sin" (8). The regular meetings of Siva and Suzanne bring them close. Suzanne's devotion for Indian ethos and Siva's Brahminic awareness confirms the affinity between them. Siva applauds her in that she has learnt Sanskrit and she is able to chant Hitopadesha or Mahabharata. Suzanne increases intellectual affinity with Siva as she understands him well. She, talking to others, never calls Siva by name and always says "you" or just "he." It presents the typical qualities of a Hindu wife. Suzanne occupies Indian rites: "She displays whole-hearted devotion to love. Her love for Indian culture is manifested in her will to be cremated like a good Hindu wife (625). She worships Siva like a god. She keeps her head on his feet as though she is worshipping God. Siva, touched by her courtesy, drowns deep into love with her. Suzanne is very much attached to him so he feels her presence everywhere. He thinks that "she was wife, and only wife," and no one could take her place, however brilliant or beautiful—"No, not even the princess" (624).

But the novel shows the differences of love between Sivaram and Suzanne. Suzanne's love for Siva appears conditional. As deserted by her husband and perturbed by the loss of her child, Robert, she wishes to have a child through Siva. But Siva does not want to have a child again. He merely expects unconditional love from Suzanne. He refers to Vedantic non-duality of Sri Sankara and wants her to get incorporated into him: "When there is no two, that is happiness, that is Truth" (314). Here we see that "she had a destiny with sorrow, she seemed pursued by melancholy or tragedy" for "even objects have hierarchies, and events are shapen by the rules of this chessgame" (195).

Now Suzanne departs away from Siva and it is Mireille who comes in his life with a sense of liberty. Everything is different with her. She does not know more about Siva. She knows a little of him. She is an emblem of chastity so she searches the experience of pure love. Siva feels that Mireille is not envious, nor possessive either. She is physically and intellectually related to him. To Siva, Mireille is the source of his enlightenment. Her love for Siva is natural, pure and devotional. When Siva falls ill she nurses him with a sense of dedication. Siva, during his ailment, is infatuated by her physical beauty. The warmth of her bosom and face and "the quiver in her very limbs" give him pleasure, comfort and calm. Mireille also declares that she has discovered, "her kingdom," her man she had been searching for since ages. She states that the prediction of Diotima, the wise woman of Greece, has become true in that she has traced out her real man in Siva. So, she adores Siva like a modest and traditional Indian woman. Siva also feels that Mireille's chastity is original. He observes, his company with her has consecrated him and changed him into a "precious jewel" (427). Mireille's 'fullness' reminds Siva of the fullness of Brahman as described in Brhad-aranyaka Upanisad. Siva recollects the soma referred to in the Upanisads. Siva finds different objects like islands and lighthouses, little bunches of lights, the shadow of soft mountains and the vast sea which state him that man has to "move softly, ontologically in this world" (368). Siva concedes that lovers can obtain perfection in love if they combine into each other. Hence, he wants Mireille to offer her individuality and get absorbed into him at the psychic plan. Mireille is aware of the fact that Siva's requirements are abstract. She is realist so she does not wish for perfection: "Perfection is the touch, no, the kiss of death. And I have no desire to die yet" (407). She wants to lead a life that is entirely hers.

We find that Siva is impressed and infatuated most by Jayalakshmi. Jaya has Brahmin like chastity and spiritual leaning. So, she ever sits against one of the pillars of the temple, closes her eyes for deep speculations. He thinks that she has got a devi mantra from her guru. Jaya also feels that she can "fly into the tower of the temple, such the lightness, the weightlessness" (101). Siva too assumes her as a goddess who gives him power. In spite of her dangerous disease, she remains lively and happy. Even after surgical operation in London hospital she appears as usual as to she is in meditation. Jaya thinks that she is ever under Siva's protection. Siva and Jaya use to meet continuously first at Ghazipur, Vilaspur and Calcutta and later in London hospital where Rani Saheba applauds the intellectual affinity between them. She also sees Siva as a son-in-law. Jayalakshmi too exposes her grief that she is wedded to unsuitable and unimaginative Surrendar. But Jaya is a Hindu woman so she maintains the holiness of age-long social convention of marriage under Indian ethos. There is one marriage for a Hindu wife. So, she wishes Siva to forget her. But Siva declares that her 'true self' belongs to him. Jaya concedes Siva as her real lord. Jaya requests Siva that if she dies, he would incarnate as Siva in the temple and their marriage will then be completed. Siva invites her to come to Paris where they will perform their marriage (174-75). The Benaras born bride, Jaya arrives her lover's place to celebrate her spiritual marriage with him. She asks him to alive for a hundred years and she assures that she will come back to him in her rebirth. This assurance of Jaya indicates her optimistic view. In a rapture of mirth, Siva compares her with an antique Pamir stone which the philosopher as well as conqueror Alexander has kissed in the presence of a crowded people from India, Egypt and Macedonia: "You are Jayalakshmi, like that ancient Pamir stone, fair with blue veins; and we come to drink of your presence for homonoia, for santam, sukham, nirmalam—for the celebration of mankind" (172). The lovers increase their intellectual affinity as :

> "Jayalakshmi was joy, and when I was 'I' (and when could I not be 'I'), Jayalakshmi was me (as 'I') so there was no J, but 'I', and finally was there an 'I'? No. 'I' could not says 'I' to itself, for saying implies he who says and he who hears the saying,

since I heard myself say myself, the saying was
myself, thus infinity slowly became zero. "There are
many infinities, but only one zero," as the scientists
say. I was supremely happy, I had seen sat as
anandam. Truth as Happiness" (330).

This affinity between Siva and Jaya is emblematic of non-dual
intellectual relationship as suggested in jnanmudra mode of Buddhist
Tantrism. In the jnanamudra ceremonial the lovers are intellectually
united with each other and man realizes his spiritual essence through
an interaction with woman.[4] In Jaya's company Siva obtains his
jiffies of gay and mirth which clarifies him that 'Truth is Happiness.'
The lovers spiritualize their love and they reside on the myth of
Siva and Kali. Siva and Jaya try to immortalize their love, as he
decides to go on with his speculations in the Himalayas while she,
unalienable from her lover, clearly states her earnest wish to merge
into him. The distance of the lovers is illustrated here resembling
with Siva and Parvati. Siva feels that Jaya, like Parvati, is unwedded
and like goddess she is everlasting bride to be awaiting her lord for
good. Siva and Jaya appear as "two peas on the same shot, two
saras birds walking in the Gangetic rice fields after monsoon rains"
(179). Their love is related to the love of Cakravaka birds, referred
to in Kalidas's "Kumarasambhavam" (VIII, 32). As the birds sail
forth in the mere, the short distances become so great that they use
to cry to get a sight of each other. Like cakravaka birds, Siva and
Jaya are perpetual lovers awaiting the fulfilment of love in their
future lives.

In one of the sections of the novel, "The Brahmin and the
Rabbi, a sub-title of the novel, as we see, an ontological discussion
takes place between the South Indian Brahmin Sivaram Sastri, and
a Jew, Michel Girome, who is a linguist at the National Centre of
Scientific Research, Paris. Michel has pride on his intellectual
supremacy while Sivaram Sastri has the same notion on his
knowledge. Michel asks Sivaram—What is wisdom, who is wise,
and how does one become a wise man? Sivaram responses that a
wise man is known as guru in Hindu mythonomy and it is guru who
answers all questions and thus removes all doubts and uncertainties
of mind. A man becomes wise as and when he comes into contact
with a guru. Wisdom is experience and it is jnana (knowledge). At

this Michel applauds Sivaram for his knowledge. Michel then asks about the importance of nine and ten in arithmetic. Siva responses that nine is the last whole number and so the forerunner of zero, the nirvana. Ten is horizontal, an indicative of infinity. "From nine you could go back to zero, or go forward to infinity" (229). Michel again raises a discourse pertaining to gods and predictors. He says that Buddha and Moses have the similar attitudes. Siva makes it clear that both the Buddha and Moses wished to liberate humanity from suffering. For this very purpose Moses has ten commandments while the Buddha has eight precepts. He refers that initially Nagarjuna, the great Buddhist philosopher orates upon the Upanisadic non-duality and later explicates Sunya (zero). Michel puts another question about the nature of the Chinese and other races in the world. Siva clarifies that there are only two races of men in the universe—one that looks the horizontal way and searches immortality and the other sees vertically and attempt to obtain nirvana—free from the recurring of birth and death. Michel has a scientific and utilitarian psyche. Michel can commit murder with a spirit of revenge. But Siva has ontological attitude. He has a metaphysical tendency towards killing. Michel thinks that life is more significant than death. He knows how to live a gay life. But Siva thinks that truth is more important than life: "Truth alone matters. Life is insignificant. Hence, my mathematical craze. For me, life comes from truth" (479). Siva appears as 'the wondering monk' in quest of Truth. He is aware of the fact that all is nothing, sunya (zero) while Michel can live a mundane life with Suzanne and so he can give back Robert to her.

Sivaram Sastri tries to explicate love as a 'being.' He defines that love is a natural sapience which brightens by itself. Siva wins Jaya's love when he is ready to lose her. So, love is an intuitive feeling. Love, apropos to him, is powerful than death. He says that God, nirvana and time are meaningful. He explains that God is no Hindu, no Christian and no Jew. If He were Hindu or Christian or Jew then He could be no God. God alone is "fullness, purnata" (605) and "the spark of dissolution" (684). This reference of God (Supreme Being) is taken from Brhad-aranyaka Upanisad which delineates Brahman as fullness.[5] Nirvana is known as moksa, emancipation, salvation, the release from the recurring of birth and death. So, time is referred as the period of birth and death (477). Sivaram says that death is an enigma. He explicates death from the Buddhist perspective. He concedes death as emptiness or zero. After death we get comprised in space: "But death is emptiness, even were there reincarnation. I carry my death with me, and I will leave nothing behind, even if being a Christian you left your bones, your skull behind" (209). Death is the result of our faith. Siva states that if we believe in death, we die. So Siva has no belief in death. He says that each dead gets immortality at Benaras where the Ganges comes down from Siva's "matted crown of hair" to make the dead alive whereas the Jews have confidence in death, hence, Jerusalem is great cemetery. Siva, according to Vedanta, says that death is attached into Siva, Kalbhairva. Death is won by Truth. He argues that if a man has jnana (knowledge) then he never dies.

In the novel, Siva says that Sunya is the great light whereby the whole world is illuminated for "all is light, all is fullness; thus essence, thus absolute" (210). Sunya (zero) has also been called void at different places in the novel. According to Mahayana Buddhism "all objects which we see about us, including ourselves are void, of void, from void, with void, and in void."[6] Sivaram rightly says that "Siva is oval and Siva is zero" (210). Siva observes that everything exists in Sunya (zero) so he says "Zero is the womb of humanity" (468).

The novel has ontological aspect and it presents symbolic meaning of the title. The 'Chessmaster' is an emblem of God, (Creator or Brahman) and the 'Chess' is presented for the world (Sansar or Jagat); and the move stands for divine play (Lila). Each move is played according to the law of Karma so that nobody's life will ever be the same again and thus the world continues for ever (501). Sivaram asserts that the performance in the chess is inevitable consequence of the rules of Karma. The narrator says that life is a chess (game or play). He says that all the incidents of our life are played by the laws of game of chess which has not "four orders of pawns, but a million" (195). Sivaram is aware of the fact that God Siva moves the world from his 'mountain retreat' and the world dances to his tune like a monkey (165). Sivaram feels himself a pawn, a piece of chess in the hands of the chessmaster, God: "Would I ever be true happy? Tell me, chessmaster, where are you taking me" (515). He knows that a piece of chess does not move by itself so he states: "He who is behind me, moves me to my next place" (644). Sivaram feels that Jayalakshmi's arrival in Paris was fixed by the will of God. He again thinks that Jaya's wedding to Surrendar is the outcome of Karma (deed). This viewpoint strengthens the ontology of the Bhagvad Gita that God alone is the doer. Sivaram thinks that birth and death have no existence when we merge into the Supreme Self. His assumption, "When I am no doer, where is bondage and liberation" (158) is taken from Bhagavad Gita. He says that the earthen pot is not different from the earth (549) which corroborates this assertion that individual self (Jiva) is not different from Brahman.

In this novel the man and the woman are presented as god and goddess. Siva feels that man is incomplete sans woman. He lays stress on this logic that man will never know himself unless he knows woman. Siva asserts that "to know woman truly is to surpass death" (182). The novel illustrates woman as a mystery. Siva concedes that woman conceals herself in greater depths even amidst her 'open nakedness' (466). The temples of Khajuraho expose the reality of the ultimate Truth. For example, the Great Liberation: Mahanirvana Tantra points out that every woman on earth represents the supreme goddess.[7] Siva feels when woman becomes sapient, she is the sage: "The hero become saint is woman, the feminine become wise, the Sage—the Truth" (194). Siva asserts that Jaya is the wisest among them all. Woman is illustrated as Mistress and Mother, and these aspect of womanhood is embodied in a single being. Sivaram's affinity with the French women Suzanne and Mireille, his seduction by Rati and his extra-matrimonial love with Jayalakshmi have a great impression on his individuality. Siva observes that man can realize God through 'the innermost recesses of woman.' He adores Jaya as goddess. His relationship with Jaya presents intellectual rapture. Sitting beside Jaya, Siva feels "sat as anandam, Truth as Happiness" (330). Jaya also observes that it is through the husband, the god, were a sweeper or a Satyavan, the woman reaches to the Supreme Being (172). Jaya believes that woman attains her ultimate destiny just by washing clothes, sweeping the floor or grinding corn (173). This concept is derived from the

Great Liberation: Mahanirvana Tantra which refers that a woman who pleases her husband attains heaven.[8]

Thus, the novel presents a saga of everlasting love between Siva and Jaya. They are inseparable that is Siva is Jaya and Jaya Siva. "The Chessmaster and His Moves" delineates ontological inquisitions on love, death and God. It also presents Siva's quest for Truth.

NOTES AND REFERENCES

1. Quoted in E.M. Forster, *A Tribute* ed., K. Natwar Singh, Delhi, 1964, 17.

2. *Ibid.*, 28.

3. Raja Rao, "Laureate's words of Acceptance," *World Literature Today*, 62, No. 4, Autumn, 1988, 528.

4. Herbert, V. Guenther, *The Tantric View of Life*, London, 1976, 73.

5. Brhad-aranyaka Upanisad, V.I.I.

6. Beatrice Lane Suzuki, *Mahayana Buddhism*, London, 1981, 42.

7. Arthur Avalon, *The Great Liberation: Mahanirvana Tantra*, 313.

8. *Ibid.*, 221.

21

The Growth of Mind and Art of Raja Rao: His Short Stories

Raja Rao has brought out two collections of his short stories "The Cow of the Barricades" (1947) and "The Policeman and the Rose" (1978). His stories need critical attention chiefly because they are "the products of an inevitable stage in the growth of a mind, in the evolution of major novelist who was cultivating his craft with the utmost care."[1] In his stories one finds his total vision of life. They are, like his novels, representative of the Indian life and attitudes, both at the social and metaphysical planes. Some of his stories have a contemporary social and political relevance. In some, he tries to unfold the metaphysical truth and symbolic reality through images and evokes India's cultural past with its continuing impact upon the present customs, conventions and attitudes. Raja Rao's short stories, however, are expressions not only of an inner joy but also something more too—a desire to satirize, a desire to reform the social scene all around. The mythological frame-work in some and the folklore technique in others also contribute to the obvious Indianness of the stories. As M.K. Naik says, "The form he experiments with here is the folk tale form or the popular legend with all simplicity and credulity, its myth-making power and the strong moralistic substratum on which it is in the popular wisdom, often grounded."[2]

Raja Rao has no doubt written fewer stories than his contemporaries but a significant variety of themes and techniques

*Head, Department of English, S.K.B.R. College, Amalapuram.

can still be seen in his stories. As Dr. C.V. Venugopal says, "Raja Rao stands out among the Indian Short Story writers in English in more ways than one. He shares with Isvaran a tenderness of approach, with Anand a deep awareness of contemporary situation, with Narayan an ease of narration and combining them, treats his themes with the objectivity of a Philosopher...."[3] Although the fewer number of the stories narrows the range, 'what he loses in range, he achieves in depth.' Raja Rao ever aims at presenting the inevitable impact of India's cultural past and its tradition, its people's attitude to life's ups and downs. He also shares with other writers of the forties a zeal for reform. As A.R. Wadia observes, like many Indians he adopts the art of the short story to Indian conditions and uses it as a vehicle of new ideas and means of accelerating reform."[4] Both 'A Client' which exposes the evils of child marriage and hardships of high caste Hindus in finding a settlement of a daughter's marriage and 'Javani' which presents the pathetic tale of a low caste widow, evidence Raja Rao's objective social concern devoid of radicalism, or ideological commitment.

The thematic development of a "A Client' centres in Hosakare Nanjundia's persuasive efforts to win the consent of Ramu, a plain-hearted school boy for marriage. Here Raja Rao hits at the institution of traditional marriage in general and child marriage in particular. "The prolonged battle between the unwilling simple youth and the crooked marriage broker, symbolising this problem of our society in a certain historical context, has been presented... like the intelligent devices of a patient hunter luring his prey into his trap."[5]

'Javani' presents a woeful tale of a low-caste widow, neglected and ill-treated by her kith and kin, serves in a middle class Brahmin family more for the affection she gets from her mistress than for the bread she earns there. She is 'Good like a Cow' to her mistress and here mistress is a 'veritable goddess' to Javani. They are bound by such a bond of love as of no caste and creed for its reciprocal 'give and take.' Ramappa, the mouthpiece of Raja Rao, could not bear to see the indignities heaped upon Javani. His vehement remarks against caste and irreligion scattered all over the story 'Javani' stand testimony to Raja Rao's aim of exposing the evils of the caste system.

In "Akkayya" he presents the story of a high caste widow in

more artistic and satisfying form. He argues for a thorough overhauling of the Indian attitude to the widow and exposes the hollowness of some of the superstitious customs down the ages. Akkayya's happiness is a 'helpless resignation to the inevitable.' Though both Akkayya and Javani belong to different castes, they share the inexorable futility of tradition-bound Indian widowhood in the same measure. Yet, as Venugopal points out "Javani is loving and is being loved, whereas Akkayya, though loving, is only tolerated."[6]

In 'The True Story of Kanakapala, Protector of Gold,' we find a blending of the homely narration and utter simplicity of ancient myths and a vivid picturization of the inevitable hatred among kinsfolk resulting from greed of wealth. It is a story of a serpent when it is a friend. Raja Rao employs folklore style and thus begins the story 'May those who read this, be beloved of Naga, King of serpents, destroyer of ills.' The lend credibility to his story and to make it appear as authentic and life-like as possible, Raja Rao gives a vivid description of the sentiments and stories with snake-motif. His graphic description of the scene and setting, results in 'the willing suspension of disbelief' and 'acceptance of fiction as truth.'

"The Little Grain Shop" is a realistic presentation of contemporary life. It depicts the rise and fall of an ambitious bania couple Motilal and Beti Bai. They amassed wealth through utter miserliness and cheating and rose to the status of moneylenders. The pathetic end of Motilal's life is a powerful reminder of the proverb "Greed brings grief." A story of realism, domestic tragedy and pathos 'Nimka' shows how Raja Rao's emotional cosmpolitanism is shaped into art. This story with its unique poetic style based on a harmonious blend of emerging sentiments of the movement and the dazzling ideas, foreshadows the typical narrative style of 'The Serpent and the Rope' and 'The Cat and Shakespeare.'

In the stories 'Narasinga,' 'The Cow of the Barricades' and 'In Kandesh,' he pioneers and pictures the spirit of the times—the theme of national resurgence and Gandhian Philosophy felt against the background of the saner and more beautiful aspects of our past tradition—simplicity and faith. 'Narasinga' is undoubtedly the best example of Raja Rao's ability to capture a whole society with sustained brilliance. 'His (Gandhiji's) fight against poverty, untouchability, drinking and illiteracy are all taken up with the thread of the narrative most naturally.'

The story 'The Cow of the Barricades,' studies a symbolic struggle against the Redman. In the Cow, 'Gauri,' he presents a powerful symbol of Mother India and also an actual cow of mysterious nature at the same time. Gauri inspires the freedom fighters as well as the soldiers with a feeling of patriotism. It dies of a police Officer's bullet and thus saves the lives of many in the village. Thus, it becomes an embodiment of the spirit of self-sacrifice, compassion and non-violence and remains in our memory for ever. Thus, 'The Cow of the Barricades,' a study of yet another facet of the Nationalist Movement, presents a 'unique combination of symbol and reality.'

In 'In Kandesh 'Raja Rao presents a witty and energetic satire on the defunct feudal system and forced loyalty expected by the then rulers. He attacks the blind adherence to false values. Commenting on the deeper implications of the story, Prof. L.S.R. Krishna Sastry adds, "The Story depicts the transition from the era of unquestioning loyalty to the British to the beginning of organized opposition to the alien rule. The pattern of broken and unconnected lines adds a visual dimension to the description of the confusion of the storm."[8] The picturesque concluding passage describing the climax has a double suggestiveness the havoc of the British rule and also the beginning of the end of loyalty to it are suggested in terms of nature's fury. M.K. Naik rightly observes "... at least one story. 'In Khandesh...' already shows the descriptive power which is a mark of Raja Rao's later and maturer works."[9]

'Companions' and 'The Police Man and the Rose' reveal Raja Rao's powers of employing symbolic structures for the most complex philosophical themes. "Companions" is a complex story full of mystery. Here he makes use of the folklore style and presents a triumph of metaphysical symbolism of redemption from the cycle of 'Karma' and the liberation from the bondage of life and death. Moti Khan and his Companion Snake each is acting as a vehicle of liberation for the other, one is redeemed in helping the other in his redemption. Here Raja Rao uses many symbols to heighten the mystical experiences in the story. "The symbolism, developed out of the legendary actuality, becomes the basis of this philosophical story of profound spiritual significance."[10]

'The Policeman and the Rose,' a story of pure metaphysical symbolism is a fantastic elaboration of the advaitic idea of Jiva and the Soul—one cased in the body and the other liberated form of a simple reality of the life principle. The 'Police Man' who arrests every man at birth is the *ahankara* (ego-sense) of the limited individual self and the 'Red Rose' is the *Rajoguna*—the passion of the mind. Man can come out of the clutches of the Police man only when he surrenders the 'Red Rose' or *Rajoguna* to the lotus of Truth (at the feet of his guru). The reverberating symbolism in some of his stories make them 'memorable metaphysical documents in fictional form without a parallel in the field of the Indian English Short Story.' "The theme and the style both evidence how philosophy can successfully be turned into art and in this respect this story is a unique example of Raja Rao's maturity as a writer."[11]

In 'India: A Fable,' the elements of fantasy and realism are combined to evoke the picture of a fabulous country which possesses a fantastic charm and magical effect. The theme of 'India: A Fable' is developed through a sweet conversation between the narrator and the French Child—Pirrot, who is fascinated and excited to learn about India—about the elephants, goddesses, and forests and rivers.

'On the Ganga Ghat' is the third collection of Raja Rao's short stories. It marks Raja Rao's return to this genre after a gap of over a decade during which time he has sharpened his old tools and added many new to his treasure. As such, his prose in this collection is exquisite, chiselled, sparse yet evocative. If the eleven short stories of this collection are read at one go, they weave themselves into a novel. These compelling stories with their photographic realism, comic and irreverent element, metaphysical and philosophical content make a delightful reading. They are paradigmatic and lovely as Mother Ganges is. In these stories Raja Rao explores the play of life as it unfolds in Benaras, the holy city to die in.

Benaras has been a cherished ultimate and final destination of millions of Indians since time immemorial. Many people from different parts of India come to Benaras as 'Ganga purifies all.'

"She gives song to songesters, limbs to brave, paddle push to the boat and child to the wife." Death and cremation on the ghats makes one immortal. Here come 'Rajas and princes from Bengal, Beggars, Jatiawari merchants, courtesans, crooks, simpletons and charlatans—seeking meaning in life or redumption in death. We find a rich variety of creatures of Beneras in Rao's 'On the Ganga Ghat'—the gentle brahmachari Madhoba and his Mohini; Bhim, the sage parrot; the Brahimini cow Jhaveri Bai; concubines like Nanna and many more and especially hard swearing, mantra chanting sadhus laughing at the foibles of others.

In these stories the Indian philosophy, ethics and metaphysics converge into a unified whole and flow along the Ganga Ghats as the mother Ganga does. These eleven short stories form the myth and reality associated with the Ganges. In these stories underneath the apparent change and human actions and reactions the "soul" of the place is witnessed.

Like 'Malgudi' of Narayan, the Ganges is the real hero of the eleven stories. The Ganges and the people swarming on the ghats for various reasons is the real theme of these stories and each story is a Jerk of the Kaledioscope when a new engaging pattern emerges to hold our attention.

Despite the variety of themes and techniques, Raja Rao's short stories presents a unity of vision of the rich and the age old yet vital and living Indian tradition. The social pre-occupations and the emotional appeals in most of his stories invariably lead to an other-worldly sense of purpose of life and as Prof. C.D. Narasimhaiah says, "The religious impulse and the metaphysical imagination are unmistakable in them."[12] Though Raja Rao, like Anand and Narayan, adopts the omniscient-author method of narration, he never describes his characters. There is a happy fusion of description and dialogue and we stare at 'Javani' or 'Narasinga' as their inner being too is unfolded gradually as the story proceeds. In the end we have a fascinating experience of the great revelation.

Raja Rao has admitted, on many an occasion, the influence of the Sanskrit classics on his writings. There are many echoes of classic lore in his works. His Indianness is mainly reflected in his experiments with the folk tale form of narration. The 'openings' and 'endings' of his stories reveal this fact. He begins his stories with a catching phrase or a clause in place of old phrase 'once upon a time' etc. In the same way, the ending of his stories are in conformity with folk tale pattern. Some-times he ends his stories with some personal comments which seem to be quite unnecessary and sound unnatural. They spoil the mood of the reader and bring him back to the mundane realities of life—a comment such as "And way, here I have written the story of Akkayya, may be her only funeral ceremony." Sometimes he ends his stories in the typical traditional manner which emphasizes the cultural impact on the average Indian's life. Such stories have about them a finality of Upanishadic or epical sayings.

Raja Rao becomes a true 'Upasaka' in having a strong desire to communicate and in achieving a mastery over the language to communicate effectively and forcefully. "Unless the author becomes an 'Upasaka' and enjoys himself in himself (which is Rasa) the enternality of the sound (Sabda) will not manifest itself and so you cannot communicate either and the word is nothing but a cacophony."[13]

His skilful use of language suits his themes and techniques. He achieves a great success in his use of English idiom by translating the purely rural and rustic Kannada speech. Like Anand, he translates oaths, adages and common sayings from his mother tongue (Kannada) and their naturalness renders them valuable contributions to the English language. Raja Rao, like Chinua Achebe, the Nigerian writer, has demonstrated the compatibility of English with the spirit of the native languages and makes it flexible enough to accommodate his varied experiences. It is his experimentation with English language and the form of the Western short story that marks his art and makes him an outstanding short story writer. As he experiments with the form, one should not really apply the criteria of the Western short story to his stories. "The concerns of the Western short story, motivation or character are not Raja Rao's concerns."[14] He personifies human virutes through fable, allegory or symbolism.

His stories, studied in the chronological order of their composition "Reveal the growth of the artist, marked in his firmer grasp of the medium and the better handling of the symbolic language."[15]

REFERENCES

1. C.D. Narasimhaiah, *Rajo Rao* 'The Short Stories, An After Word,' New Delhi: Arnold Heinemann, 127.

2. M.K. Naik, *Raja Rao*, New York, 1972, 50.

3. C.V. Venugopal, *The Indian Short Story in English* (A Survey), Bareilly: Prakash Book Depot. 74.

4. A.R. Wadia, *The Future of English in India*, Bombay, 1954, 118.

5. Narasingh Srivastava, *The Mind and Art of Raja Rao*, Bareilly: Prakash Book Depot, 1980, 122.

6. Venugopal, 64.

7. *Ibid.*, 66.

8. L.S.R. Krishna Sastry, 'Raja Rao,' *Triveni*, Jan. 1968.

9. M.K. Naik, Narrative Strategy in Raja Rao's 'Cow of the Baricades and Other Stories' (U.P.P.).

10. Srivastava, 135.

11. *Ibid.*, 136.

12. Narasimhaiah 2.

13. Raja Rao, 'The Writer and the World,' *The Literary Criticism*, Vol. VIII, No. 1, Winter, 1965.

14. Muralidas Melwani, 'Themes in Indio-Anglian Literature,' 54.

15. Srivastava, 140.

22

Sri Rama Rides again: Hindu and Raj views of Holy Benares

ALESSANDRO MONTI*

The eleven brief stories featuring the volume *On the Ganga Ghat* published by Raja Rao in 1989[1] deal with the staple theme of timeless and holy Benares, seen through the eyes of an old expatriate professor, back to India for a short time and introducing the city to a young American friend.

Apparently Raja Rao takes up again the time-honoured question of the meeting of the West with the East, to the exclusion of any didactic overtone though: any possible hint of a *guru-shishya* (pupil) relationship between the two introductory *personae* is just nipped in the bud, and the tales are narrated by a fleshless voice, possibly the communal "I" of the people living in Benares.

Similarly the slightly disturbing charm of the travelogue (including the up-to-date version of the controversial return or visit to the forgotten *desa*, *i.e.* the Indian homeland) is dropped in favour of a straight narrative steeped in myth and told as the folk reshaping of a holy book, a Benares Purana.

However the sacred Hindu character of the city has been a must for a long time, since Bishop Heber and his *Journey through India* (1824-25) up to the writers of the Raj, Rudyard Kipling and Flora Annie Steel among them. To the British mind Benares was a nightmare of disorder and estrangement, the abode of the thousand creeds (and stenches), in Kipling's his own words. The saddest city

*University of Turin, 10124 Turin, Italy.

on God's earth, according to Mrs. Steel, with its sunless alleys and
its endless shrines and worn stone.[2] The benighted character of the
city could only be redeemed from its unsavoury aspects through the
agency of the picturesque, actually a simplified Orientalist lore
lending stereotyped meaning and second-hand significance to the
individual response of European sensibility in front of Eastern
difference.

In his modern Benares tales Raja Rao shifts the traditional
Orientalist viewpoint of the East as a land without progress since
its ancient history to the search for a past that lives on in the
present. To attain his aim he devises a technique of bifocal vision
after the *dhwani* theory of "echoing what is ideal by what it is."[3]
Thus Raja Rao blurs away any a priori boundary between the things
as they are and the things as they ought to be, or as they are not;
in the first tale he writes that "in Benares no act has any
consequence," with the result that "everything benefits from all
acts."[4] This statement may reflect the debate on the "Self-evidence
of the Self" in the Indian theologies of identity or non-difference;
Prakasananda writes that "it has been shown to imply that actions
forfeit, and non-actions appropriate, fruition."[5]

In simpler terms one may assume that Benares is viewed as an
inter-entity connecting the above and the below, as a mirror (more
than a bridge) between heaven and earth. To quote again tale 1,
"The world is indeed the city seen in a mirror, and, upside down."[6]
A further issue at hand is suggested when one reads that in Vedic
tradition *tapas* (or ascetic heat) possess the "connecting capacity."
To make the point clear I will focus my attention on a single tale,
to indicate how Raja Rao operates on the Indian heritage. The
uneventful and almost plotless tale 3 features Chhota Munna Lal, a
young vendor of firewood for the burning ghat of Benares. He is
a bachelor and a wrestler within the pale of the divine monkey
Hanuman, a god presiding not only over physical strength but also
implying the essential qualities to salvation: wisdom, service and
perfection. Munna Lal meets a Mohini in his room; she is perhaps
an *apsrara's* figure (a dancer or a courtesan of heaven) and comes
through the mirror to sing and to dance, invisible to everybody
except him. The Mohini "is not of the world of the dead" but
belongs to an unspecified number of heavenly creatures (halfway

between the above and the below) who "cannot approach a god directly" but "have to go through a man...who has never touched a woman."[7] The seminal point worth discussing is that Munna Lal is given as a *brahmachari* (to follow Raja Rao's spelling of the word); the glossary at the end of the book translates the term as "celibate." However, in ancient India a *brahmacharin* was a Vedic student, whose ascetic career coincided with the *brahmacharya asrama*, namely the first stage in life, which could last up to twelve years. It required bachelorhood, the other three stages being those of householder, forest hermit and *sannyasin*, or one who renounces the world (nowadays, *bramachari* is the current term to indicate a wrestler like Munna Lal). Among the many *vratas*, or vows of austerity, a *brahmacharin* was devoted to chastity, in order to generate *tapas,* a fertilizing and life-maintaining heat (The word derives from a Sanskrit root, *tap,* which means to give out heat, to make or to be hot).

Vedic *tapas* was seen as a power giving unity to every aspect of reality, as a force operating homologies. According to Vedic commentators, "Through the connecting capacity of *tapas,* above and below, then and now, macrocosm and microcosm are vowed into a sacred whole."[8] *Tapas* and the *brahmacharin* are closely associated with fire; Vedic texts draw a homology between the two actions of "placing fuel upon the fire" and of "enkindling the mind." "To tend the fire well" is a common Vedic expression to indicate either meditation or the act of teaching (Agni, the god of fire, is the *guru* of the *brahmacharin*).

The characterization of Munna Lal fits essentially this mould; the vendor is a confirmed bachelor dealing with fuel and the tending of fire. He shares his capacity with the Doms, who inherited the art of arranging firewood for a pyre from Shiva himself, Lord of the crematorium, and practice it "as a heaven-ordained right."[9] However humble his role may seem, one has to understand that Munna Lal is under the protection of the god of fire for pushing down to the ghat the cart with the firewood. In fact a Vedic hymn to Agni sings, "He who carries fuel for you...do you be his self-strong protector, O Agni!."

The Vedic paradigm might also be applied to the uncanny and baffling relationship of Munna Lal with the Mohini, perhaps an expurgated and modified reminiscence of the *Mahavarata* rite, in which a *brahmacharin* and a prostitute (*pumscali*) exchanged sexual verbal abuse as a part of a ritual meant to promote fertility through rain. In ancient times the chastity of the *brahmacharin* was seen as a "reservoir of fecundating power," which could be discharged to effect rainfall and fertility.[10] The rainy weather of the winter monsoon prevails in the tale, probably as a counterpoint to the association which equates through sympathy liquid fertility with the generating power of heat or fire.

A final inference may be suggested to understand the apparition of the Mohini. The devotee of Agni is viewed as a "head-heated" (*tapurmurdhan*) seer, endowed with a strong capacity of vision. Carrying wood and sweating for Agni is in the Vedic language a way to acquire wisdom and the direct knowledge of the supernatural in its visible form: a similar underlying rationale may explain the figure of the Mohini. However she is related on her account to the mythological lore of India: in the *Vishnu Purana* the God adopts the female form of the courtesan Mohini (from a Sanskrit root *mo*, roughly meaning passion, love) to trick the demons of the *amrita* and give it to the gods. Consequently she is to some extent a dispenser of the nectar or drink that confers immortality.[11]

The Mohini herself introduces a further and most important mythological reference, when she turns the sight of Munna Lal the wrestler going to the temple into the vision of Sri Rama travelling back to Ayodhya (the capital of his kingdom) with a gorgeous train of elephants and horses. This piece of traditional Indian pageantry calls forth the image of a *sawari*, a cavalcade of mounted riders attending a person of high rank.[12]

The sober evocation of a mythic *sawari* reshapes in terms of inner vision (nurtured by purified love) a colourful display, often enlisted by the early British representation of India as a particularly apt instance of the "native" picturesque. In Miss Eden's *Letters from India* (1837-40) an excursion leaving Benares for the nearby country-house of the local raja requires fifteen elephants and crowds of attendants. The magnificent but somewhat fanciful grandeur of the scene elicits from the writer a phony atmosphere of stage Orientalism: "We went on to elephants through the great gateway, in a Timour the Tartar fashion, into the court. Such torches and spearmen and drums and crowds, like a melodrama...," reminiscent *via* parodic memory of the operatic Western representations of the East, "It was the sort of scene where Ellen Tree would have snatched up a doll from under Farley's sword, and said, 'My boy, boy, my rescued Agib!,' or words to that effect, while the curtain fell slowly."[13]

Rudyard Kipling's Benares replaces mock-heroic Orientalism with middle-class philistinism, already redolent of the pioneer spirit of modern tourism. In "The Bride's Progress" (a sketch first published in 1888 and featuring the Indian honeymoon of a young English couple) the exotic view of the great umbrellas covering the *ghats* of Benares reminds the bride of some capering mushrooms seen at a Brighton pantomime.[14]

Each culture has its own landmarks, however funny they may seem to us. Perhaps a cardboard picturesque or a dancing mushroom are less enticing than the stately vision of Sri Rama riding again in holy Benares. But a Mohini is better company than any Lalla Rookh.[15]

NOTES

1. Raja Rao, *On the Ganga Ghat* (New Delhi & Bombay: Vision Books, 1989).
2. Flora Annie Steel, "The Squaring of the Gods" in *In the Guardianship of God* (London: William Heinemann, 1903).
3. *Dhwani* or *dhvani* means reverberation, *i.e.* the suggestion or incantation of words and phrases. It implies more than the bare meaning of a word, it is a sort of connotation. The notion of *dhwani* is seminal to understand the fictional rendering of reality in contemporary Indian novel in English.
4. Raja Rao, *On the Ganga Ghat*, *cit.*, 9-10.
5. Jose Pereira, *Hindu Theology, Themes, Texts & Structures* (Delhi: Motilal Banarsidass Publishers, 1976), 209-13.
6. Raja Rao, On the Ganga Ghat, cit., 12.
7. *Ibid.*, 37.
8. Walter O. Kaelber, *Tapta Marga. Asceticlsm and Initiation in Vedic India* (Delhi: Sri Satguru Publications, 1989), 1-4.
9. Raja Rao, *On the Ganga Ghat*, cit., 32.
10. Walter O. Kaelber, *Tapta Marga*, cit., 17-20.
11. According to Ivor Lewis *Mohini* is from the Sanskrit *much*, to confuse, to bewilder. He calls the *Mohini* the supreme seductress of Hindu mythology and remembers a *Mohini Attam*, a graceful solo dance for women, originally

from Kerala. See Ivor Lewis, *Sahibs, Nabobs and Boxwallahs—A Dictionary of the Words of Anglo-India* (Bombay & Delhi: Oxford University Press, 1991), 166.

12. See Ivor Lewis, *Sahibs, Nabos and Boxwallahs*, cit., 223.

13. Emily Eden, *Up the Country, Letters from India*, London, Virago Press, 1984, 27-28.

14. Rudyard Kipling, "The Bride's Progress," 8 February 1888, "Pioneer Mail," collected in *From Sea to Sea*, 1899.

15. Thomas Moore, *Lalla Rookh*, 1817. The Oriental poem by Moore is an early instance of the British interest in the Eastern picturesque.

SELECT BIBLIOGRAPHY

PRIMARY SOURCES

I. Novels

Kanthapura. London: George Allen & Unwin, 1938, New York: New Directions, 1963: Bombay: Oxford University Press, 1947, Rpt. Delhi: Oxford, 1974. Introduction by C.D. Narasimhaiah. Rpt. Delhi: Oriental Paperback, n.d.

The Serpent and the Rope. London: John Murray, 1960. New York: Pantheon Books, 1968. Delhi: Oriental Paperbacks, 1963, 1968. Rpt. Delhi: Hind Pocket Books, 1968.

The Cat and Shakespeare: A Tale of Modern India. New York: The Macmillan Company, 1965. Delhi: Hind Pocket Books, 1971.

Comrade Kirillov. Delhi: Oriental Paperbacks, 1976.

The Chess Master and His Moves. Delhi: Vision Books, 1988.

II. Short Stories

The Cow of the Barricades and Other Stories. London: Oxford University Press, 1947. Bombay: Oxford University Press, 1978.

The Policeman and the Rose. Delhi: Oxford, 1978.

On the Ganga Ghat (Short Stories). New Delhi: Vision Books, 1989.

III. Non-Fiction

A. *Books*

The Meaning of India: The Collection of Essays. New Delhi: Vision Books, 1996

The Best of Raja Rao Ed. Makarand Paranjape. New Delhi: Katha Publications, 1998.

B. *Articles*

"Pandit Taranath." *Asia* Jan. 1935: 10-15.

"The Premier of Shakuntala." *Asia* June 1943: 365-368.

"Jupiter and Mars." *Pacific Spectator* 8 (1954): 369-379.

"Aurobindo Ghosh: An Anniversary Meeting Address." *Arts and Letters: Journal of the Royal India and Pakistan Society* 31.2 (1957). 4-6.

"Out of Step with Shiva." *Book Week* 29 Aug. 1965: 4.

"The Gandhian Way: Replies to questionnaire on Gandhi." *Illustrated Weekly of India* 14 Feb. 1965: 39.

"Irish Interlude." *Saturday Review* 49.26 (1966): 32, 37-38. Also in *Illustrated Weekly of India* 9 Apr. 1967: 21.

"The Climate of Indian Literature Today." *Literary Criterion* 10.3 (1972): 1-7.

"Aru and Toru." Preface to Toru Dutt's *Ancient Ballads and Legends of Hindustan*. Calcutta: Writers Workshop, 1972.

"The Caste of English." *Awakened Conscience: Studies of Commonwealth Literature*. Eds. Narasimhaiah *et al*. New Delhi: Sterling Publishers, 1978. 420-422.

"Autobiography: Entering the Literary World." *Journal of Commonwealth Literature* 13.3 (1979): 28.

"The Word." *Colonial Consciousness in Commonwealth Literature*. Eds. G.S.Amur and S.K. Desai. Bombay: Somaiya Publications, 1984.

"The Ultimate Word." *Temenos* (London) 9 (1988).

"The Cave and the Conch: Notes on the Indian Conception of the Word." *The Eye of the Beholder: Indian Writing in English* Ed. Maggie Butcher. London: Commonwealth Institute, 1983: 45.

Interviews

Balu, Shakuntala. "Meeting Raja Rao." Interview. *Economic Times* 25 Jan. 1987: 3.

Bhattacharji; Shobana. Interview with Raja Rao (Letter). *Citizen and Weekly Review* (India) 11 Oct. 1969: 37.

Brierre, Annie. Interview with Raja Rao. *Illustrated Weekly of India* 10 Mar. 1963: 26.

Eskay. "Raja Rao: Man and the Mask." Interview. *Patriot* (Mag.) 25 Apr. 1982: IV.

"The Gandhian Way." Replies to a Questionnaire on Gandhi. *Illustrated Weekly of India* 14 Feb. 1935: 39.

Kaushik, Asha. "Meeting Raja Rao." *Literary Criterion* 18.3 (1983): 33-38.

Kohli, Suresh. "Raja Rao: Ambivalence and Individuality: Interview." *Indian and Foreign Review* 15 June 1969: 11.

——. Interview with Raja Rao. *Times Weekly* 13 Sep. 1970: 4.

——. "Views of an Indian Novelist." Interview. *Times Weekly* 18 Apr. 1972.

Maeindroo, Vaiju. "Raja Rao: A.Y.T. Interview." *Youth Times* 12-27. May, 1978: 13.

Niranjan, Shiva. Interview with Raja Rao. *Indian Writing in English.* Ed. Krishna Nanda Sinha. New Delhi: Heritage Publishers, 1979. 19-28.

O'Brien, A.P. "Meeting Raja Rao." *Praja* (Benares) 11.2 1966.

Pais, Arthur and Radhika Radhakrishnan. "Award Winning Raja Rao Likened to Joyce, Proust." *India Abroad* 27 May 1988: 134-135.

Paniker, Ayyappa. "A Conversation with Raja Rao on *The Cat and Shakespeare.*" *Chandrabhaga* 2 (1979): 14.

Paranjape, Makarand. "Art of the Matter: Raja Rao's *The Meaning of India: The Collection of Essays.*" An Interview. *Indian Review of Books* 16 Nov.-15 Dec. 1976: 6-7.

Parthasarathy, R. "The Future World Is Being Made in America: An Interview with Raja Rao." *Span* (New Delhi) Sep. 1977: 29-30.

"Raja Rao: A Brief Encounter." *Indian Express* 28 April 1982: 3.

Raman, A.S. "Chiaroscuro: A Meeting with Raja Rao Recalled." *Illustrated Weekly of India* 25 Sep. 1966: 15. 25 Oct. 1966: 13.

Ranchan, Som P. "A Meeting with Raja Rao." *Thought* (Delhi) 13 July 1968: 14-16. 20 July 1968: 14-16. 27 July 1968: 14-16. 3 Aug. 1968: 14-16.

Rangra, Ranvir. "I Write to Myself: An Interview." *Indian Literature* July-Aug. 1988: 113-123.

——. "Beyond the Body and Mind: An Interview with Raja Rao." *Interview with Indian Writers*. Delhi: B.R. Publishing Corporation, 1992.

Reddy, P. Bayapa. "A Conversation with Raja Rao." *Studies in Indian Writing in English*. New Delhi: Prestige Books, 1990. 88-92.

Replies to the Questionnaire." *Kakatiya Journal of English Studies* 3.1 (1978): 69-70.

S.V.V. "Raja Rao: Face to Face." *Illustrated Weekly of India* 5 Jan. 1964: 44-45.

Shankardass, Rama. "Face to Face." *Weekend Review* 15 June 1968: 16-17.

Subrahmanian, K. "Meeting Raja Rao." *Kakatiya Journal of English Studies* 3.1 (1978): 70A.

Wohl, Elizabeth. "Raja Rao on America." *Span* (New Delhi) Jan.

SECONDARY SOURCES: CRITICAL WORKS

I. Bibliographies

Bhattacharya, P.C. "Select Bibliography." *Indo-Anglian Literature and the works of Raja Rao*. Delhi: Atma & Sons, 1983. 379-395.

Celly, Anee. "A Selected Bibliography." *Women in Raja Rao's Novel: A Feminist Reading of The Serpent and the Rope*. Jaipur: Printwell, 1995. 117-124.

Dey, Esha. "Bibliography." *The Novels of Raja Rao*. New Delhi: Prestige Books, 1991. 256-264.

Jamkhandi, Sudhakar Ratnakar. "Raja Rao: A Selected Checklist of Primary and Secondary Material." *Journal of Commonwealth Literature* 15.1 (1981): 132-139

Naik, M.K. "Bibliography." *Raja Rao*. Madras: Blackie & Sons, 1982. 157-160.

Nanda, Nivedita. "Bibliographies" *Raja Rao and Religious Traditions*. New Delhi: Anmol 1992. 115-119.

Narayan, Shyamala A. "Selected Bibliography." *Raja Rao: Man and His Works.* New Delhi: Sterling Publishers, 1988. 134-139.

Niranjan, Shiva. "Select Bibliography." *Raja Rao: Novelist as Sadhaka.* Ghaziabad (Delhi): Vimal Prakashan, 1985. 139-148.

Parthasarathy, R., comp. "Selected Bibliography (1931-1988)." *World Literature Today* (1988): 556-560.

Rao, K. R. "Select Bibliography." *The Fiction of Raja Rao.* Aurangabad: Parimal Prakashan, 1980. 156-160.

Sharma, K.K. "Select Bibliography." Sharma, *Perspectives on Raja Rao.* Ghaziabad: Vimal Prakashan, 1980. 231-234.

Sharrad, Paul. "Bibliography." *Raja Rao and Cultural Tradition.* New Delhi: Sterling Publishers, 1989. 171-189.

Singh, Paraminder. "Bibliography." *Semiotic Analysis of Raja Rao's The Serpent and The Rope.* Delhi: Bahri Publications, 1991.

Srivastava, Narasingh. "A Select Bibliography." *The Mind and Art of Raja Rao.* Bareilly: Prakash Book Depot, 1980. 154-157.

Srivastava, Ramesh K., comp. "Selected Bibliographies: Raja Rao." Srivastava, R.K., *Six Indian Novelists in English.* Amritsar: Guru Nanak Dev University, 1987: 329-333.

II. Special Issues

World Literature Today 62.4 (1988). A special issue on Raja Rao as an award winner of the tenth Neustadt International Prize for literature, 1988.

III. Books

Abraham, T.J. *A Critical Study of Novels of Arun Joshi, Raja Rao and Sudhin Ghose,* New Delhi: Atlantic Publishers. 1998.

Agnihotri, G.N. *Indian Life and Problems in the Novels of Mulk Raj Anand and Raja Rao and R.K. Narayan.* Meerut: Shalabh Book House 1984, 1993.

Belliappa, K.C. *The Image of India in English Fiction: Studies in Kipling, Myers and Raja Rao.* Delhi: B.R. Publishing Corporation, 1991.

Bhattacharya, P.C. *Indo-Anglian Literature and the Works of Raja Rao.* Delhi: Atma Ram & Sons, 1983.

Celly, Anee. *Women in Raja Rao's Novel: A Feminist Reading of the Serpent and the Rope.* Jaipur: Printwell, 1995.

Dayal, P. *Raja Rao: A Study of His Novels.* New Delhi: Atlantic Publishers, 1991.

Dey, Esha. *The Novels of Raja Rao.* New Delhi: Prestige Books, 1991.

Hardgrave, Robert L., ed. *The Art of Raja Rao.* New Delhi: Katha Publications in associations with University of Texas, Austin, 1998.

Naik, M.K. *Raja Rao.* Twayne's English Authors Series. New York: Twayne Publishers, 1972. Rpt. Indian edition with a chapter on *Comrade Kirillov.* Madras: Blackie and Sons, 1982.

Nanda, Nivedita. *Raja Rao and the Religious Traditions: Study of The Serpent and the Rope.* New Delhi: Anmol, 1992.

Narasimhaiah, C.D. *Raja Rao.* Indian Writer's Series. New Delhi: Arnold Heinemann, 1973.

Narayan, Shyamala A. *Raja Rao: Man and His Works.* New Delhi: Sterling Publishers, 1988.

Niranjan, Shiva. *Raja Rao: Novliest as Sadhaka.* Ghaziabad: Vimal Prakashan, 1987.

Niven, Alastair. *Truth Within Fiction: Raja Rao's The Serpent and the Rope.* Calcutta: Writers Workshop, 1979.

Pallan, Rajesh K. *Myth and Symbols in Raja Rao and R.K. Narayan.* Jalandhar: ABS Publications, 1994.

Paranjpe, Makarand, ed. *The Best of Raja Rao.* Delhi: Kath Association, 1998.

Rao, K.R. *The Fiction of Raja Rao.* Aurangabad: Parimal Prakashan, 1980.

Rao, Sudhakar. *Socio-Cultural aspects of Life in The Selected Novels of Raja Rao* New Delhi: Atlantic Publishers. 1999.

Shankaran, Chitra. *The Mythic Connection: The Use of Hindu Mythology in Some Novels of Raja Rao and R.K. Narayan.* New Delhi: Allied Publishers, 1993.

Sharma, Jai Prakash. *Raja Rao: A Visionary of Indo-Anglian Fiction.* Meerut: Shalabh Book House, 1980.

Sharma, K.K., ed. *Perspectives on Raja Rao.* Ghaziabad: Vimal Prakashan, 1980.

Sharrad, Paul. *Raja Rao and Cultural Tradition.* New Delhi: Sterling Publishers, 1987.

Singh, Paraminder. *Semiotic Analysis of Raja Rao's The Serpent and the Rope.* New Delhi: Bahri Publications, 1991.

Singh, R.S. *Raja Rao's Kanthapura: A Critical Study.* Delhi: Doaba House, 1973.

Srivastava, Narasingh. *The Mind and Art of Raja Rao.* Bareilly: Prakash Book Depot. 1980.

VI. Research Articles

Agnihotri, G.L. "Raja Rao—The Distinguished Philosopher Novelist." Agnihotri 61-83.

Aithal, S. Krishnamoorthy and Rashmi Aithal. "Inter-racial and Inter-cultural Relationship in Raja Rao's *The Serpent and the Rope*." *International Fiction Review* 7.2(1980): 94-98.

——. "East-West Encounter in Four Indo-English Novels." *ACLALS Bulletin* 6.1 (1982): 1-7.

Alam, Qaiser Zoha. *"Kanthapura's* Style: A Point of View." *Language Forum* 5.2 (1979): 27-37. Rpt. in Alam, *Language and Literature* 1-13.

Ali, Ahmed. "Illusion and Reality: The Art and Philosophy of Raja Rao." *Journal of Commonwealth Literature* 5 (1968): 16-28.

Alphonso-Karkala, J.B. "Myth, Matrix and Meaning in Literature and Raja Rao's Novel, *Kanthapura*." Sharma, K.K., *Perspectives on Raja Rao* 67-83.

Amur, G.S. "Raja Rao: The Kannada Phase." *Journal of Karnatak University* (Humanities) 10 (1966): 40-52. Also in Amur, *Critical Spectrum* 7-16.

——. "Marriage as Symbolic Strategy of Cultural Encounter in *Seeta, Esmond in India* and *The Serpent and the Rope*." *Journal of Literature and Aesthetics* 1.3 (1981): 5-14. Rpt. in Amur, *Forbidden Fruit.*

——. "Self-Recognition in Raja Rao's *The Serpent and the Rope*."

Kakatiya Journal of English Studies 3.1(1978): 71-82. Rpt. in Amur, *Images and Impressions* 1-15. Aslo in Prabhakar 97-105.

Anand, Mulk Raj. "Roots and Flowers: Two Lectures on the Metamorphosis of Technique and Content in the Indo-English Novel." *Littcrit* 8.1(1982): 47-60

Anjaneyulu, D. "The Art of Raja Rao." *Thought* 9 May 1964: 12-14.

———. "Towards an Image of India: Nirad C. Chaudhari and Raja Rao." *Triveni* 49.2 (1980): 40-50.

———. "The Art of Raja Rao." *Triveni* 66.3 (1997): 58-62.

Arora, V.N. "The Use of Myth in *Kanthapura*." Saxena, *Glimpses* Vol. 3. 80-94.

Badve, V.V. "The Use of Mythology in Raja Rao's *Kanthapura*." *Journal of Shivaji University* 10.16 (1977): 45-51.

———. "Raja Rao's *Comrade Kirillov*." *New Quest* Mar.-Apr. 1979: 21-28.

Beatrice, Menezes. "Female Characterization in Raja Rao's Novel, *Th Serpent and the Rope*." *Journal of South Asian Literature* 16.2 (1981): 5-15.

Belliappa, K.C. "The Question of Form in Raja Rao's *The Serpent and the Rope*." *World Literature Written in English* 24.2 (1948): 407-416. Rpt. in *Journal of Commonwealth Literature* 26.1 (1991): 158-168.

———. "Raja Rao." Belliappa 191-301.

Bhalla, Brij M. "Quest for Identity in Raja Rao's *The Serpent and the Rope*." *Ariel* 4:4 (1973): 59-105.

Bhatnagar, K.C. "Raja Rao: Poetry as Prophecy." Bhatnagar, K. C., *Realism* 209-248.

Birji-Patil, J. "*Kanthapura* from an African Perspective." Narasimhaiah, *Commonwealth Literature* 102-106.

Chaddah, R.P. "Raja Rao" *Thought* 15 June 1974.

Chakravorthy, D.K. "The Ganges in Raja Rao's Novel, *The Serpent and the Rope*." Chakravorthy, 10-15.

———. "Phases of Transition: An Approach to Raja Rao's novel, *Kanthapura*." Chakravorthy 6-9.

Chandrika B. "Gender and Resistance: A Reading of Raja Rao's *The Cat and Shakespeare." Indian Journal of English Studies* 32 (1993-94): 80-86.

Chari, V.K. "Rama's Tragic Quest: A Reading of *The Serpent and the Rope* in the light of *Rasa* theory." *Littcrit* 36 & 37, 19. 1-2 (1993): 5-20.

Chaturvedi, S.P. "Raja Rao as a Short-Story Writer." Sharma K.K., *Perspectives on Raja Rao.* 109-119.

Chellappan, K. "Voices in Exile: 'Journey' in Raja Rao and V.S. Naipaul." Nelson, *Reworlding* 25-34.

Curtis, Chantal. "Raja Rao and France." *World Literature Today* 62.4 (1988): 595-598.

Daniel, Ezra M. "A Writer of Purana." *Tribune* 8 March 1987.

Das, Elizabeth. "The Choric Element in *Kanthapura*." *Panjab University Research Bulletin* (Arts) 15.1(1984): 53-58.

Davies, M. Bryn. "Raja Rao's *The Serpent and the Rope:* A New Literary Genre." Niven, *The Commonwealth Writer Overseas:* 265-269.

Dayal, B. "Minor Indo-Anglian Short Story Writers: Kaleidoscopic View." Dayal 207-254.

Dayal, Prabhu. "The Influence of Vendanta on Raja Rao." *Panjab University Journal Medieval Indian Literature* 7.12 (1983): 62-74.

———. "The Image of Woman in the Novels of Raja Rao." *Panjab University Research Bulletin* (Arts) 16.1 (1985): 45-53.

———. "All Brides be Benares Born: An Interpretation of *The Serpent and the Rope*." *Journal of Indian Writing in English* 13.1 (1985): 64-68.

———. "The Tantric Elements in the Novels of Raja Rao." *Literary Half-Yearly* 28.1 (1987): 105-118.

———. "Raja Rao and Romain Rolland." *Literary Criterion* 22.3 (1987): 65-72.

———. "Raja Rao and Fyodor Dostoevsky" *Panjab University Research Bulletin* (Arts) 18.1 (1987): 11-18.

———. "Raja Rao and the Charles Baudelaire: An Affinity." *Literary Half Yearly* 30.2 (1989): 54-65.

———. "The Concept of 'Shivoham' in Raja Rao's *The Serpent and Rope.*" *Journal of Religious Studies* 12.1 (Spring 1984): 109-117.

Desai, S.K. "Transplantation of English: Raja Rao's Experimentation with English in His Work of Fiction." Desai, *Experimentation with Language* 1-32.

Devi, D. Deena. "From Quiescence to Self-Action: A Study of Raja Rao's *Kanthapura* in the Light of Gandhian Thought." *Commonwealth Quarterly* 11.32 (1986): 31-49.

Dey, Esha. "Hindu Critic on *The Serpent and the Rope.*" *Bharati* 6.10 (1972): 27-36.

———. "Myth and Metaphysics in *The Serpent and the Rope.*" *Journal of the Dept. of English* (Utkal University) 2.1 (1973-74): 1025.

———. "Fissures in Being: Anguish and Alienation in *The Serpent and the Rope.*" *Littcrit* 12, 7.1 (1981): 62-73.

———. "Raja Rao's India: The Axis of *Comrade Kirillov*—An Anti-Novel." *Commonwealth Quarterly* 5.20 (1981): 24-43.

———. "A Baroque Stylization: A Note on *The Serpent and the Rope.*" *Language Forum* 6.3-4 (1980-81): 1-15.

———. "Woman as Object: The Feminine Condition in a Decadent Patriarchy (Raja Rao's *The Serpent and the Rope* and Shouri Daniels's *The Salt Doll.*)" *Literary Criterion* 20.4 (1985): 9-19.

———. "*The Serpent and the Rope:* A Structure of Discord." Typescript article. 1980.

Dhawan, Neeta R. "The Colonizer and the Colonized in Raja Rao's *Kanthapura.*" Srivastava, Ramesh K., *Colonial Consciousness* 107-112.

Dissanayake, Wimal. "Questing Self: The Four Voices in *The Serpent and the Rope.*" *World Literature Today* 62.4 (1988): 598-602.

Dooley, Gillam. "Attitudes to Political Commitment in Three Indian Novels: *Kanthapura, Train to Pakistan* and *Rich Like Us.*" *Littcrit* 39, 20.2 (1994): 30-39.

Dutta, Sujit Kumar. "A Stylistic Study of Raja Rao's English" *Journal of the Maharaja Sayaji Rao University of Baroda* 31-32.1 (1982-83): 17-27.

Dwivedi, A.N. "The Serpent in the Rope: Symbolism in *Kanthapura.*" *Ravenshaw Journal of English Studies* 6.2 (1996): 1-17.

———. "Symbolism in Raja Rao's *Kanthapura.*" Srivatsava, R.K., *Symbolism* 37-49.

Eng, Ooi Boo. "Making Initial Innocent Sense of *The Serpent and the Rope.*" *Journal of Indian Writing in English* 8.1-2 (1980): 53-62. Rpt. in Singh, Kirpal, *Through Different Eyes* 72-86.

Frost, Christine-Mangala. "'Fleshing the Bones'; Conducting Inter-Faith Dialogue in Fiction." *Literature and Theology* (IRD, England) 10.3 (1996). 216-223.

Galante, Loretta Lynn. "Nativization and Characterization in Raja Rao's *Kanthapura,* Amos Tutuolas *The Palm-wine Drunkard* and Chinna Achebe's *A Man of the People.*" *Journal of Indian Writing in English* 14.2 (1986): 21-31.

Gemmill, Janet Powers. "Rhythm in *The Cat and Shakespeare.*" *Literature East and West* 13.1-2 (1969): 27-42.

———. "Dualities and Non-duality in Raja Rao's *The Serpent and the Rope.*" *World Literature Written in English* 12.2 (1973): 247-259.

———. "The Transcreation of Spoken Kannada in Raja Rao's *Kanthapura.*" *Literature East and West* 18.2-4 (1974).

———. "Raja Rao: Three Tales of Independence." *World Literature Written in English* 15.1 (1976): 135-146.

———. "Raja Rao's *The Cow of the Barricades:* Two Stories." *Journal of South Asian Literature* 13.1-4 (1977-78): 23-30.

———. "Elements of Folktale in *The Cow of the Barricades* and Other Stories." *World Literature Written in English* 20.1 (1981): 149-161.

248   THE FICTION OF RAJA RAO: CRITICAL STUDIES

———. "*Kanthapura:* India *en route* to Independence." *CEA Critic* 44.4 (1982): 30-38.

Ghosh, Sadhan Kumar. "Raja Rao's Magnum Opus: *The Serpent and the Rope.*" Sharma, K.K., *Perspectives on Raja Rao* 84-92.

Gondal, Yogesh. "Raja Rao: Obscure but Rhythmic Writer." *New Delhi* 3.7 (18-31 Aug, 1988): 60-64.

Gorlier, Claudio. "See What I am: The Figure of Beatrice in *The Serpent and the Rope.*" *World Literature Today* 62.4 (1988): 606-607.

———. "Raja Rao's *The Cat and Shakespeare*: A Western View." *Jounal of Indian Writing in English* 26.2 (1998): 1-9.

Gowda, H.H. Annaiah. "Raja Rao's *The Serpent and the Rope.*" *Literary Half-Yearly* 4.2 (1963): 36-40.

———. "Phenomenal Tradition: The Case of Raja Rao and Wilson Harris." *ACLALS Bulletin* 9 (1972): 28-48.

Goyal, Bhagwat S. "Raja Rao's *Comrade Kirillor.*" Goyal, *Culture and Commitment* 117-118.

Gregor, Arthur. "An Introduction to Raja Rao's *The Cat.*" *Chelsea Review* 5 (1954): 16.

Gupta, A.N. *"Comrade Kirillov:* An Appraisal." Sharma, K.K., *Perspectives on Raja Rao* 120-139.

Gupta, G.S. Balarama. " *Kanthapura* as a Political Novel." Dinesh & Joshi 10-15.

Guruprasad, Thakur. "Reflections on Rama: India as Depicted in *The Serpent and the Rope.*" *Journal of Indian Writing in English* 1.1 (1973): 19-28.

Guzman, Richard R. "The Saint and the Sage: The Fiction of Raja Rao." *Virginia Quarterly Review* 56.1 (1980): 32-50.

Harrex, S.C. "Companion of Pilgrimage." Narasimhaiah and Nagarajan, *Studies* 277-298. Also in Harrex, *The Fire and the offering* Vol. 2. 147-200.

———. "The Fascination of What's Difficult: Some Students Response to Raja Rao." Sharma, K.K, *Indo-English Literature* 177-192.

———. "Typology and Modes: Raja Rao's Experiment in Short Stories." *World Literature Today* 62.4 (1988): 591-595.

Harris, Wilson. "Raja Rao's Inevitable Style and Art of Fiction." *World Literature Today* 62.4 (1988): 587-590.

——. *"The Serpent and the Rope."* Harris, *The Womb of Space* 78-83. "The Whirlingstone."

Hema, M.S. "Care of the Self: Raja Rao's *The Chessmaster and His Moves* and *On the Ganga Ghat.*" Kirpal, *Postmodern Indian English Novel* 71-83.

Hemenway, Stephen I. "Raja Rao's *Kanthapura* and *The Serpent and the Rope.*" Hemenway 71-109.

Hiatt, Shennon T. "Oral Tradition as a Nativization Technique in Three Novels." *Journal of Indian Writing in English* 14.1 (1986): 10-20.

Issac, Shanty. "Two French Elements in *The Serpent and The Rope.*" *Journal of Karnatak University* (Humanities) 18 (1974): 138-147.

Iyengar, K.R. Srinivasa. "Literature as "Sadhana": A Note on Raja Rao's *The Cat and Shakespeare.*" *Aryan Path* 40.7 (1969): 301-305. Rpt. in Sharma, K.K., *Perspectives on Raja Rao.* 103-108.

——. "Raja Rao." Iyengar, *Indian Writing in English* 386-411.

——. "On Re-Reading *The Serpent and the Rope.*" Naik, *Perspectives* 72-92.

Jamkhandi, Sudhakar Ratnakar. *"The Cat and Shakespeare:* Narrator Audience and Message." *Journal of Indian Writing in English* 7.2 (1979): 25-40.

Jha, Ashok K. "Identity and Its Quest in Raja Rao's Later Fiction." *Language Forum* 18.1-2 (1992): 29-37. Rpt. in Pathak, *Quest for Identity* 29-37.

Jha, Rama. "Raja Rao: Quest for spiritual Regeneration through Gandhian Thought." Jha 87-116.

Jhanji, Rekha. "Cultural Encounter and Realization of Traditional Identity: Some Comments on *The Serpent and the Rope.*" Kaul, and Jaidev 146-150.

John, Joseph. "Ramaswamy's Quest: Explorations of Love in *The Serpent and the Rope.*" *Journal of South Asian Literature* 26. 1-2 (1991): 277-292.

Juneja, Punim. "The East-West Theme: *Some Inner Fury, The Serpent and the Rope* and *A Dream in Hawaii.* Dhawan, *Commonwealth Fiction.* Vol. 1. 178-197.

Kachru, Braj B. "Toward Expanding the English Canon: Raja Rao's 1938 Credo of Creativity." *World Literature Today* 24 (1988): 582-586.

Kalinnikova, E.J. "Ancient Indian Philosophy and Raja Rao's Works." Sharma, K.K., *Perspectives on Raja Rao* 23-31.

———. "The French Brahmin: Raja Rao." Kalinnikova, *Indian English Literature: A Perspective* 133-148.

———. "Russian-Indian Literary Connection: Dostoevsky and Raja Rao: A Comparative Analysis of Two novels: *The Possessed* and *Comrade Kirillov.*" Yaravintelimath, *et al.* 137-146.

Kamath, M.V. "The Brahmin and the Rabbi." *Illustrated Weekly of India* 24 Aug. 1980: 47.

Kantak, V.Y. "The Language of *Kanthapura.*" *Indian Literary Review* 3.2 (1985): 15-26. Rpt. as "Raja Rao's *Kanthapura*" in *Chandrabagha* 13 (1985): 35-45.

Karnani, Chetan. "From Sense to Nonsense: The Case of Raja Rao." *Thought* 17 Aug. 1974: 15.

Katamble, V.D. "*Kanthapura* and *Things Fall Apart* as Sthalapuranas." *Littcrit* 22 & 23, 12.1-2 (1986): 56-78.

Kaul, R.K. "*The Serpent and the Rope* as a Philosophical Novel." *Literary Criterion* 15.2 (1980): 32-63.

———. "The Problem of Speech in Indo-Anglian Writing: R.K. Narayan and Raja Rao." *Quest* 85, Nov.-Dec. 1973: 65-87.

Kirpal, Vineypal Kaur. "Raja Rao's *Comrade Kirillov.*" *Journal of Indian Writing in English 5.2* (1977): 46-48.

Knippling, Alpana Sharma. "R.K. Narayan, Raja Rao and Modern English Discourse in Colonial India." *Modern Fiction Studies* 39.1 (1993): 169-186.

Krishna Kutty, Gita. "From Indulekha to Shanta: A Lineage of Coconuts." *Literary Criterion* 20.4 (1985): 26-68. Also in Narasimhaiah, *Women in Fiction, Fiction by Woman* 62-68.

Krishnaswami, Shanta. "Raja Rao: The Indian Pattern of Saved Males and Doomed Females." Krishnaswamy, 22-59.

Kumar, Bimal. "Theosophy in the Fiction of Raja Rao." *Contour* 1.2-3 (1992): 16-19.

Kumar, Shiv K. "In Search of Excellence: A Tribute to Raja Rao on Receiving Neustadt International Prize." *Hindustan Times,* 4 Dec. 1988: 13. Also in *Indian Book Industries* Jan.-Feb. 1989: 58-59.

Kumar, Sudhir. "Reading Raja Rao's The Meaning of India." *New Quest* 126, Nov.-Dec. 1997: 337-340

Lalitha, J. "Politics of Freedom: Gandhi in *Kanthapura* and *A Bend in the Ganges.*" *Kakatiya Journal of English Studies* 10 (1989-90): 32-40.

"Raja, Rao's use of English Language." *The Critic's Horn Book: Reading for Interpretation.*

Latha, K.S. "Rural Ethos in Indian Novels in English: Kamala Markandaya's *Nectar in a Sieve,* Raja Rao's *Kanthapura,* Mulk Raj Anand's *The Village.*" *Triveni* 61.2 (1992): 53-56.

Laxmana Murthy, S. "Raja Rao: A Note on the Philosophy." *Journal of English Studies* (Warangal) 8 (1987-88): 9-18.

——. "Self-Knowledge and Grace in Raja Rao." Rao, Ramakrishna & Sivaramkrishna 98-105.

Larson, Charles. "Revolt and Rebirth: Cultural Renewal: Raja Rao's *Kanthapura* and Markandaya's *Two Virgins.* Larson 131-151.

Laxmi Mani. "Voices and Vision in Raja Rao's Fiction." *Journal of South Asian Review* 4.1 (1980): 1-11.

Lehmann, Winfred P. "Literature and Linguistics: Text Linguistics" *Literary Criterion* 17.1 (1982): 18-29.

——. "The Quality of Presence." *World Literature Today* 62.4 (1988): 578-582.

Maini, D.S. "Raja Rao's vision, Values and Aesthetics." Sharma, K.K, *Perspectives on Raja Rao* 1-22. Rpt. in Narasimhaiah, *Commonwealth Literature* 90-101.

Mani, Raghunath. *"The Cat and Shakespeare:* Dialectics of Inclusiveness. *Language Forum* 24.1-2 (1998): 193-199.

Mani, K. Ratna Shiela. "The Use of Myth in Raja Rao's *The Serpent and the Rope.*" *Triveni* 60.3 (1991): 9-17.

———. "Mythic Form in Raja Rao's *The Cat and Shakespeare.*" *Triveni* 67.2 (1998): 42-44

Mansur, Rajshekar. "Why does *The Cat and Shakespeare* Fail: A Linguistic Approach." *Journal of Karnatak University* (Humanities) 26 (1982): 68-75.

———. "*Kanthapura* and *The Princes:* A Study in Contrasting Modes of Political Fiction." *Journal of Karnatak University* (Humanities) 30 (1986): 43-56.

Maratha, S. Menon. "Three Indian Novelists." *Life and Letters* Dec. 1948: 187-192.

Mathur, O.P. "The Serpent Vanishes: A Study in Raja Rao's Treatment of East-West Theme." Sharma, K.K., *Perspectives on Raja Rao* 44-54. Rpt. in Mathur, *The Modern Indian English Fiction* 98-108.

———. "The East-West Theme in *Comrade Kirillov.*" *New Literary Review* 4 (1978): 25-29. Rpt. in Mathur, *The Modern Indian English Fiction* 109-116.

Mathur, O.P. and G. Rai. "Existential Overtones in Raja Rao's *Comrade Kirillov. Journal of South Asian Literature* 17.1 (1982): 264. Also in Mathur, *The Modern Indian English Fiction.* 117-125.

McCutchion, David. "The Novel as Sastra." McCutchion *Indian Writing in English* 69-82. Rpt. in Mukherjee, *Considerations* 90-101.

Meera Bai, K. "The Theme of Marital Disharmony in *The Serpent and the Rope* and *The Guide.*" *Triveni* 64.3 (1995): 23-25.

Melwani, M.D. "The Experimental Story in English." *Thought* 15 May 1971: 14-15.

Menon, A.M. "Indian Writers in English Literature: Raja Rao." *Akasavani* 4 July 1971: 344.

Menon, K.P.K. "*Kanthapura* as a Political-Religious Novel." Paniker, *Contemporary Indian Fiction in English* 68-75.

Mishra, Ganeswar. "The Search for an Idiom: A Study of

Kanthapura and *Nectar in a Sieve.*" Mishra 36-54. Also in *Mahanandi Review* 3.2 (1983).

——. "The Novel as Purna: A Study of the Form of *The Man-Eater of Malgudi and Kanthapura.*" *Journal of Literary studies.* (1978): 1-24. Rpt. in Mishra 18-35.

Mondal. Anshuman. "The Ideology of Space in Raja Rao's *Kanthapura*," *Journal of Commonwealth Literature* 34.1 (1999): 103-114.

Monti, Alleggandro. "A Ples and a Cheer for Indian English: A Note on Raja Rao." *Journal of Literature and Aesthetics* 7.1 (1999): 7-11.

Moorthy, S.S. "Beyond the Gandhian Dimension: Mythical and Folklore Elements in *Kanthapura.*" *Commonwealth Novel in English* 5.1(1992): 20-26.

Mukherjee, Meenakshi. "Raja Rao's Shorter Fiction." *Indian Literature* 10.3 (1967): 66-76.

Muller, Ulrich and William C. McDonald. "Tristan in Deep Structure: Raja Rao's *The Serpent and the Rope*—A Paradigmatic Case of Intercultural Relations." *Tristania: A Journal Devoted to Tristan Studies* 12.1-2 (1986-87): 44-47.

Nagarajan, S. "An Indian Novel: *The Serpent and the Rope.*" *Sewanee Review* 72.3 (1964): 521-517. Rpt. in Mukherjee, *Considerations* 84-89.

——. "A Note on Myth and Ritual in Raja Rao's *The Serpent and the Rope.*" *Journal Commonwealth Literature* 4.1 (1972): 45-48.

——. "Little Mother in *The Serpent and the Rope.*" *World Literature Today* 62.4 (1988): 609-611.

Nagpal, L.R. "Home Coming in *Comrade Kirillov*" Awasthi 123-131.

Naik, M.K. *"Kanthapura:* The Indo-Anglian Novel as Legendary History." *Journal of Karnatak University* (Humanities) 10 (1966): 26-39.

——. "Raja Rao as a Short Story Writer: *The Cow of the Barricades.*" *Books Abroad* 40.4 (1966): 391-96.

———. "The Kingdom of God is Within Man: A Study of *The Cat and Shakespeare*." *Journal of Karnatak University* (Humanities) 12 (1968): 123-150. Rpt. as *"The Cat and Shakespeare: A Study"* in Narasimhaiah, *Indian Literature of the Past Fifty Years* 147-176. Also in Naik, *Raja Rao*. Chapter IV, 113-141.

———. *"The Serpent and the Rope:* The Indo-Anglian Novel as an Epic Legend." Naik, *et. al., Critical Essays* 272-306.

———. "The Achievement of Raja Rao." *Banasthali Patrika* 12 (1969): 44-56.

———. "Influences on Raja Rao." *Triveni* 41.1 (1972): 68-75.

———. "Narrative Strategy in Raja Rao's *The Cow of the Barricades and Other Stories*." *Indian Writing Today* 5.3 (1971). Rpt. in Mohan 47-55.

———. "In Native Accents,The Juvenilia of Raja Rao." *Aryan Path* 43 (1972): 74-80.

———. "Feline Felicity: On the Meaning of *The Cat and Shakespeare*." Sharma, K.K., *Perspectives on Raja Rao* 93-102.

———. "The Short Story as Metaphycial Parable." Raja Rao's *The Policeman and the Rose." Language Forum* 7.1-4 (1981-82): 110-122. Rpt. in Dhawan, *Explorations* 110-122.

———. "Coils of the Serpent: Raja Rao and the Unreal World." Naik, *Studies* 34-45. Also in Dwivedi, *Studies in contemporary Indian Fiction in English* 163-174.

———. "Raja Rao's *Comrade Kirillov*." *Indian Journal of English Studies* 21 (1981-82): 107-116.

Naikar, Basawaraj S. "Coming Togehter: The Central Problem in *The Serpent and the Rope*." *Journal of Karnatak University* (Humanities) 22 (1978): 114-122.

Nair, Rama. "Maya as Narrative Structure: A Study of Raja Rao's *The Cat and Shakespeare*." *Osmania Journal of English Studies* 25 (1989): 18-29.

Narain, Lakshmi. "Raja Rao: Indian Novel in Three Languages." *Asian Student* 6 Feb. 1972.

Narasimhaiah, C.D. "Raja Rao's *The Serpent and the Rope*: A Study." *Literary Criterion* 5; 4 (1963): 62-83.

——. "Raja Rao's *Kanthapura:* An Analysis." *Literary Criterion* 7.2 (1966): 15-77. Rpt. in Naik, *et al. Critical Essays* 246-271. Also in Narasimhaiah, *Fiction and the Reading Public* 270-296.

——. "*The Cat and Shakespeare:* An *ad hoc* Assessment." *Literary Criterion* 8.3 (1968): 65-95.

——. "National Identity in Literature and Language: Its Range and Depth in the Novels of Raja Rao." Paper delivered at the Commonwealth Literary Conference on National Identity at University of Queensland, Brisbane on August 9th-15th, 1968. Published in Goodwin 153-164

——. "The Metaphysical Novel: *The Serpent and the Rope.*" Narasimhaiah, *The Swan and the Eagle* 150-202. Rpt. in Walsh, *Readings* 39-50.

——. "Raja Rao: Novel as Magic Casement of Celestial Concerns and Social transactions." *Literary Criterion* 33.3 (1998): 37-47.

Narayan, Shyamala. "Social Concerns in the Fiction of Raja Rao." *Gray Book* 3 (1973): 42-46.

——. "East-West Encounter in Raja Rao's *The Serpent and the Rope* and Victor Anant's *The Revolving Man.*" *Indian Literary Review* 1.5-6 (1978): 50-55.

——. "Ramaswamy's Euridition: A Note on Raja Rao's *The Serpent and the Rope.*" *Ariel* 14.4 (1983): 6-15. Rpt. in Rajan, *Changing Traditions* 69-80.

——. "Tender Confrontation between East and West." *Hindu* 20 Nov. 1983: 18.

——. "Women in Raja Rao's Fiction." *Literary Criterion* 20.4 (1985): 35-47. Rpt. in *Islamic Culture* 20.4 (1985): 35-45. Also in Narasimhaiah, *Women in Fiction* 35-47.

Nasimni, Reza Ahmad. "*Kanthapura:* Language as Convultions of Consciousness." *Nasimi* 56-75.

Nath, Suresh. "Gandhi and Raja Rao." Sharma, K.K., *Perspectives on Raja Rao* 55-66.

Nelson, Cecil. "Syntactic Creativity and Intelligibility." *Journal of Indian Writing in English* 12.2 (1984): 1-14.

——. "My Language, Your Culture: Whose Communicative Competence." Kachru. 327-339.

Niranjan, Shiva. "The Nature and Extent of Gandhi's Impact on the Early Novels of Mulk Raj Anand and Raja Rao." *Commonwealth Quarterly* 3.2 (1979): 36-66.

——. "Myth as a Creative Mode: A Study of Mythical Parallel is in Raja Rao's Novel." *Commonwealth Quarterly* 4.13 (1980): 49-68.

——. "Philosophy into Fiction: A Study of the Thematic Aspects of Raja Rao's Novels." Prasad, H.M., *Response* 112-126.

Niven, Alastair. "Any Row over Rao?" *Commonwealth Newsletter* 6 (1974): 34-35.

Pai, Arthur and Radhika Radhakrishnan. "Award-Winning Raja Rao Likened to Joyce Proust." *India Abroad* 27 May 1988: 134-135.

Pallan, Rajesh K. "The Feminine Principle in Raja Rao's *The Cat and Shakespeare*." Bande, *Mothers and Mother-figures* 70-86.

Paniker, Ayyappa. "The Frontiers of Fiction: A Study of Raja Rao's *The Cat and Shakespeare*." *Journal of Literary Studies* 2.2 (1979): 39-56. Rpt. in Nagarajan *et al.* 84-91.

——. "Man and God in Indian and African Fiction: A Study Based on *Kanthapura, Arrow of God* and *Mookajji's Vision*." Narasimhaiah, *Commonwealth Literature* 107-116.

——. "On Translating Raja Rao's *The Cat and Shakespeare*," Rajan, *Changing Traditions* 13-22.

Parameswaran, Uma. "Karma at work, The Allegory in Raja Rao's *The Cat and Shakespeare*." *Journal of Commonwealth Literature* 7 (1969): 107-145.

——. "Without Women the World Is Not: Shakti in Raja Rao's Novels." *ACLALS Bulletin* 9 (1972): 4-72.

——. "Excelsior—Raja Rao." Parameswaran, *A Study of the Representative Indo-English Novelists* 141-171.

——. "Siva and Shakti in Raja Rao's Novels." *World Literature Today* 62.4 (1988): 574-577.

Paranjape, Markarand R. *"The Chessmaster and His Moves:* A Review of Reviews and an Introduction." Rao, A. Ramakrishna, *Comparative Perspectives on Indian Literature* 81-102. Rpt. in Bharucha and Sarang. 185-206.

———. "Critique of Communism in Raja Rao's *Comrade Kirillov*" Pandey & Raj Rao 69-83.

———. "Raja Rao." *Critical Survey of Long Fiction*. Ed. Frank N. Magnill. Englewood Cliff (New Jersy): Saleem Press, 1983. Vol. 6. 2205-2215.

Parashar, B.P. "The Cow and the Herd: The Image of Plurality in *Kanthapura.*" *Ken* 2 (1986): 35-54.

Parera, Senath W. "Towards A Limited Emancipation: Women in Raja Rao's *Kanthapura.*" *Ariel* 23.4 (1992): 99-110.

Parthasarathy, R. "*The Chessmaster and His Moves*: The Novel as Metaphysics." *World Literature Today* 62.4 (1988): 561-566.

———. "Tradition and Creativity: Stylistic Innovations in Raja Rao." Smith 157-165.

Parvathi Devi, M. "Threefold Path to Fulfilment: A Note on Raja Rao's Fiction." *Triveni* 53.1 (1984): 46-52.

Pati, M.S. "Rope in the Serpent." *Sambhalpur Studies in Language and Literature* 2 (1981): 10-30.

Patil, Chandrasekhar B. "The Kannada Element in Raja Rao's Prose: A Linguistic Study of *Kanthapura.*" *Journal of Karnatak University* (Humanities) 13 (1969): 143-167.

Pousse, Michel. "So Many Freedoms" *Commonwealth Essays and Studies* 12.1 (1989): 30-38.

Powers, Janet M. "Raja Rao." *Encyclopaedia of World Literature in the 20th Century.* Ed. Wolfgang Bernard Fleischamann. New York: Frederick Ungar, 1985.

———. "Initiate Meets Guru: *The Cat and Shakespeare* and *Comrade Kirillov.*" *World Literature Today* 62.4 (1988): 611-616.

Prabhat, Swarna. "The Use of Myth in *Kanthapura.*" *Quest* (Ranchi) 5.2 (1991): 25-27.

Prakash, Ravendra. "Indian Element in the Style of *The Serpent and the Rope.*" *Rajasthan University Studies in English* 13 (1980): 96-102.

Prasad, Baidya Natha. "The Language of Raja Rao's *The Serpent and the Rope.*" Sinha, K.N., *Indian Writing in English* 92-41. Rpt. in Prabhakar 112-121.

Prasad, V.V.N. Rajendra. "Raja Rao and the Imperial Self." Prasad, V.V.N. Rajendra 43-70.

Raizada, Harish. "Literature as Sadhana: The Progress of Raja Rao from *Kanthapura* to *The Serpent and the Rope.*" Sharma, K.K., *Indo-English Literature* 157-176.

———. "Point of View, Myth and Symbolism in Raja Rao's Novels." Sharma, K.K., *Perspectives on Raja Rao* 189-204.

Raine, Kathleen. *"The Serpent and the Rope." World Literature Today* 62.4 (1988): 603-605.

Rajan, B. *"Kanthapura."* King, *Literature of the World* 87-97.

Rajan, P.K. "An Introduction to *Comrade Kirillov." Littcrit* 3.1 (1977): 51-54.

"Raja Rao." *World Authors, 1950-1970.* 1183-1185.

Ram, Atma. "Peasant Sensibility in *Kanthapura." Sharma, K.K., Indian English Literature* 193-200. Also Ram, *Essays* 26-33.

———. "Raja Rao: The Philosopher Novelist." *Perspective* May 1978: 49-50.

———. "The Linguistic Devices in Indian English of Raja Rao and Mulk Raj Anand." Ram, *Essays* 8-25.

Ramachandraiah, P. "The Journey Motif in *Kanthapura." Indian Review of English Studies* 1.1 (1989): 61-65.

Ramamurthi, K.S. "Kanthapura, Kedaram, Malgudi and Trinidad as India in Miniature: A Comparative Study." Srivastava, A. K., *Alien Voices* 61-74.

Rama Moorthy, P. "Death in Raja Rao's *The Policeman and the Rose* and Witi Ihimaera's *Pounamu Pounamu.*" Narasimhaiah, *Commonwealth Literature* 127-136.

Ramaswamy, S. "Self and Society in Raja Rao's *The Serpent and the Rope.*" Naik, *Aspects* 199-208.

———. "India and France in Raja Rao's *The Serpent and the Rope.*" Ramaswamy, *Explorations* 179-185. Rpt. in Ramaswamy, *Commentaries* 183-188.

———. "'The Sanskrit Charge' in Raja Rao: The Word and 'Sabbda Tattva.'" Rao, A. Ramakrishna, *Comparative Perspectives* 103-112.

Ranchan, Som P. "Ramaswamy's Dilemma: An Analytical Interpretation of *The Serpent and the Rope*." *Language Forum* 7-14 (1981-82): 101-109. Rpt. in Dhawan, *Explorations* 101-109.

———. "*The Serpent and the Rope:* India Made Real." *Illustrated Weekly of India* 13 Mar. 1966: 45-47. 3 Apr. 1966: 33-35. 10 Apr. 1966: 33-35.

Rao, A. Ramakrishna. "Kirillov in the First Circle." *Literary Endeavour* 6.1-4 (1985): 45-54.

Rao A.V., Krishna. "Raja Rao: The Novel of Prophecy." Rao, A.V. Krishna *The Indo-Anglian Novel* 107-133.

Rao, J. Srihari. "Concept of Time and Death in Raja Rao's *The Cat and Shakespeare*." *Littcrit* 3, 2.2 (1976): 35-38.

———. "Image of Truth: A Study of Raja Rao's *The Cat and Shakespeare*." *Journal of Indian Writing in English* 5.1 (1977): 36-41.

Rao, K. Ramachandra. "Raja Rao's *Kanthapura*." Raghavacharulu, *Two Fold Voice* 99-113.

———. "The Novelist as a Marxist: A Study of Raja Rao's *Comrade Kirillov*." *Triveni* 49.1 (1980): 47-50.

———. "Raja Rao and the Metaphysical Novel." Amur *et al. Indian Readings* 87-93.

Rao, N. Madhava. "*Kanthapura:* An Appreciation." *Triveni* 44.3 (1975): 55-59.

———. "The Experiences of Renaissance in *Kanthapura*." *Triveni* 49.4 (1981): 29-32.

Rao, M. Subba. "Raja Rao: The Path Breaker." Rao, M. Subba Vol. 1. 130-140.

Rao, C. Vimala. "Love and Marriage in Raja Rao's *The Serpent and the Rope*." *Littcrit* 33, 17.2 (1981): 12-21.

Ray, Robert J. "The Novels of Raja Rao." *Books Abroad* 40.4 (1966): 411-414. Rpt. in *World Literature Today* 63.2 (1985): 197-199.

Reddy, K. Venkata. "An Approach to Raja Rao's *The Cat and Shakespeare*." *World Literature Written in English* 20.2 (1981):

344-350. Rpt. as "A Tale of Modern India." in Reddy, Venkata *Major Indian Novels* 51-59.

Riemenscheider, Dieter. "Mulk Raj Anand, Anita Desai, G.V. Desani, P. Lal, Kamala Markandaya, R.K. Narayan, Raja Rao, Salman Rushdie and Khushwant Singh." *Lexikon der Welt Literature.* Dortraund: Harenberg Kommunikations, 1988.

Rothfork, John. "Religion and Culture in Raja Rao's *The Serpent and the Rope.*" *Journal of Literary Studies* 4.2 (1981): 25-44.

Sambamurthy, Indira. "The Divine in their Human Abode: Mythical Lore and Metaphysical Quest in the Novels of Raja Rao." *Quest* (Ranchi) 4.2 (1990): 25-33.

Sankaran, Chitra. "Misogyny in Raja Rao's *The Chessmaster and His Moves.*" *Journal of Commonwealth Literature* 30.1 (1995): 87-95.

Sanyal, Samres. "Gandhi as Prominent Myth in *Kanthapura.*" Sanyal, *Indianness in Major Indo-English Novels* 128-130.

——. "Raja Rao and His Experiment with New Technique and Vision in Style." Sanyal, *English Langauge in India* 77-85.

Sarachchandra, Edirwira. "Illusion and Reality: Raja Rao as Novelist." Amirthanayagam and Harrex 107-117.

Sastry, L.S.R. Krishna. "Raja Rao" *Triveni* 36.4 (1968): 16-30.

Seshachari. Chandadai. "The Gandhian Dimension: Revolution and Tragedy in *Kanthapura.*" *South Asian Review* (Jackson Ville, Fl) 5.2 (1981): 82-87.

Shahane, Vasant A. "Raja Rao's *The Cat and Shakespeare:* A Study in the Form of Fiction." *Journal of Indian Writing in English* 3.1 (1975): 7-91.

——. "Quest for Reality in Patrick white and Raja Rao: A Comparative Appraisal." *Orbit* 1.1 (1982): 1-12.

——. "Raja Rao's *The Serpent and the Rope* and Patrick White's *The Solid Mandala.*" Nageswara Rao 177-192. Rpt. in *Language forum* 11.1-4 (1985-86) 128-145. Also in Dhawan, *Comparative Literature* 128-145.

——. "Raja Rao's *Kanthapura.*" Pradhan, 22-40.

——. "Fiction and Reality in Raja Rao." *Journal of South Asian*

Literature 22.2 (1987): 34-42. Rpt. in Naik, *Perspectives* 58-71.

Sharma, Atma Ram. "Raja Rao: Cats, Serpents and Comrades of the Human Condition." *Perspective* 1.1 (1978): 59.

——. "Raja Rao's Prose Style." Sharma, K.K., *Perpsectives on Raja Rao* 204-214.

Sharma, Brahma Dutta. "Mothers and Mother Figures in Raja Rao's Fiction." Bande, *Mothers and Mother-figures* 87-94.

——. "Victim of Colonial Oppression in Raja Rao's *Kanthapura.*" Bande, *Victim Consciousness* 17-27.

Sharma, Jatindra Kumar. "Responses to Alien Culture in Henry James and Raja Rao: Comparative Observations on *The American* and *The Serpent and the Rope.*" *Panjab University Research Bulletin* 15.1 (1984): 11-25.

Sharma, K.K. "The Philosopher as Novelist: Raja Rao's Preoccupation with Philosophy." *Rajasthan Journal of English Studies* 13 & 14 (1981): 40-41. Rpt. in Bhatnagar *Essays in Criticism.*

——. "Introduction." Sharma, K.K., *Perspectives on Raja Rao* i-xiv.

——. "Raja Rao: A Reappraisal." Pathak, *Indian Fiction in English* 55-70.

Sharma, P.P. "Quest for Wholeness: A Central Pre-occupation of Raja Rao's Fiction." Sharma, K.K., *Perspectives on Raja Rao* 32-43.

Sharma, R.S. "The Rope without the Serpent: Reading Raja Rao's Classic." *Osmania Journal of English Studies* 25 (1989): 1-17.

Sharma, Roshanlal. "The Enlightenment Theme: A Study of the Motifs in Raja Rao's *On the Ganga Ghat.*" *Revaluations* 6.1 (1995): 43-54.

Sharma, Som P. "Raja Rao's Search for the Feminine." *Journal of South Asian Literature* 12. (1977): 95-101. Rpt. in Sharma, K.K. *Perspectives on Raja Rao* 180-188.

Sharrad, Paul. "Aspects of Mythic Form and Style in Raja Rao's *The Serpent and the Rope.*" *Journal of Indian Writing in English* 12.2 (1984): 82-95.

——. "A Sense of Place in Raja Rao's *The Serpent and the Rope*." Nightingle 86-96.

Shepherd, Ron. "The Character of Ramaswamy in Raja Rao's *The Serpent and the Rope.*" *New Literary Review* 4 (1978): 17-24.

——. "Symbolic Organization in *The Serpent and the Rope.*" *Southern Review* (Adelaide) 6.2 (1973): 93-107.

——. "Raja Rao: Symbolism in *The Cat and Shakespeare*." *World Literature Written in English* 14.2 (1975): 347-356.

——. "The Conservative Rebel: A Type of an Indian Hero." Sharma, K.K., *Perspectives on Raja Rao* 171-180. Rpt. in Dhawan, *Commonwealth Fiction* Vol. 1. 135-145.

Shirwadkar, K.R. "Literature as Ideology: Raja Rao's *Serpent and the Rope*." Pandey and Raj Rao 1-12.

Singh, Avtar. "Raja Rao's *Kanthapura:* A Study on Technique." Sinha & Sinha 123-135.

Singh, Brij Raj. "Looking for a Classic in Indian English Writing." *Humanities Review* 2.1 (1980): 15-21.

Singh, J.P. "The Serpent and the Rope Dancer." *Indian Journal of English Studies* 16 (1982): 53-76.

Singh, R.S. "Raja Rao's India: Fact or Fiction?" *B.I.E.T. English Association Journal* (1971): 14.

——. "A European Brahmin." Singh, R.S., *Indian Novel in English* 73-95.

Singh, Satyanarain. "A Note on Raja Rao's World View in *The Serpent and the Rope*." *Kakatiya Journal of English Studies* 3.1 (1978): 253-256.

Singh, Sunaina. "*The Cat and Shakespeare:* Metaphysical Reality or Surrender to Destiny." *Kakatiya Journal of English Studies* 8 (1987-88): 156-162.

Sinha, R.K. "Oral Tradition in *Kanthapura* and *Arrow of God*." Sinha & Sinha, 136-143.

Sitaramayya, K.B. "The Narrator in Raja Rao's *Kanthapura*." *Journal of Literature and Aesthetics* 2.2-3 (1982): 67-73.

Sivaraman, S. (Mrs.). "Archetypal Experience in *The Serpent and the Rope*." Pathak, *Indian Fiction in English* 71-78.

Soni, N.C. "The Achievement of Raja Rao." Sharma, K.K., *Perspectives on Raja Rao* 215-230.

Srinivas, V. "Tradition and Experiment in *The Cat and Shakespeare.*" *Kakatiya Journal of English Studies* 11 (1991): 119-124.

——. "Myth and Experiment in *Kanthapura.*" *Kakatiya Journal of English Studies* 13 (1993): 74-80.

Srivastava Narasingh. "Love and Divorce in *The Serpent and the Rope.*" *Quest* Sept.-Oct. 1975: 58-62.

——. "Image of India in the Novels of Raja Rao." *Indian Scholar* 2.1 (1980): 57-69.

——. "Raja Rao's *Comrade Kirillov:* The Dilemma of a Divided Consciousness." *Journal of Commonwealth Literature* 16.1 (1981): 8-15.

——. "The Narrative Technique of Raja Rao." Dwivedi, *Studies in Contemporary Indian Fiction in English* 173-190.

Srivastava, Ramesh. "Structure and Theme in Raja Rao's Fiction." Sharma, K.K., *Perspectives on Raja Rao* 140-170. Rpt. in Srivastava, R.K., *Six Indian Novelists* 47-54.

——. "Raja Rao's *Kanthapura:* A Village Revitalised." Srivastava, R.K., *Six Indian Novelists* 3-16. Rpt. in Dhawan, *Commonwealth Fiction* Vol. 1. 122-134.

Subramanyam, Ka. Naa "On Reading Raja Rao's *The Cat and Shakespeare.*" *Thought* 16 Apr. 1966: 16-17.

——. "Raja Rao and Current Literature." *Hindustan Times* 6 June 1969: 7-4.

Sundaram, P.S. "Single and Double Vision: Anand, Raja Rao and R.K. Narayan." *Rajasthan University Studies in English* 7 (1974): 68-78.

Taranath, Rajeev. "A Note on the Problem of Simplification." Narasimhaiah, *Fiction and the Reading Public* 205-212.

Thumboo, Edwin. "Raja Rao: *The Chessmaster and His Moves.*" *World Literature Today* 62.4 (1988): 567-578.

Tiffin, Helen and Arvind Sharma. "Advaita Vedanta in Three Novels of Raja Rao." *Religion* 13 Oct. 1983: 359-379.

——. "The Word and the House: Colonial Motifs in *The Double Hook* and *The Cat and Shakespeare.*" *Literary Criterion* 20.1 (1985): 204-226.

Tikoo, Swaraj Krishna. "Raja Rao's *The Serpent and the Rope:* The East-West Cocktail." Rao, Visheswara 83-94.

Tiwary, R.S. "Tolerance and Accommodation in *The Serpent and the Rope"* *Language Forum.* 24.1-2 (1998): 177-191.

Usha, V.T. "Raja Rao and Jhabvala Two Variant Visions of Indian Widow." *Journal of Indian Writing in English* 21.1 (1993): 13-20.

Vanita, Ruth. "Ravana Shall be Slain and Sita Freed—The Feminine Principle in *Kanthapura."* Chatterjee 188-193.

Venkatachari, K. "Raja Rao's *The Serpent and the Rope:* A Study in Advaitic Affirmation." *Osmania Journal of English Studies* 8.1 (1971): i-xii.

——. "The Feminine Principle in Raja Rao's *The Serpent and the Rope.*" *Osmanial Journal of English Studies* 8.2 (1971): 113-120. Also in Gupta, *Studies* 152.

Venugopal Rao, C.V. "Raja Rao: A Short Story Writer—A Study" *Journal of Karnatak University* (Humanities) 14 (1970): 159-170.

Verghese, C. Paul. "Raja Rao, Anand, R.K. Narayan and Others." *Indian Writing Today* 3.1 (1969): 31-38.

——. "Raja Rao: An Assessment." Verghese, *Problems of Indian Creative Writing in English* 142-154.

Vijayasree, C. "The Philosophy of Womanhood in Raja Rao's *The Serpent and the Rope.*" Rao, Ramakrishna & Sivaramkrishna 106-114.

Visweswariah, H.S. "*The Serpent and the Rope:* A Stylistic Approach." *Literary Endeavour* 1.1 (1979): 49-62.

Wasi, Jehanara. "Metaphysical Novelist." *Link* 19 May 1985: 41.

——. "Metaphysical Quest." *Economic Times* 16 Nov. 1986. 4.1.

Westbrook, Perry D. "Raja Rao." *Contemporary Novelists.* 5th ed. (1991): 756-757.

——. "Theme and Inaction in Raja Rao's *The Serpent and the Rope*." *World Literature Written in English* 14.2 (1975): 385-398.

——. "Raja Rao's *Comrade Kirillov*: Marxism and Vedanta." *World Literature Today* 62.4 (1988): 617-620.

White, Ray Lewis. "Raja Rao's *The Cat and Shakespeare* in the U.S.A." *Journal of Indian Writing in English* 7.1 (1979): 24-29.

——. "Raja Rao's *The Serpent and the Rope* in the U.S.A." *Journal of Indian Writing in English* 10.1-2 (1982): 41-50.

Williams, Haydn Moore. "Raja Rao: The Idea of India." *Miscellany* 61 (1973): 10. Rpt. in Williams, *Studies in Modern Indian Fiction* Vol. 2. 95-125.

——. "Raja Rao's *The Serpent and the Rope* and the Idea of India." *Rule, Protest, Identity: Aspects of Modern South Asia.* Eds. Peter G. Robb and David D. Taylor. London: Curzon, 1978: 206-212. Rpt. in Williams, *Galaxy* 91-97.

Yok, Choi Kim. "The Concept of Love in Raja Rao's *The Serpent and the Rope*." *Triveni* 44.4 (1976): 39-47.

V. Reviews

Advani, G.J. "Philosophical Novel." Rev. of *The Serpent and the Rope." Baltimore Sun* (MD) 14 April 1963.

——. "Pseudo Profundities." Rev. of *The Cat and Shakespeare. Baltimore Sun* (MD) 14 Feb. 1965.

B.J. "Contrasts." Rev. of *The Serpent and the Rope. Des Moines Register* (IA) 16 June 1963.

B.J.R. "Rao Explores Oriental Mind" Rev. of *The Cat and Shakespeare. Birmingham News* (AL) 4 Apr. 1965.

Badve, V.V. Rev. of *Comrade Kirillov. New Quest* Mar.-Apr. 1979: 121-128.

Bagai, Leona Bell. "A Many-Peopled Tragedy." Rev. of *The Serpent and the Rope. Los Angeles Times* (CA) 10 Feb. 1963.

Barkham, John. "Hindu Widens Gulf Between East West." Rev. of *The Serpent and the Rope. Philadelphia Bulletin* (PA) 17 Feb. 1963.

——. "India's Gifted Raja Rao Wins Acclaim with Brilliant *The Serpent and the Rope*." Rev. of *The Serpent and the Rope*. *Youngstown Vindicator* (OH), 2 Mar. 1963.

Bergamo, Ralph. "A Piquant Fable About India in War." Rev. of *The Cat and Shakespeare*. *Atlanta Journal and Constitution* (GA) 31 Jan. 1965.

——. "Book About India." Rev. of *The Serpent and the Rope*. *Hickory Review* (NC) 4 Apr. 1963.

Bloom, Edward A. Rev. of *The Serpent and the Rope*. *Providence Journal* (RI) 10 Mar. 1963.

Bosworth, Grace. "Near East Revealed." Rev. of *The Cat and Shakespeare*. *Norfolk Pilot* (VA) 31 Jan. 1965.

Bowman, Harry. "Tale of Quite Living." Rev. of *The Cat and Shakespeare*. *Dallas News* (TX) 24 Jan. 1965.

Brandt, J. Donald. "Wedding of Two Worlds." Rev. of *The Serpent and the Rope*. *Wilmington News* (DL) 11 Mar. 1963.

Clifford, William. Rev. of *Kanthapura*. *Saturday Review* 11 Jan. 1964: 62.

Dance, Jim. Rev. of *The Serpent and the Rope*. *Detroit Free Press* (MI) 24 Feb. 1963.

Dimar, Edward C. Jr. "The Garden Wall Between Worlds." Rev. of *The Cat and Shakespeare*. *Saturday Review* 16 Jan. 1965: 48-27.

Fremont-Smith, Eliot. "Books of the Times." Rev. of *The Cat and Shakespeare*. *New York Times* 20 Jan. 1965.

Glauber, Robert. "A Story of Two Worlds." Rev. of *The Serpent and the Rope*. *Chicago Daily News* (IL) 15 June 1963.

Godsell, Geoffrey. "Novels From India and Japan." Rev. of *The Serpent and the Rope*. *Christian Science Monitor* (Boston, MA) 14 Feb. 1963.

H.I. "May Be It'll Go Big in India." Rev. of *The Cat and Shakespeare*. *Columbus Bispatch* (OM) 31 Jan. 1965.

Hartley, Lois. Rev. of Raja Rao's *The Serpent and the Rope*. *America* 4 May 1963: 645.

Hill, William, B. Rev. of Raja Rao's *The Serpent and the Rope.*
Best Sellers: The Monthly Book Review 15 Feb. 1963: 429-430.

"Indian Writer Honoured." Rev. of *The Serpent and the Rope. New
York Times* 4 Apr. 1964.

Jackman, F.P. "The Flower of India." Rev. of *The Serpent and the
Rope. Worcester Telegram* (MA) 17 Feb. 1963.

Keat, Betty Y. "Books in Review." Rev. of *The Cat and Shakespeare.
Baltimore Sun* (MD) 28 Jan. 1965.

King, Terry Johnson. "Tender Love Story in Eastern Setting." Rev.
of *The Serpent and the Rope. Miami News* (FL) 17 Feb. 1963.

Krishnama, B.G.R. Rev. of *The Policeman and the Rose. Hindu* 8
Aug. 1978: 5.

Leland, Jack. "Indian Novelist Raja Rao's Book Gains High Praise."
Rev. of *The Serpent and the Rope. Cherleston; News and
Courier* (S5) 10 Mar. 1963.

Mann, Charles, W. Jr. Rev. of *The Serpent and the Rope. Library
Journal* 1 Feb. 1963.

———. Rev. of *Kanthapura. Literature East and West* 8.4 (1964):
154-155.

Maurer, Robert. "Landing Right Side Up" Rev. of *The Cat and
Shakespeare. Book Week* (Chicago, IL) 31 Jan. 1965: 16.

May, Carl. "Novel with East Flavor Ranks High." Rev. of *The
Serpent and the Rope. Nashville Tenessean* (TN) 2 June 1963.

McLaughlin, Richard. *"The Serpent and the Rope:* A Notable
Indian Novel." *Spring Field Republican* (MA) 10 Mar. 1963.

McMurtry, Larry. "Subtle East-West Tale." Rev. of *The Serpent
and the Rope. Houston Post* (TX) 27 Jan. 1963.

Morgan, John G. "Conflict Between Cultures." Rev. of *The Serpent
and the Rope. Charleston Gazette* (SC)17 Feb. 1963.

Nagarajan, S. "An Indian Novel: *The Serpent and the Rope.*"
Sewanee Review 72.3 (1964): 512-517. Rpt. in *Considerations.*
ed. Meenakshi Mukherjee, Bombay: Allied Publishers, 1971:
84-89.

Naik, M. K. "The Unwise Thrush." Rev. of *The Chess Master and
His Moves. Indian Literature* Mar.-Apr. 1989: 173-178.

———. "Not Quite Pandit Jagannath." Rev. of *On the Gangaghat*. *Indian Literature* 136, 33.2 (1990): 151-155.

Narasimhan, Raji. Rev. of *The Policeman and the Rose*. *Hindustan Times* 11 June 1978: IV.1.

"Notice" Rev. of *The Serpent and The Rope*. *St. Paul Pioneer Press* (MN) 24 June 1962.

Orth, Jan. "New Novel Is Strange Experience." Rev. of *The Serpent and the Rope*. *Charlotte Observer* (NC) 24 Feb. 1963.

Panikar, A.K.C. Rev. of *The Cat and Shakespeare*. *Quest* 57, Apr.-Jun. 1967: 101-102.

Ray, Robert. Rev. of *The Serpent and the Rope*. *Mahfil* 1.3 (1965): 47-51.

Ray, Robert. Rev. of *The Cat and Shakespeare*. *Mahfil* 2.3 (1966): 47-50.

Reif, Jane. "Hindu Mysticism Sets Mood." Rev. of *The Serpent and the Rope*. *Norfolk Pilot* (VA) 3 March 1963.

Rev. of *The Cat and Shakespeare*. *Chicago Tribune Books Today* 31 Jan. 1955.

Rev. of *The Cat and Shakespeare*. *Booklist* 15 Mar. 1965.

Rev. of *The Cat and Shakespeare*. *Times* 5 Feb. 1965: 85-114.

Rev. of *On the Ganga Ghat* (Short Stories). *Times of India* 10 Dec. 1989: 3.

Rev. of *On the Ganga Ghat*. *Economic Times* 7 Jan. 1990: 6.

Rogers, Mary. "Novel from India." Rev. of *The Cat and Shakespeare*. *Louisville Courier Journal* (KY) 7 Feb. 1965.

Ross, Nancy Wilson. "Subtle Marriage of East and West." Rev. of *The Serpent and the Rope*. *New York Herald Tribune Books* 7 Apr. 1963.

Ross, Nancy Wilson "Where Myth and Fact Meet." Rev. of *The Cat and Shakespeare*. *New York Times Book Review* 17 Jan. 1965: 5.

Rothchild, Sylvia. "The Book Shelf." Rev. of *The Cat and Shakespeare*. *Jewish Advocate* [Boston (MA)] 16 Sep. 1965.

Ryan, Charles. "Of Brahmins and Bromides." Rev. of *The Serpent and the Rope*. *San-Francisco Chronicle* (CA) 17 Feb, 1963.

Schroetter, Hilda N. "Indian Author Produces Quiet Warm Simple Tale." Rev. of *The Cat and Shakespeare. Richmond Times-Dispatch* (VA) 14 Mar. 1965.

Shamlal. Rev. of *The Chessmaster and His Moves. Times of India* 21 May 1988: 6.

Singh, K. Natwar. "Return Passage to India." Rev. of *The Serpent and the Rope. Saturday Review* 16 Mar. 1963: 88-89.

"Slow Burners." Rev. of *The Serpent and the Rope. Times Literary Supplement* 9 Dec. 1960: 793.

Soni, N.C. Rev. of *The Policeman and the Rose. Journal of Indian Writing in English* 7.2 (1979): 110-111.

Sykes, Gerald. "An Indian Man of Our Time." Rev. of *The Serpent and the Rope. New York Times Book Review* 14 Apr. 1963.

Thorpe, Michael. Rev. of *The Policeman and the Rose. Literary Half-Yearly* 29.2 (1978): 160-162.

"Truth and All that" Rev. of *The Serpent and the Rope. Times* 22 Feb. 1963.

Tucker, Martin. "Cultures in Conflict." Rev. of *The Serpent and the Rope. Commonweal* 25 Jan. 1963.

Watts, Anne. "Indian Novel Has Metaphysical Bent." Rev. of *The Cat and Shakespeare. Fort Worth Star* (TX) 7 Feb. 1965.

Wills, K.T. Rev. of *The Cat and Shakespeare. Library Journal* 1 Feb. 1965: 90. 668.

Wood, Percy. "Beautifully Written Tale of Brahmin Folkways." Rev. of *The Serpent and the Rope. Chicago Tribune* (IL) 10 Mar. 1963.

Yadav, R.S. "Cat Gut" Rev. of *The Cat and Shakespeare. Thought* (India) 3 Aug. 1974: 18.

VI. Dissertations

Agnihotri, Gopinath. "On the Treatment of Indian Life and Problems in the Novels of M.R. Anand, Raja Rao and R.K. Narayan." Meerut U, 1973.

Atchutaraman, S. "Short Stories of Raja Rao." Diss. (M.Phil.). Andhra U,19?.

Badve, V.V. "Narrative Techniques in Indian Fiction in English with Particular Reference to the Works of Raja Rao, R.K. Narayan, M.R. Anand and Manohar Malgonkar." Shivaji U, 1979.

Bhat, Nithunantha "Themes and Techniques in the Short Stories of Mulk Raj Anand, Raja Rao and R.K. Narayan." Calicut U, 1988.

Bhattacharya, P.C. "Study of the Works of Raja Rao with a View to Assess his Contribution to Indo-Anglian Literature." U of Gorakhpur, 1978.

Chakrapani, Y.S. "Man-Woman Relationships in Indian English Fiction of R.K. Narayan, Raja Rao, Kamala Markandaya and Anita Desai." Karnatak U, 1991.

Choudhury, Shashikala, "Raja Rao's Novels: A Transmutation of Philosophy." IIT Delhi, 1988.

Desai, S.N. "Women Characters in Raja Rao's Novels." Diss. (M.Phil.). Shivaji U, 19?.

Deshpande, J.P. "A Stylistic Analysis of Raja Rao's Novels." Poona U, 1988.

Devasia, S.D. "Indian English and the Indian Spirit: Analysis of Three Novelists: R.K. Narayan, Raja Rao and Mulk Raj Anand." Diss. (M.A.). U of Calicut, 1979.

Devi, Deena. D. "Raja Rao: A Study in the Light of Indian Thought." Banaras Hindu U, 1981.

Dey, Esha. "Crisis of Identity in the Novels of Raja Rao: An Indian Writer in English: With the Emphasis on the Problems of Form and Style." U of Calcutta, 1981.

Dutta, Sujit Kumar Hriday Rajan. "Comparative Stylistic Analysis of Raja Rao and Chinua Achebe's English." Maharaja Sayaji Rao U of Baroda, 1984.

Gemmill, Janet P. "Narrative Technique in the Novels of Raja Rao." U of Wisconsin (Md.), 1971. DA 33 (1972): 6309A-10A.

George, M.P.C. "Raja Rao as a Fiction Writer." Barkatullah U, 1987.

George, Raju. "The Mythical Elements in the Novels of Raja Rao." U of Kerala, 19?.

Gupta, Chamanlal. "Vedanta Vision of Raja Rao." M.D. Univ. (Rohtak).

Guzman, Richard Ramirez. "Bandematara: Nationalism, Personality and Literary Style in Four Third World Writers (Raja Rao, Chinua Achebe, N.V.M Gonzalez and Bienvenido W. Santos). U of Virginia, 1977. DA 38.71 (1978): 4180A.

Jain, J.P. "Philosophical Dimensions in Raja Rao's Fiction." U of Delhi, 19?

Janaki Devi, P. "East-West Encounter in the Indo-Anglian Literature (A Selected Study of Raja Rao, R.K. Narayan, Kamala Markandaya)" Andhra U, 19?.

Juneja, Om Prakash. "Colonial Consciousness in Recent Black American, Indian and African Fiction with Special Reference to the Novels of Richard Wright, Ralph Ellison, James Baldwin, Raja Rao, R.K. Narayan, M.R. Anand, Chinua Achebe, T.K. Aluko and James Nquqi." Maharaja Sayaji Rao U of Baroda, 1980.

Kaur, Davinder. "Raja Rao: A Study of His Fiction with Special Reference to the Treatment of Ideas." U of Malaya, 1983.

Kumar, Hansa Mohan. "A Comparative Study of the History in the Novels of Raja Rao and Alijo Carpentier." Diss. (M.Phil.). Maharaja Sayaji Rao U of Baroda, 1986.

Kulbhusan. "The Fictional Art of Raja Rao: A Formalistic Approach." Guru Nanak U, 1991.

Kumar, Rajesh. "The Use of Myth in the Novels of Raja Rao and R.K. Narayan." Himachal Pradesh U, 1987.

Mukhajoadhayay, Esha. "Crisis of Identity in the Novels of Raja Rao." U of Calcutta, 1983.

Misra, Lalji. "The Impact of Gandhi on Indian English Fiction with Special Reference to M.R. Srivastava, R.K. Narayan, Anand and Raja Rao." Diss (D.Phil.). Gyanpur,1992.

Mishra, S.K. "The Destiny of Man in the Novels of Raja Rao." Banaras Hindu U, 1988.

Nagpal, L.R. "Theme of Self in the Novel of R.K. Narayan and Raja Rao" U of Himachal Pradesh, 1984.

Narayan, Shyamala A. "Raja Rao and the Indian Novel in English." U of Mysore, 1974.

Niranjan, Shiv. "Raja Rao: Novelist as Sage." U of Bihar, 1983.

Oberoi, Narender Kumar. "Sociology of Indo-Anglian Novel with Special Reference to the Novels of Mulk Raj Anand, R.K. Narayan, Raja Rao." Panjab U, 1980.

Pandey S.C. "The Novels of Raja Rao: A Study of His Philosophical and Mythical Themes." U of Kumann, 1983.

Prabh Dayal, "The Philosophical Vision of Raja Rao: A Study of His Fiction in English." Punjabi U, 1986.

Pradhan, Shanta. "Modern Element in Indian English Fiction with Special Reference to the Novels of Raja Rao, Anita Desai, and Arun Joshi." Gauhati U, 1990.

Prakash, Ravindra. "A Stylistic Study of Raja Rao's *The Serpent and the Rope.*" Central Institute of English and Foreign Languages (Hyderabad),1973.

Prasad, V.V.N. Rajendra. "Self, Family and Society in the Novels of Rajan, Raja Rao, R.K. Narayan, Arun Joshi and Anita Desai." U of Krishnadevaraya, 1986, New Delhi: Prestige, 1986.

Rai. Lajpat. "The Theme of Self in the Novels of Raja Rao And R. K. Narayan." U of Himachal Pradesh, 1986.

Rao, K. Ramachandra. "The Fiction of Raja Rao." Marathwada U (Aurangabad), 1976.

Rao, A.V. Krishna. "The Indo-Anglian Novel and the Changing Tradition: A Study of the Novels of M.R. Anand, Kamala Markandaya, R.K. Narayan and Raja Rao." U of Mysore, 1964. Mysore: Rao & Raghavan, 1972.

Sambamurthy, V. Indira. "The Use of Myth in Indo-Anglian Fiction with Special Reference to R.K. Narayan, Raja Rao and Sudhin Ghose." Osmania U, 1984.

Sethi, R. "Literary Representation of National Identity and the Rhetoric Nationalism in Raja Rao's *Kanthapura.*" U of Cambridge, 1992. IT 42.2 (1993): 475.

Sharma, Alpana. "Indian Nationalism and Indo-Anglian Literature: A Critical Re-evaluation of Writing Race into the English language." U of Pittsburgh, 1990. DA 51 (1991): 3749A.

Sharma, Ishwar Dass. "Semantic Universe of Raja Rao: A Study of His Stories." U of Himachal Pradesh, 1989.

Sharma, Jai Prakash. "Raja Rao as a Novelist and Short Story Writer." Meerut U, 1975.

Sharrad, Paul. "Open Dialogue: Metropolitan Provincial Tensions and the Quest for a Post-Colonial Cultures in the Fiction of C.J. Koch, Raja Rao and Willson Harris." Flinders U (South Australia), 1985. DA 47 (1986): 2152A.

Shepherd, Ronald. "Aspects of Identity in the Indo-English Novel: A Study of Three Novelists: Raja Rao, R.K. Narayan and Mulk Raj Anand." U of Adelaide, 1974.

Singh, Ashok Kumar. "Quest for Truth in the Novels of Raja Rao." Magadh U, 1988.

Singh, Parminder. "The Cultural Myth as Defense Mechanism in The Serpent and the Rope of Raja Rao." Punjabi U, 1989.

Sreenivas Reddy, P. "Treatment of Myth in the Novels of Raja Rao." Barkatullah U, 1990.

Sreeramachandra Murthy, K. "Raja Rao: A Critical Study." Andhra U, 1974.

Srivastava, Girish Chandra. "Raja Rao as a Novelist: A Study of Themes and Techniques in His Novels." U of Gorakpur, 1983.

Suresh Kumar, A.V. "Non-Indian Characters: Anglo-American and European in the Novels of Mulk Raj Anand, Raja Rao, R.K. Narayan, B. Rajan, Markandaya and Anita Desai." Osmania U, 1990.

Thomas, Polanna. "Role et statut de la femme dans l'ocuvre de Raja Rao." DA 1979: 200A.

Venkateswaran. Shyamala. "Raja Rao and the Indian Novel in English." U of Mysore, 1974.

Wali, Ahmed. "Stylistic Study of The Cat and Shakespeare." Diploma Thesis. Central Institute of English and Foreign Languages (Hyderabad), 1972.